S0-DTB-163

DISCOVERIES IN THE JUDAEAN DESERT · V

QUMRAN CAVE 4

I

DISCOVERIES IN THE JUDAEAN DESERT · V

QUMRAN CAVE 4

I

BY

JOHN M. ALLEGRO

WITH THE COLLABORATION OF

ARNOLD A. ANDERSON

CLARENDON PRESS · OXFORD

Oxford University Press, Great Clarendon Street, Oxford OX2 6DP
Oxford New York
Athens Auckland Bangkok Bogota Bombay
Buenos Aires Calcutta Cape Town Dar es Salaam
Delhi Florence Hong Kong Istanbul Karachi
Kuala Lumpur Madras Madrid Melbourne
Mexico City Nairobi Paris Singapore
Taipei Tokyo Toronto
and associated companies in
Berlin Ibadan

Oxford is a trade mark of Oxford University Press

Published in the United States
by Oxford University Press Inc., New York

© Oxford University Press 1968

All rights reserved. No part of this publication may be reproduced, stored in a retrieval system, or transmitted, in any form or by any means, without the prior permission in writing of Oxford University Press. Within the UK, exceptions are allowed in respect of any fair dealing for the purpose of research or private study, or criticism or review, as permitted under the Copyright, Designs and Patents Act, 1988, or in the case of reprographic reproduction in accordance with the terms of the licences issued by the Copyright Licensing Agency. Enquiries concerning reproduction outside these terms and in other countries should be sent to the Rights Department, Oxford University Press, at the address above

British Library Cataloguing in Publication Data
Data available

Library of Congress Cataloging in Publication Date
Data available

ISBN 0–19–826314–7

1 3 5 7 9 10 8 6 4 2

Printed in Great Britain on acid-free paper by
St Edmundsbury Press, Bury St Edmunds

FOREWORD

THE manuscripts of Qumrân Cave 4, the richest of all the caves, have been allocated to several editors and have been given a continuous numeration, in a logical sequence. It was hoped to start publication with the Biblical manuscripts. But delay on the part of one of the editors and the possibility of delay in the preparation of other volumes have made it advisable to publish first those texts which had been allotted to Mr. John M. Allegro, Lecturer in the University of Manchester, and which were ready for press. However, the original numeration has been preserved. This volume contains manuscripts 4**Q158** to 4**Q186**: paraphrases and commentaries on books of the Bible, collections of Biblical quotations, and various other texts.

R. DE VAUX, O.P.

Jerusalem
September 1966

PREFACE

THE following pages contain that part of the extensive Fourth Cave material from Qumrân for which I undertook responsibility when invited to join the international editing team in Jordan in 1953. Most of these documents have already appeared in provisional editions in learned journals since that date. Both in these preliminary publications and here it has been my practice to offer no more than the basic essentials of photographs, transliteration, translation of non-Biblical passages where this might serve some useful interpretative purpose, and the minimum of textual notes. This should give the specialists at least the raw material for their work of elucidating the Qumrân texts.

It was originally intended that my section of the Fourth Cave material should form only part of a larger volume to which one or more of my colleagues of the team should contribute. However, a change of editorial policy in this regard has now required completion of my section as a separate publication with its own index. In this additional work I have enjoyed the cooperation of my academic colleague, Mr Arnold Anderson, who has also been kind enough to check all the texts against the photographs and has proffered many useful suggestions for correcting or alternatively reading the documents. Most of these suggestions have been gratefully incorporated and to a considerable degree this volume must be regarded as our joint work. However, the original work on the sorting and piecing together of the manuscripts and the initial identification and decipherment of the texts was mine alone, and I must bear full responsibility for any faults that may be detected in this regard.

JOHN M. ALLEGRO

Manchester
September 1966

CONTENTS

LIST OF PLATES

158. Biblical paraphrase: Genesis, Exodus 1
159. Ordinances 6
160. The vision of Samuel 9
161. Commentary on Isaiah (A) 11
162. Commentary on Isaiah (B) 15
163. Commentary on Isaiah (C) 17
164. Commentary on Isaiah (D) 27
165. Commentary on Isaiah (E) 28
166. Commentary on Hosea (A) 31
167. Commentary on Hosea (B) 32
168. Commentary on Micah (?) 36
169. Commentary on Nahum 37
170. Commentary on Zephaniah 42
171. Commentary on Psalms (A) 42
172. Commentaries on unidentified texts 50
173. Commentary on Psalms (B) 51
174. Florilegium 53
175. Testimonia 57
176. *Tanḥûmîm* 60
177. Catena (A) 67
178. — 74
179. Lamentations 75
180. The Ages of Creation 77
181. — 79
182. Catena (B) 80
183. — 81
184. — 82
185. — 85
186. — 88

INDEX OF HEBREW WORDS APPEARING IN NON-CANONICAL TEXTS 92

LIST OF PLATES

I. **158** Biblical Paraphrase: Genesis, Exodus
II. **159** Ordinances
III. **160** Vision of Samuel
IV. **161** pIsa[a]
V. **161** pIsa[a]
VI. **162** pIsa[b]
VII. **163** pIsa[c]
VIII. **163** pIsa[c]
IX. **164** pIsa[d] **165** pIsa[e]
X. **166** pHos[a] **167** pHos[b]
XI. **167** pHos[b]
XII. **168** pMic(?) **169** pNah
XIII. **169** pNah
XIV. **169** pNah **170** pZeph **171** pPss[a]
XV. **171** pPss[a]
XVI. **171** pPss[a]
XVII. **171** pPss[a]
XVIII. **172** pUnid **173** pPss[b] **181**
XIX. **174** Florilegium
XX. **174** Florilegium
XXI. **175** Testimonia
XXII. **176** *Tanḥûmîm*
XXIII. **176** *Tanḥûmîm*
XXIV. **177** Catena[a]
XXV. **177** Catena[a] **178**
XXVI. **179** Lamentations **183**
XXVII. **180** The Ages of Creation **182** Catena[b]
XXVIII. **184**
XXIX. **185**
XXX. **185**
XXXI. **186**

(*Copyright of the Palestine Archaeological Museum*)

158. BIBLICAL PARAPHRASE: GENESIS, EXODUS

(PL. I)

1–2: Gen 32^{25-32} Ex 4^{27-28}

]ץ למען[
]שרית ופ[
] 25 וי[ותר י]עק[וב ל]בדו שמה ויאבק[
]בהאבקו עמו [ו]יאחזהו 27 ויאמ[ר] אל[יו 26
]אלי 28 ויאמר לו מה שמכה [ויגד] לו[
]אנשים ותוכל 30 ויש^א^ל י[ע]קוב [ו]יאמ[ר הגי]ד ^נא^ לי מ[ה 29
ויבר]ך אותו שם ויאמר לו יפרכה יה[וה וירב]כה[
ד]עת ובינה ויצילכה מכול חמס ו°[
עד היום הזה ועד דורות עולם[
וילך לדרכו בברכו אותו שם וי[
32 לו השמש כאשר עבר את פנוא[ל
ביום ההואה ויאמר אל תוא[כל
33 על שתי כפות הירך עד ה[יום הזה
Ex 4^{27} אל אהרון לאמור לך לקרא[ת
28 דברי יהוה אשר ש[לח]ו ואת כול [האותות
יהוה לי לאמור בהוציאכה את[
ללכת עבדים והנה המה שלושי[ם
יהוה אלוהים[ ]ל[
נשל[ ]ל[ ]°[

L. 3, Gen 32^{25}: שמה. Addl. to MT.
L. 4, v. 26: ויאחזהו. Addl. to MT.
v. 27: אלי. Addl. to MT.
L. 5, v. 28: לו. MT has אליו.
שמכה. The *plēnē* script in the suffixes is normal in this document, against MT's defective writing.
[ויגד] לו? MT has ויאמר יעקב.
L. 6, v. 30: וישאל. The *'āleph* has been inserted above the line.
יעקוב. MT defectively written.
הגיד נא. The last two letters have been written above the line. MT has הגידה נא.
לי (as LXX Syr Vulg). Additional to MT.
מה. Addl. to MT.
L. 7: ויברך אותו שם. So the end of v. 30, but our document must have been considerably expanded from MT.
אותו. MT defectively written.

'And he said unto him, May Yah[weh] make thee fruitful [*and multiply*] thee . . .' Cf. Gen. 28^{3}.
L. 8: 'kn]owledge and understanding, and that he may deliver thee from all violence *and* [. . .'
L. 9: 'unto this day and for everlasting generations [. . .'
L. 10: 'And he went on his way when he had blessed him there, and [. . .'
L. 12: 'in that day, and he said, Thou shalt not ea[t. . .'
L. 13, v. 33: שתי כפות. MT has כף.
L. 14, Ex 4^{27}: אהרון. MT defectively written.
לאמור. Addl. to MT.
L. 15, v. 28: כול. The *plēnē* writing of this word is normal for this document, against MT's defective script.
L. 16: 'Yahweh to me, saying, When thou hast brought forth[. . .' Cf. Ex 3^{12}.
L. 17: 'to go (as) *slaves*, and behold they were thirt[y . . .'
L. 18: 'Yahweh, God[. . .'

3: Gen $32^{31(?)}$

ויקרא יעקוב[
בארץ הזות מ◦[
אבותי לבוא אל֯[

L. 1: 'And Jacob called[. . .' (cf. Gen 32^{31}).
L. 2: 'in this land[. . .'
L. 3: 'my fathers to come *to*[. . .'

4: Ex 3^{12} 24^{4-6}

]צוה לכה֯[
3^{12} העם ממצרים תעבד֯[ון
24^{4} למספר שנים עשר֯ שבט֯י֯[ישראל
5 ויעל את העולה֯ על המזב[ח
6 באגונות וחצ[י ה]דם זרק על ה֯[מזבח
אשר היראתי אל אברהם ואל ◦◦◦◦◦[
אתם להי֯[ות] להמה֯ ול[ע]ם לאלוהים ◦[
ע]ד֯ עול[ם . . .]ת֯ ע֯[◦]ל[. . .]◦ יהוה ◦[

L. 2, Ex 3^{12}: cf. ff. 1–2, l. 16.
L. 3, 24^{4}: למספר. Addl. to MT.
L. 4, v. 5: ויעל את העולה. MT has ויעלו עלת.
על המזבח. Addl. to MT.
L. 5, v. 6: באגונות. MT has באַגָּנֹת.
L. 6: 'which I *showed* to Abraham and to [. . .'. Cf. Gen 12^{1} Deut 34^{4}.
היראתי for הראיתי?
ואל is followed by an erasure.
L. 7: 'with them to b[e] for them and for the [peo]ple gods . . .'
L. 8: '*fo*]*r* eve[r . . .] *Yahweh* [. . .'

5: Ex 19^{17-23}

17 בתח]תית

19]השופר

21]◦ ויאמר יהוה אל

22 פ]ן יפרוץ בהמה

23]◦ ההר וק[דשתו

L. 2, Ex 19^{19}: השופר. MT defectively written.
L. 4, v. 22: יפרוץ בהמה. MT has יפרץ בהם.

6: Ex 20^{19-22} Deut 5^{29} $18^{18-20, 22}$

]א֯תה[

20^{19} ול]וא ידב֯ר֯ ע֯[מנו

20 בא הא֯[לוהים ובע]בו[ר] תהיה י[ר]את[ו

21 האלהים 22 ו֯[יאמר] יהוה אל מוש֯ה֯ ל[אמור

Deut. 5^{29} והיה הלבב הזה להמה ליראה[

את קול דברי אמו[ר] 18^{18} ל֯המה נביא[

19 א֯שר לוא ישמע֯ [א]ל ד֯ב֯ר֯[י

20 לד]בר או אשר י֯ד֯[בר

22 א]ש֯ר ידבר֯ [הנביא

]ל ◦◦[

L. 2, v. 19: ולוא. MT has ואל.
L. 4, v. 22: מושה. *Plēnē* script as 4Q *Testimonia* (**175**) l. 1. MT defectively written.
L. 5, Deut 5^{29}: הלבב הזה. MT (and 4Q *Testimonia*, l. 3) has לבבם זה.
L. 6: 'the sound of my words, sa[y] to them, "A prophet [. . ."' This introductory passage to the quotation of Deut 18^{18} is missing from both Sam (Ex 20^{21}) and 4Q *Testimonia*.
L. 7, 18^{19}: לוא, in *plēnē* script as elsewhere in this document (and 4Q *Testimonia*, l. 7). MT defectively written.
L. 8, v. 20: או אשר. MT has ואשר.

7–8: Ex $20^{12, 16, 17}$ Deut $5^{30, 31}$ Ex 20^{22-26} $21^{1, 3, 4, 6, 8, 10}$

12 את אבי]כ֯ה ואת א֯מ֯כ֯ה֯[

16 ברע]כ֯ה עד שקר 17 לוא תחמוד אשת ר֯[עכה

Deut. 5^{30} ויאמר יהוה אל מושה לך אמור להמה שובו ל֯[כמה

31 ואת המשפטים אשר תלמדם ועשו בארץ אשר֯[

וישובו העם איש לאהליו ויעמוד מושה לפני[

Ex. 20^{22} ראיתמה כי מן השמים דברתי עמכמה 23 לוא תעש[ון

[24] עליו את עולותיכֹה ואת שלמיכֹה את צואניכֹה[

[25] תעשה לי לוא תבנה אתהנה גזית כי חרבכה[

[26] עֹליו [21¹] אלה המשפטים [אשר] תֹשֹׂ[ים

[3] אם] בֹגֹפיו בא בגפיו יצא אֹ[ם

[4]]ל[א]דֹוֹנֹוֹ וֹהֹוֹאֹ[

[6(?)] וֹהֹ[גישו

[6] אזנו במרצעֹ[

[8] והפ]דה לע[ם

[10] ועונתה] ל[וא

L. 1, 20^{12}: אמכה . . . אביכה, *plēnē* spelling of the suffixes as regularly in this document against MT's defective writing.

L. 2, v. 17: לוא written *plēnē* as regularly, against MT's defective writing.

תחמוד. MT defectively written.

אשת (= LXX). MT has בית (cf. Deut 5^{21}).

L. 3: 'And Yahweh said to Moses'. Addl. to MT.

אמור להמה. MT defectively written.

L. 4, v. 31: ואת המשפטים. MT omits את.

L. 5: 'And the people returned, each man to his tents, and Moses stood before . . .' Addl. to MT.

L. 7, v. 24: עולותיכמה . . . שלמיכמה . . . צואניכמה. The sing. suffixes have been made plural (= LXX Vulg) by the addition of a *mēm* above the line.

צואניכמה. MT has צאנך.

L. 9, v. 26: עליו. Thus MT, although אליו with Sam is possible. 21^1: אלה (= Sam Vulg). MT has ואלה.

L. 10, v. 3: בגפיו . . . בגפיו (= Sam). MT has בגפו.

L. 11, v. 4: לאדונו. Reconstruction is not certain but traces remaining will not allow לאדניה of MT; cf. Sam (ניו'') Syr LXX^B Vulg.

L. 12, v. 6: והגישו. Reconstruction and position of fragment not certain.

L. 15, v. 10: ועונתה. MT defectively written.

9: Ex $21^{15, 16, 18, 20, 22, 25}$

[15]]יֹוֹמֹתֹ [16] גֹוֹנֹבֹ[

[18] אי]ש את רעהו באבן[

[[20] יכה איש את עבד[ו

[22] וכ]יא ינצו[

[[22] בפליליים[

[[25] תֹחֹתֹ[

L. 1, Ex 21^{16}: גונב. MT has וגנב.

L. 4, v. 22: כיא, as regularly in this document, against MT's כי.

L. 5, v. 22: בפליליים. A scribal error for MT's בפללים.

10–12: Ex 21[32, 34, 35–37] 22[1–11, 13]

32 כס]ף שלוש[ים

34]הבור יש[לם

35 כ]ספו וגם [את המת יחצון] 36 אם נוד[ע] כ[יא שור נג]ח[

] 37 אם יגנוב איש שור או שה וטבחו או מ[כרו

22 1]והוכה ומת אין לו דמים 2 אם זרחה השמש עליו דמים[

3]חמור עד שה חיים אחד שנים ישלם 4 וכי יבעה[

4 כת]בואתו אם כול השדה יבעה מיטב שדהו ומיטב

כרמו י[שלם

ש]לם ישלם המבער את הבערה 6 כיא יתן

איש אל[

7 בע]ל הבית לפני האלוהים אם לוא ילח ידו

במלאכ[ת

8 א]שר יואמר עד ˹כיא הואה זה˺ יהוה יבוא דבר שניהמה[

9]או שור או שה או כול בהמה לשמור[

10]במלאכת [רע]הו ולקח בעליו ולוא

יש[לם 11 ואם] גנוב יגנב[

13 ו]כיא ישאל אי[ש מעם] רעהו בהמה

[ונשבר או מת] בעל[יו

L. 1, Ex 21[32]: שלושים. MT defectively written.
L. 3, v. 36: אם; similarly LXX Vulg Syr. MT has או.
L. 4, v. 37: אם. MT has כי.
יגנוב. MT defectively written.
L. 5, 22[1]: והוכה. MT defectively written.
L. 6, v. 3: אחד. So Sam Syr; addl. to MT.
v. 4: וכי, written, unusually for this MS, defectively, as MT which omits the conjunction, shown also in Kenn Sam Syr. יבעה. MT has יבער.
L. 7, v. 4: כתבואתו אם כול השדה יבעה; similarly Sam (כתבואתה ואם כל השדה יבעה) and LXX; addl. to MT.
מיטיב. The second *yōdh* has been inserted above the line. MT has מֵיטַב.
L. 10, v. 7: לפני האלוהים. MT has אל האלהים.
ילח. A scribal error for ישלח? MT has שלח.
L. 11, v. 8: יואמר; a *plēnē* writing for MT's יאמר.
כיא הואה זה; inserted above the line.
יהוה (= Sam). MT has האלהים.
יבוא. MT defectively written.
L. 12, v. 9: או כול (= Sam; cf. LXX Syr). MT has וכל.
לשמור. MT defectively written.
L. 15, v. 11: גנוב. MT defectively written.
L. 16, v. 13: בהמה, as Syr (cf. LXX ed. Lagarde); addl. to MT.

13: Ex 30[32, 34]

]◦ ◦◦[

30[32] ק]וׄדש הוא קודש קדשים

[34]ול]בׄנׄה זכה ב[ד] בב[ד

L. 2, v. 32: קודש קדשים. MT has קדש.

14

Col. I

ה[

]ר וכול הרוחות

]לברכה להארץ

]שׄה ובארץ מצרים

]◦◦ול יד מצרים וגאלתים

]ה בׄמצרים ואת [רש]ע

]לבב ים במצ[ל]ות

]אשׄר יישבו

]◦◦לי ◦[

Col. II

נ]

[2] . . .] and all the spirits [[3] . . .] for a blessing to the earth [[4] . . .] and in the land of Egypt [[5] . . .] the power of Egypt, and I shall redeem them [[6] . . .] in Egypt, and the [*wick*]*ed* [[7] . . .] the midst of the sea in the depths [[8] . . .] who dwell [. . .

L. 2: הרוחות. The first *wāw* has been inserted above the line.
L. 5: יד has been inserted above the line.
L. 6: the *hē* appearing at the edge of the fragment has been inserted above the line.
L. 7: cf. Ex 15[4–8].

15

]◦ע◦דה[

]ר ה[

159. ORDINANCES

(PLATE. II)

(Already partly published in *Journal of Semitic Studies* 6, i (1961) 71–73)

1

Col. I

ט[

אׄ[

◦ל[

Col. II

]הׄו אל ◦[ ]נׄחל ליׄ[

]◦ל אׄתׄ ◦[ ]ותיו ולכפר לכול פשעיה[ם

ו]עשה איש ממנה גורן וגת הבא לגור[ן

אשׄר ביׄ[שר]אל אשר אין לו יאוכלנה וכנס לו ולב[יתו

השדה יאׄכׄל בפיהו ואל ביתו לוא יבוא להניחו[
ע]ל[ ]כסף הערכים אשר נתנו איש כפר נפשו מחצית[השקל
רק פׄ[עם] אחת יתננו כול ימיו עשרים גרה השקל ב[שקל הקודש
לשש מא[ו]ת האלף מאׄת ככר לשלישית מחצית הככר[
ולחמשים מחצית המׄ[נ]הׄ [עשרים ו]חמשה שקל הכולׄ[
המנה שׄ[◦]מׄ[ ]ל[של]וש לעשרת המנים[
חמ]שה כׄסׄף מעשר הׄ[מנה
שק]ל הקודש מחצ[ית
]האיפה והבת תכון אׄ[חד
ש]לושת העשרונים ◦[

ע]ל העם ועל בׄ[ג]די[הם
י]שראל שרף מוש[ה

[1]. . .] *apportion* to [[2] . . .] his [. . .] and to make atonement for all *the*[*ir*] sins [[3] . . . and if] one should make of it a threshing [-floor] or winepress: he who comes to the threshing-fl[oor . . .] [4] who is in *I*[*sr*]*ael*, who has nothing, shall eat and gather for himself and for [*his*] house-[hold . . .] [5] the field he shall eat for himself but shall not bring (it) to his house to deposit it. [[6] *Con*]*cerning* [. . .] money of Valuations that a man gives as a ransom for his soul: half a [shekel.] [7] Only once shall he give it during his lifetime—the shekel is twenty gerahs according to [the shekel of the Sanctuary.] [8] For the Six Hundred Thousand: one hundred talents; for The Third: half a talent; [. . .] [9] and for The Fifty: half a mi[n]a—[*twenty*]-five shekels; the *total* [. . .] [10] the mina [. . . *th*]*ree* for ten minas [[11] . . . *fi*]*ve* (shekels) of silver: a tenth of a [mina . . . [12] shek]el of the Sanctuary, hal[f . . . [13] . . .] The ephah and the bath are of the s[ame] measure [[14] . . . th]ree tenths [. . . [16] . . . *con*]*cerning* the people and concerning [*their*] *gar*[*ments* [17] . . . I]srael, Moses burnt[. . .

L. 3: גורן וגת for גורן ויקב of Deut 15^{14} 16^{13}, as in CD xii 9–10.
L. 4: אשר אין לו. Cf. Ex 22^{2}.
L. 6: cf. Ex 30^{12} Lev 27^{1-8}.
כפר. The *kaph* has been inserted above the line.
L. 7: עשרים גרה השקל. Cf. Ex 30^{13} Nu 18^{16}.
L. 8: שש מאות האלף. Cf. Ex 12^{37} Nu 11^{21}.
שלישית, 'The Third', the half-a-talent levy for which implies a force of 3,000 men. Cf. II Sam 18^{2} and $23^{18, 19}$ where the dubious שלשה (Ktb v. 18 שלשי) may possibly conceal our word.
L. 9: עשרים וחמשה שקל. I.e. the mina = 50 shekels, as in Ezek 45^{12} (LXX); cf. l. 11.
L. 13: האיפה. The *yōdh* has been inserted above the line. For the equation of ephah and bath, cf. Ezek 45^{11} and 4QD[c] I. ii. 2.
תכון: MT Ezek 45^{11} has תֹּכֶן.
L. 14: cf. Lev 14^{10} Nu 15^{9} $28^{12, 20, 28}$ $29^{3, 9, 14}$.
L. 16: בגדיהם. Reconstruction suggested by ff. 2–3, ll. 6–7.
L. 17: cf. possibly, Ex 32^{20}.

2–4

ואם[ ]גׄדׄאו שׄוקד משפׄח[ה
לעיני ישׄרׄ[אל ל]וׄאׄ יעבודו הגויים בזר[ים
מצרים ויצו עליהיהם לבלתי ימכרׄ ממכרת עבד ו◦[עשר]הׄ אנשים
וכוהנים שנים ונשפטו לפני שנים העשר האלה ◦[
דבר בישראל על נפש על פיהם ישאלו ואשר ימרה[
יומת אשר עשה ביד רמה אל יהיו כלי גבר על אשה כול [
יכס בשלמות אשה ואל ילבש כתונתׄ אשה כיא [ת]ועבה הוא
כי יוצו איש שם רע על בתולת ישׄראל אם ב[ ] קחתו אותה יואמר ובקרוה
נאמנות ואם לוא כחש עליה והומתה ואם ב◦[ ] ענה בה ונענש שני מנים
ושלח כול ימיו כול[ ]אׄשׄרׄ[ ]ל◦◦ית ◦◦◦[

[1] And if [. . .] they *cut off* the guardian of a famil[y . . .] [2] before Isra[el] they shall [n]ot serve Gentiles among *stra[ngers* . . .] [3] Egypt, and he commanded them that one should not be sold as a slave is sold. And [. . . te]n men [4] and two priests, and they shall be judged before these twelve [. . .] [5] spoke in Israel against anyone, according to their evidence they shall inquire and whoever rebels [. . .] [6] shall be put to death since he has behaved arrogantly. Let not a man's garb be upon a woman. Every [. . .] [7] be covered with a woman's mantles, but let him not be dressed in a woman's tunic, for such is an abomination. [8] If they defame a man concerning a virgin of Israel, if his taking her was by [. . . ,] let him say so, and they shall examine her [9] as to (her) trustworthiness, and if he has not lied about her, she shall be put to death. But if by [. . .] he humbled her, he shall be fined two minas [10] and be expelled all his life. All [. . .] who [. . .

L. 1: **גדאו**. If this is a correct reading, possibly an error for **גדעו**.
Ll. 2–3: cf. Lev 25^{42}.
Ll. 3–4: **עשרה אנשים וכוהנים שנים**. F. 3 is only tentatively positioned. In CD x 4 ff. the judiciary body consists of ten members, four of them priests, and in 1QS viii 1 ff. of twelve laymen and three priests (cf. also ix 10 and perhaps 4QpIsa^{d} (**164**) f. 1 l. 4).
Ll. 5–6: **יומת . . . ימרה**. Cf. Jos 1^{18}.
L. 6: **יהיו כלי גבר**. MT of Deut 22^{5} reads **כלי** as singular with **יהיה**, and **לא** for **אל**.
Ll. 6–7: **יכס בשלמות אשה [. . .] כול** is additional to MT.
L. 7: **ואל ילבש כתונת אשה**. MT has **ולא ילבש גבר שמלת אשה**.
כיא תועבה הוא. MT has **כי תועבת יהוה אלהיך כל עשה אלה**.
L. 8: **יוצו** for **יוצאו**; cf. Deut $22^{14,19}$.
Ll. 8–10: cf. Deut 22^{28-29} and Ex 22^{15-16}.
L. 9: **ונענש שני מנים**. The fine is the amount required by Deut 22^{19} from a husband falsely accusing his wife of unchastity.

5

]םׄ אל וימותו פשר[
בני לוׄ[י
]בׄמשפט ואשר אמׄ[ר

9

]בקחת מושה את [

]יצאו שמה פשר הדבר[

ד]רוש התורה בצוקה ו◦[

אש]ר דבר מושה[

]כול[

[1] . . .] God, and they died. The interpretation of [. . . [2] . . .] The *Levi*[*tes* . . . [3] . . .] in judgement. As it sa[ys . . . [4] . . .] when Moses took [. . . [5] . . .] they went out thence. The interpretation of the passage is [. . . [6] . . . in]terpret the Law in distress and [. . . [7] . . . *a*]*s* Moses spoke [. . . [8] . . .] *all* [. . .

L. 1: possibly derived from Lev 16^{1}.
L. 6: cf. Deut 4^{29-30} (Sam).

6

]להק[

7

]◦ קל◦[

8

]שה א[
]ל[

9

י]שרא[ל

160. THE VISION OF SAMUEL

(PL. III)

1: I Sam 3^{14-17}

כ]יא נשב[עתי ל]בית [עלי

]◦[ ]שמע שמוא[ל א]ת דב[רי

]שמואל שכב לפני עלי ויקום ויפתח את ד[לתות

]להגיד את המשא לעלי ויען עלי ו[

הו]דיעני את מראה האלוהים אל◦[

]אם תכחד ממני ד[בר

]שמואל ◦[

[1] . . . f]or I have swor[n to] the house of [Eli . . . [2] . . .] Samuel heard the wo[rds of . . . [3] . . .] Samuel lay down before Eli, and he arose and opened the d[oors . . . [4] . . .] to tell the oracle to Eli. And Eli answered and [. . . [5] . . . Let] me know the vision of God, do not [. . . [6] . . .] if you hide from me a w[ord . . . [7] . . .] Samuel [. . .

L. 1, I Sam 3^{14}: כיא. MT has לכן.
L. 3, v. 15: שמואל שכב. MT has וישכב שמואל.
לפני עלי is additional to MT, but cf. f. 7, l. 4.
ויקום is additional to MT, but cf. LXX (ὤρθρισεν τὸ πρωὶ).
L. 4: להגיד. MT has מהגיד.

המשא. MT has המראה.
לעלי. MT has אל עלי.
ויען. MT (v. 16) has ויקרא.
L. 5: MT has מה חדבר אשר דבר אליך.

2

]אותם ולהבר כפים לֹ[

. . .] them, and to cleanse hands [. . .

3–4

Col. III	Col. II	Col. I
מחלה את[	]עֹבֹדכה לוא עצרתי כוח עד זואת כיא	
שמוֹ[	]קֹוו אלוהי לעמכה ועזרתה היה לו והעלהו	
	אל ה]שֹׁמים הואהֹ [. . .] ל[ו]הֹעמד להמה סלע למרואש כיא תהלתכה	
	בֹּארצות ובימיםֹ[ ]דֹשׁ◦ ובזעם שונאי עמכה תגביר תפארת	
	אתה בראתה[ ]וממלכה וידעו כול עמי ארצותיכהֹ[	
	וה◦[י]בֹינו רבים כיא עמכה הואהֹ[	מ]רֹאה
	קדו]שׁיכה אשר הקדשתֹ[ה	

Col. I. [6] . . . vi]sion

Col. II. [1] . . .] thy *servant*, I retained no strength until this, for [. . . [2] . . .] they waited, O my God, for thy people. But he was a help to him and he lifted him up [[3] to the] heavens, he [. . . and] will raise up for them a rock for a *headstone* for thy renown is [4] in lands and in seas [. . .] and in the indignation of them that hate thy people thou shalt prevail gloriously. [5] Thou hast created [. . .] and a kingdom that all the peoples of thy lands shall know [. . .] [6] and [. . .] many shall [un]derstand that thy people are (he is with thee) [. . . [7] . . . thy [*ho*]*ly ones* whom thou hast sanctified [. . .

Col. III. [1] *makes sick* [. . .

F. 3–4. col. II. L. 1: לוא עצרתי כוח. Cf. Dan $10^{8, 16}$.
L. 3: the placing of f. 3 is only tentative. העמד, probably defectively written for העמיד.

5

]מטיט יון[
]עֹוז עמכה ומ[
]יֹראתכה על ◦◦ל[

[1] . . .] from the miry bog [. . . [2] . . .] *strength* of thy people (with thee) and [. . . [3] . . .] thy fear is upon [. . .

6

]לכה̊ ואתה תהיה להמה ות◦[
כי]א אתה למרישונה ב◦[

[1] . . .] thine and thou shalt be theirs, and [. . . [2] . . . *fo*]*r* thou at the beginning [. . .

7

]פ̊נ̊י יה̊י ע[
]◦גרתי עמו מוע̊ד̊י ונלויתי ^לו^ מ◦
]יחלתי פניה רכוש והון ומחיר[
]◦דוני ובחרתי לשכוב לפני יצוע̊[

[1] . . .] *may there be* [. . . [2] . . .] I *stayed* with him for *my appointed time* and joined myself to him [. . . [3] . . .] I did [*not*] seek her favour with property or wealth or purchase-price [. . . [4] . . .] they [. . .] me but I chose to lie before the couch of . . .

L. 2: לו, inserted above the line.
L. 3: יחלתי, presumably a *pē-yōdh* bi-form of the normal חלה.
L. 4: לשכוב for BH לשכַב, cf. 1QS vii 10.
לפני יצוע. Cf. f. 1, l. 3, n.

161. COMMENTARY ON ISAIAH (A)

(PL. IV–V)

(Partly published already in *JBL* lxxv (1956) 177–82)

1: Quotation from Isa 10[21] and *pešer* on vv. 20–21

שאר ישוב שאר יעקוב] אל א̊[ל גבור
שאר י]ש̊ראל היאה[
]א̊ילי אנשי חילו ופ◦[
מו]ע̊ד̊י הכוהנים כיא היא[ה

[1] . . . A remnant will return, the remnant of Jacob,] to the [mighty] Go[d . . . [2] . . . '*remnant of* I]srael': it is [. . . [3] . . .] the *leaders* of his warrior band, and [. . . [4] . . . *assembly*] *places* of the priests, for it [. . .

L. 2: שאר ישראל. The reconstruction is based on v. 20, the gender of היאה notwithstanding, the gender of the pronoun having been attracted into that of the following word, perhaps עדת.

L. 3: אילי, or the remnant of גאולי or the like. The fragment here appended has shrunk a little, but the join seems certain.

2–4: Quotation of Isa $10^{22, 24-27}$ and *pešer*

]◦י בני[
א]שׁר אמר אם הי̊[ה עמכה ישראל כחול הים
שאר ישוב בו כליון חר]וץ ושוטף צד[קה
]גׄה ורבים יוב[דו
]◦◦[...]מט[ה...ב]ארץ באמת ◦[
[לכן כׄ[ה אמ]ר אד[וני 𐤉𐤄𐤅𐤄 צבאות אל תירא עמי
יש]ב ציוןׄ[מאשור ב]שׁבט [יככה ומטהו ישא עליך בדרך מצרים
כיא] עוד מע[ט מזער וכלה זעם ואפי על תבלית]ם̊ ויעׄ[ורר עליו
𐤉𐤄𐤅𐤄 צבאות שוט כמכת מדין בצור עו]רב ומטׄ[הו על הים
ונשאו בדרך מצרים והיה ביום ההואה] י̊סור סב[לו מעל שכמך

[1] . . .] of the children of [. . . [2] . . .] as he said, 'If [thy people Israel be like the sand of the sea, [3] only a remnant of them will return. Destruction is dec]reed, and overflowing with righteous[ness . . . [4] . . .] and many will per[ish . . . [5] . . .] *ro*[*d* . . . *in* the] land in truth [. . . [6] . . .] 'Therefore th[us say]s the Lo[rd, Yahweh of hosts, Be not afraid, my people [7] who dwe]ll in Zion, [of the Assyrians when with the] rod [they smite you and lift up their staff against you as did the Egyptians. [8] For] in a very little [while my indignation will come to an end and my anger will be directed to] their [destruction.] And [Yahweh of hosts] will wi[eld against them [9] a scourge as when he smote Midian at the rock of O]reb; and [his] rod [will be over the sea, [10] and he will lift it as he did in Egypt. And in that day his] burden will depart [from thy shoulder . . .

L. 2, Isa 10^{22}: אם היה. MT has כי אם יהיה.
L. 3: ושוטף. MT omits the conjunction.
L. 8, v. 26: ויעורר. MT has ועורר.

5–6: Quotation of Isa 10^{28-32} and *pešer*

]◦◦ ◦[
]בׄשובם ממדבר הע[מים
]נשיא העדה ואחר יס[ו]ר מעלה̊[ם

]בׄא אל עיתה עבר [במגרון] למכמ[ש
יפקיד כליו עברו] מׄעברה גבעׄ מלון למו חר[דה הרמה גבעת
שאול נסה צהלי] קׄולכי בת גלים הקשיב[י לישה עניה ענתות
נדדה]מׄדמנה ישבי הגׄבים הׄעיזו עוד [היום בנב לעמד
ינפף]יׄדו הר בת ציון גבעת ירושלים[
]פתגם לאחרית הימים לבוא ◦[
חר]דׄה בעלותו מבקעת עכו ללחם בׄי ◦[
]דׄה ואׄין כמוהוׄ ובכול ערי ה ◦[
]ועד גבול ירושלים[

[2] . . .] when they return from the Desert of the *Peo*[*ples* . . . [3] . . .] Prince of the Congregation, and afterwards [. . .] will depart from [*them* . . . [5] . . .] 'he has come to Aiath; he has passed [through Migron,] at Michma[sh [6] he stores his baggage; they have crossed over] the pass, at Geba is their lodging; [Ramah] tre[mbles, Gibeah of [7] Saul has fled. Cry] aloud, O daughter of Gallim! Hearken, [O Laishah! Answer her, O Anathoth!] [8] Madmenah [is in flight,] the inhabitants of Gebim flee for safety. This very [day he will halt at Nob, [9] he will shake] his fist at the mount of the daughter of Zion, the hill of Jerusalem. [' [10] . . .] a decree at the end of days to come [. . . [11] *tre*]*mbles* when he goes up from the Vale of Accho to war against [. . . [12] . . .] and there is none like him, and among all the cities of the [. . . [13] . . .] and unto the boundary of Jerusalem [. . .

Ll. 2–4: presumably the *pešer* on v. 27 quoted in f. 4.
L. 2: ממדבר העמים. Cf. 1QM i 2–3, and possibly 4QpIsa^{e} (**165**) f. 5, l. 6.
L. 3: נשיא העדה. Cf. 1QSb v 20; CD vii 20.
L. 5. The beginning of v. 28 was perhaps preceded by the end of v. 27, as commonly conjectured.
אל. MT has על.
עיתה. MT has עית.
L. 6: למו. MT has לנו.
L. 7: קולכי. MT has קולך.
L. 9: בת = MT Qre; Ktb has בית.
ירושלים = MT Qre *perpetuum*; Ktb has לם״.

7

נש]ברי ל[ב
]שׂפל ◦[

[1] . . . *bro*]*ken hear*[*ted* . . . [2] . . .] low [. . .

On this fragment's tentative positioning, see the note to line 1 of f. 8.

8–10: Quotations of Isa $10^{33, 34}$ 11^{1-5} and *pešer*

ורמי הקו]מ֯ה [גדועי]ם֯
והגבהים ישפלו וניקפו] ס֯בכי [היער] בברזל ולבנון באדיר
יפול   פשרו על הכ]ת֯יאים אש֯[ר] י֯כ֯ת֯[ו] ב֯י֯ת֯ י֯שראל ועניי
]כ֯ול הגואים וגבורים יחתו ונמס ל[בם
רמי] הקומה גדועים המה גבורי כת֯[יאים
ואשר אמ]ר ונ̓קפו סובכי [ה]י֯ער בברזל ה[מה
]◦ם למלחמת כתיא֯י֯ם֯ ולבנון בא[דיר
יפול   פשרו על ה]כתיאים אשר ינת[נו] ביד גדולו[
]◦י֯ם בברחו מלפ֯נ֯י֯ ל◦[. . .]מ֯[

ויצא חטר מגזע] י֯שי ונצר משר֯[שיו יפרה ונח]ה עלו ר֯[וח

רוח חכמ]ה ובינה רוח עצ[ה וגבורה] רוח דע[ת 𐤉𐤄𐤅𐤄
ויראת 𐤉𐤄𐤅𐤄 והריחו ביראת] 𐤉𐤄𐤅𐤄֯ [ולוא] למראה ע֯[יניו
ישפוט ולוא למשמע אוזניו יוכי]ח֯ ושפ֯ט֯ [בצדק דלים והוכיח
[במישור לענוי ארץ והכה ארץ בשבט פיו וברוח שפתיו ימית]
רשע והיה צדק אזור מ]ת֯ניו וא֯[מונה אזור חלציו
פשרו על צמח] דויד העומד באח֯[רית הימים
או]יבו ואל יסומכנו ב֯[...ה]ת֯ורה[
כ]סא כבוד נזר ק[ודש] ובגדי רוק֯מ֯ו֯[ת
]ן֯ בידו ובכול הג֯[וא״]ם ימשול ומגוג
כו]ל֯ העמים תשפוט חרבו ואשר אמר לוא
]ולוא למשמע אוזניו יוכיח פשרו אשר
]וכאשר יורוהו כן ישפוט ועל פיהם
]עמו יצא אחד מכוהני השם ובידו בגדי֯[

[1] . . . the great in hei]ght [will be hewn down, [2] and the lofty will be brought low.] The thickets of [the forest will be cut down] with an axe, and Lebanon by a majestic one [[3] will fall. *Its interpretation concerns* the Ki]ttim who will *beat down* the House of Israel and the poor ones of [. . . [4] . . .] all the Gentiles and warriors will be dismayed, and [their he]arts will melt [. . . [5] . . . 'the great] in height will be hewn down': they are the warriors of the Kitt[im [6] . . . *and as it say*]*s*, 'the thickets of [the] forest will be cut down with an axe', th[ey are [7] . . .] to the war of the Kittim; 'and Lebanon by a ma[jestic one [8] will fall': *its interpretation concerns the*] Kittim who will be given into the hand of his great one [[9] . . .] when he flees from before [. . . [11] 'And there shall come forth a shoot from the stump of] Jesse, and a branch [shall grow out of his] roots. And the spi[rit of Yahweh shall re]st upon him, [[12] the spirit of wisd]om and understanding, the spirit of coun[sel and might,] the spirit of knowled[ge [13] and the fear of Yahweh, and his delight shall be in the fear of] Yahweh. [And he shall not judge] by the sight of [his] ey[es, [14] or dec]ide [by what his ears shall hear;] but he will judge [the poor with righteousness, and decide [15] with equity for the meek of the earth. And he shall smite the earth with the rod of his mouth, and with the breath of his lips he shall slay [16] the wicked. Righteousness shall be the girdle of] his waist, and fai[thfulness the girdle of his loins.' [17] *Its interpretation concerns the Shoot of*] David who will arise at the e[nd of days . . . [18] . . .] his [*ene*]*mies*, and God will sustain him with [. . . *the*] Law [. . . [19] . . . th]rone of glory, a ho[ly] crown, and garments of variegat[ed stuff . . . [20] . . .] in his hand, and over all the *G*[*entile*]*s* he will rule, and Magog [[21] . . . al]l the peoples shall his sword judge. And as it says, 'Not [[22] . . .] or decide by what his ears shall hear': its interpretation is that [[23] . . .] and according to what they teach him so shall he judge, and according to their command [[24] . . .] *with him*, one of the priests of repute shall go out with garments of [. . .] in his hand [. . .

In the preliminary publication f. 8 was treated as two separate fragments, but later recognized as belonging together. Shrinkage and darkening of the skin had disguised their relationship, and the depredation of worms has left an actual contact only possible at one place (l. 5).

L. 1. This reconstruction assumes that this and the previous line contained the text of Isa 10^{33}, probably following straight on after the *pešer* of v. 32 contained in ff. 5–6. If, however, f. 7 stands correctly in the position tentatively assigned to it in Pl. V, i.e. its שפל of the 2nd line corresponding with ישפלו in the reconstructed l. 2 of f. 8, then the preceding line does not represent any part of v. 33 according to MT.

L. 2, v. 34: סבכי; cf. סובכי in l. 6. The remains of the letter before the *bēth* do not easily permit of the reconstruction of a *plēnē wāw*.

ולבנון. MT has והלבנון.

L. 6: וניקפו. The *yōdh* has been inserted above the line. MT has ונקף.

סובכי. MT has סבכי (cf. שובך of II Sam 18⁹ and סְבכו of Jer 4⁷).

L. 7: לבנון. Cf. 4QpNah (**169**) ff. 1–2, ll. 7–8.

L. 11, 11²: עלו. MT has עליו.

L. 16, 11⁵: MT has והאמונה.

L. 17: צמח דויד. Cf. Jer 23⁵ etc., 4QFlorileg. (**174**) ff. 1–2, col. I, l. 11; 4QpGen ('Patriarchal Blessings': *JBL* lxxv (1956) pp. 174–76, ll. 3–4.

162. COMMENTARY ON ISAIAH (B)

(PL. VI)

(Published already in *JBL* lxxvii (1958) pp. 215–21)

Col. I: Quotations from Isa 5⁵, ⁶ and *pešer*

הסר משוכתו ויהי לבער פר]ץ גדרו ויהי למרמס אשר
אמר ...   ]◦ פשר הדבר אשר עזבם
]דׄ ואשר אמר יעלה שמיר
ושית ...   ]עת ואשר וֹאֹשֹׁרֹ
אמר ...   ]◦נת דרך
]עׄיניהם

[1] I will remove its hedge that it may be for burning; I will break] down its wall that it may be for trampling'; as [[2] *it says* . . .] The interpretation of the phrase is that he forsook them [[3] . . .] and as it says, 'there shall come up briers [[4] and thorns . . .'] and as [[5] *it says* . . .] the way of [[6] . . .] their eyes

L. 1, Isa 5⁵: ויהי. MT has והיה; cf. עזבם in l. 2.
L. 3, v. 6: יעלה. MT has ועלה.
L. 4: the second ואשר (*wāw* inserted above the line) has been erased with dots placed above and below the letters.

Col. II: Quotations from Isa 5¹¹⁻¹⁴, ²⁴⁻²⁵ and *pešer*

פשר הדבר לאחרית הימים לחובת הארץ מפני החרב והרעב והיה
בעת פקדת הארץ הוי משכימי בבקר שכר ירדפו מאחרי בנשף יין
ידלקם והיה כנור ונבל ותוף וחליל יין משתיהם ואת פעל יהוה
לא הביטו ומעשי ידו לא ראו לכן גלה עמי מבלי דעת וכבדו מתי רעב
והמנו צחי צמא לכן הרחיבה שאול נפשה ופערה פיה לבלי חוק
וירד הדרה והמנה ושאנה עליז בא אלה הם אנשי הלצון

אשר בירושלים הם אשר מאסו את תורת יהוה ואת אמרת קדוש
ישראל נאצו על כן חרה אף יהוה בעמו ויט ידו עליו ויכהו וירגזו
הה֯ר֯י֯ם֯ ותהי נבלתם כסחה בקרב החוצות בכל זאת לא שב
אפו ועוד ידו נטויה] היא עדת אנשי הלצון אשר בירושלים

1 The interpretation of the phrase concerns the end of days, at the doom of the earth before the sword and famine; and it shall be 2 in the time of the earth's visitation. 'Woe to those who rise up early in the morning, that they may follow strong drink; that tarry late into the night till wine 3 inflames them! And there shall be harp and lute and tabret and pipe (and) wine of their feasts; but the deed of Yahweh 4 they have not regarded, neither have they considered the works of his hand. Therefore my people have gone into captivity for lack of knowledge; and the honourable men are famished, 5 and their multitude are parched with thirst. Therefore Sheol has enlarged her gullet and opened her mouth without measure; 6 and her glory and multitude have descended, and her tumult and he who exalts in her.' These are the Men of Scoffing 7 who are in Jerusalem. Those are they who 'have rejected the law of Yahweh, and the word of the Holy One of 8 Israel they have despised. Therefore is the anger of Yahweh kindled against his people and he has stretched forth his hand against them, and has smitten them, and the hills 9 trembled, and their carcases were as refuse in the midst of the streets. For all this his anger is turned not away 10 and his hand is stretched out still.' That is the congregation of the Men of Scoffing who are in Jerusalem.

Ll. 1–2: *pešer* on Isa 5^{10}.
ברעב. Cf. pHos[a] (**166**) ii 12; pPs[a] (**171**) ff. 1–2, ii 1; iii 3, 4; (**172**) f. 1, l. 2.
L. 3, v. 11: ידלקם. MT has ידליקם.
v. 12: ותוף. MT has תף.
יין. MT has ויין.
L. 4: הביטו = 1QIsa[a]; MT has יביטו.
ומעשי. MT has ומעשה.
ידו. MT has ידיו.
v. 13: וכבדו. MT has וכבודו.
L. 5: והמנו. MT has והמונו.
צחי. MT has צחה.
v. 14: חוק. MT has חק.
L. 6: והמנה. MT has והמונה.
ושאנה. MT has ושאונה.
עליז בא. MT has ועלז בה.
אנשי הלצון. Cf. l. 10; Isa 28^{14} CD xx 11 (i 14: ״איש הל).
L. 7, v. 24: יהוה. MT adds צבאות.
L. 9, v. 25: כסחה. MT has כסוחה.
החוצות. MT omits the article.

Col. III: Quotations from Isa 5^{29-30} 6^{9} (?) and *pešer*

ואין מ[ציל .;; וינהם עליו ביום ההוא 5^{29-30}
כנהמ[ת ים ... ונבט לארץ והנה חשך צר ואור חשך v. 30
בער֯[יפיה
הוא]

האלה[

הבאי̇[ם

אמר[

ראו ר̇[או ואל תדעו ? $6^{9(?)}$

תבי ∘[

The width of this column was either considerably shorter than the second or something other than a simple statement of MT filled the lacuna.

163. COMMENTARY ON ISAIAH (C)

(PL. VII–VIII)

(Already partly published in *JBL* lxxvii (1958) 215–21)

1

]∘∘[

]∘ הואה[

]ו̇בלע דרך̇[

כאשר כ]ת̇וב עלי̇ו̇ בי̇ר̇[מיה

L. 3: cf. Isa 3^{12}.
L. 4: 'as it is wr]itten concerning *him* by *Jere[miah. . .*'

2–3: Quotation from Isa $8^{7, 8, 9(?)}$ and *pešer*

ולכן הנה אדני מע]לה עליה̊[ם] את מ̇י̇ הנהר ה[עצומים והרבים את מלך אשור

ואת כל כבודו ועלה] על כל אפיקו והלך על כל גדו[תיו וחלף ביהודה שטף] ועב[ר

עד צואר יגיע וה]יו מטות כנפו מלא רחב ארצכ̊[ה

]ע̇[∘∘]ם̊ התרה היא ר̇צי̇ן̇ רע̇[ו

כ]ת̇וב ב[

]ם̊ ולא[

L. 2, Isa 8^7: **אפיקו**. MT has **אפיקיו**.
L. 3, v. 8: **והיו**. MT has **והיה**.
כנפו. MT has **כנפיו**.
L. 4: 'the Torah is Rezin', a *pešer* on v. 6.
רעו. Possibly the beginning of a statement of v. 9.

4–7

Col. I: Quotations from Isa 9[11(?), 14–20] and *pešer*

]כתוב
]ליהמה
י]שׄרׄאל בׄכול
]בׄוא והואה
]םׄ ובׄיום אחד זקן
]הואה הזנב
מב]לעים על כן
אל]מׄנותו לוא ירחםׄ

]בׄשׄתםׄ
]∘∘ נפש[
כיא בערה כאש רשע]ה שמיר [ושית ת]אכל ותצית
בסבכי היער ויתאבכו גא]ות עשן [בעברת יהוה צ]באות [נת]עׄם
איש אל אחיׄ]ו לו]א
]שמאול ולוא יׄשׄבתׄ
]אׄפרים ואפרי[ם] אׄת
מנש]הׄ יחדיו[המה על יהודה בכול זאת לוא] שב אפו

L. 3: cf. Isa 9[11].
L. 5: apparently the end of a *pešer* on v. 13 and the beginning of the statement of v. 14.
L. 6, v. 14: הואה. MT has הוא.
L. 8, v. 16: אלמנותו לוא. MT has אלמנתיו לא.
L. 13, v. 17: ותצית. MT has ותצת.
L. 14, v. 18: נתעם = 1QIsa[a]. MT has נעתם.
L. 16, v. 19: ולוא. MT has ולא.
ישבת 'will cease'? MT has שבעו to which our reading may have more closely corresponded before it was apparently amended with a heavily written *tāw* over the last two letters.
L. 18, v. 20: יחדיו. MT has יחדו.

Col. II: Quotations from Isa 10[12 13, 19(?), 20–24] and *pešer*

והיה] כיא יבצע [אדוני את כול מעשהו בהר ציון ובירושלים אפקד על פרי
גד]ל לבב מלך א[שור ועל תפארת רום עיניו כיא אמר בכח ידי עשיתי
ובחכמת]יׄ כיא [נבנותי ואסיר גבולת עמים ועתידתיהם שושתי
— פשר הדבר על חׄבׄלׄ בבל[
— חקות עמים הׄ[∘]תׄ∘[
— לׄבגוד רבים הוא[

— ישראל ואשר אמׄרׄ [ושאר עץ יערו מספר יהיו ונער יכתבם
פשרו למעוט האדם[

והיה ביום ההואׄה [לוא יוסיף עוד שאר ישראל ופליטת
בית יעקוב להשׁׄ[ען על מכהו ונשען על יהוה קדוש
ישר]אל באמת ש[אר ישוב שאר יעקוב אל אל גבור
כי אם יהיה עמכה יׄ[שראל כחול הים שאר ישוב בו
— פשר הדבר לאחרית הׄ[ימים
— ילכו בשׁׄ[בי
אמ◦[
— פשרו לׄמׄיׄעׄטׄ[
כאשר כתוב[כליון חרוץ שוטף צדקה כיא כלה ונחרצה
אדוני יהוה [צבאות עשה בקרב כול הארץ

לכן כוה אמר אדוני י[הוה

L. 1: the placing of f. 7 here depends on the correspondence of מלך אשור of Isa 10^{12} with בבל in the second line of f. 6. Note also the possible relevance of חקות עמים with גבולת עמים of v. 13.
כיא. MT has כי.
L. 3, v. 13: כיא. MT has כי.
L. 4–7: 'the interpretation of the passage concerns the *territory* of Babylon [. . .] [5] decrees of peoples [. . .] [6] to deal treacherously with many, he [. . .] [7] Israel. And as it says [. . .'
L. 8: 'its interpretation concerns the diminution of mankind [. . .'
L. 10, v. 20: ההואה. MT has ההוא.
L. 11: יעקוב. MT has יעקב.
L. 13, v. 22: עמכה. MT has עמך.
L. 14–18: 'The interpretation of the phrase: at the end of [days . . .] they will go into *cap*[*tivity* . . .] [17] its interpretation concerns the reduction [. . .] [18] as it is written [. . .'
L. 19, v. 23: אדוני. MT has אדני.
L. 21, v. 24: כוה. MT has כה.
אדוני. MT has אדני.
The marginal markings are of interest: the short horizontal line seems to relate only to *pešer* passages, but l. 8 has a kind of large 'comma' which is found at l. 16 against a biblical quotation to judge from the *pešer* following in the next line. The signs at ll. 10 and 11 may be compared with those found in 1QIsa^{a} at v 22 (cf. also 1QS v. 1) and viii 9 respectively, only in reverse. The sign at l. 18 is very indistinct.

8–10: Quotations from Isa $14^{8,\ 26-30}$ and *pešer*

פשר הדב]רׄ על כלׄה בבל[. . . גם ברושים
שמחו ל]כה ארזי לבנון מאזׄ[שכבת לוא יעלה
הכרת] עלימו הברושים וארזׄ[י לבנון הם
]לׄבׄנׄוׄןׄ ואשר אמר זׄוׄאׄ[ת העצה היעוצה על

כול] הׄא̊רׄץ̊ ווזאת היד [הנטויה על כול הגוים
כיא יהו]ה צבאות יעׄ[ץ ומי יפר וידו הנטויה
ומי ישי]בנה היאה מׄ◦[
כתו]בׄ בׄספר זכׄריה מׄפׄ[

vacat

vacat

בשנת מו]ת המלך אחׄ[ז היה המשא הזה אל תש]מׄחׄ̊י̊
פלשת כ]ו̊ל̊ך כיא נשבר שבט [מכך כיא משרש נ]חש י[צא
צפע ופריו שרף] מׄעׄו̊פׄף בׄ[כורי דלים ו]אביו̊נים
לבטח ירבצו והמתי ברעב שרשך וש]אׄרׄיׄתׄ[ך יהרג

L. 1: '*The interpretation of the passa*]*ge* concerns the destruction of Babylon [. . .', presumably the *pešer* on Isa 14^{4-7}.
L. 2, 14^{8}: לכה. MT has לך.
L. 3: עלימו. MT has עלינו.
L. 4, v. 26: זואת = 1QIsa^{a}. MT has זאת.
L. 5: ווזאת. MT has וזאת.
L. 8: 'writt]en in the book of Zechariah [. . .'
L. 12, v. 29: כולך = 1QIsa^{a}. MT has כלך.
כיא. MT has כי.
L. 13, vv. $^{29-30}$: the letter following מעופף appears to be a *bēth* apparently indicating that ורעו of MT has been omitted.

11
Col. I

בׄ [. . .]◦מׄ
]ה עובדי
]הׄמׄה
]◦ציה◦◦
]הׄזׄאׄתׄ

Col. II: Quotations from Isa 19^{9-12}

ואורגימׄ[חורי והיו שתתיה מדכאים כול עושי
שכר אגמׄ[י נפש אך אולים שרי צען חכמי יועצי
פרעוה ע[צה נבערה איך תאמרו אל פרעוה בני חכמים
אניׄ בני מ[לכי קדם אים אפוא חכמיכה ויגידו נא
ל[כה וידעו

L. 1, Isa 19^{9}: ואורגים = 1QIsa^{a}. MT has וארגים.
L. 3, v. 11: פרעוה = 1QIsa^{a}. MT has פרעה.
L. 4: אני, although the following plural בני might indicate that NH אנו should be read here.

12

]ר בואו[

]◦ בׄרׄאׄשׁ[

]◦די ◦◦◦[

]ויתר יותר ◦[

]הׄאבן אש[

כ]והנים וא[

] למשקלת וׄ[

כא]שר צוׄהׄ[

] רעות הׄ[

]הׄ ◦[...]האׄ[...]◦◦ ◦

]הׄוׄאׄ[

L. 4: 'and a remnant will remain . . .'
L. 5: **האבן**. Cf. Isa 28[16].
L. 7: **למשקלת**. Cf. 28[17].

13

]◦◦◦◦[...]◦

]כׄי הׄרׄחׄקוׄתׄ ◦[

לאחר]ית הימים עׄלׄ[

]בׄיׄוׄםׄ הׄ[הו]אׄה יבק[שו

]◦ צׄיׄ ◦[

Ll. 2–4: '. . .] distant [. . . [3] . . . at the en]d of days *concerning* [. . . [4] . . .] in *that day* [they] will *seek* [. . .
A close study of the fibres has suggested to Dr. John Barnes, the papyrologist, that this fragment came originally from a position in a vertical plane with f. 15 and 'fairly close'.

14

]תׄוׄמים[

אח]רׄית הימי[ם

]הׄוׄא אבדׄןׄ ◦[

]מׄה לוא תי[

]◦מה כפרם[

]בׄה אתרוׄ◦[

]את נפשו[

]◦◦◦◦◦[

]◦ תׄו֯[

]לׄ ◦[

The position of this fragment, in a vertical plane with f. 16, is thought by Dr. Barnes to be 'not certain, but almost so'.

15–16: Quotation from Isa 29[10–11]

עליכ]מה י֯ה֯ו֯ה֯ [רוח ת]ר֯דמה וי֯ע֯צ֯ם א֯ת֯[עיניכמה את הנביאים ואת

ר]אשיכמה הח֯[זים] כסה ותהי לכמה ח֯[זות הכול כדברי הספר

הח]תום אשר [יתנו א]ותו אל יודע ספר לא֯[מור קרא נא זה

ואמר לוא אוכל כיא] ח֯תו֯ם הוא֯[

L. 1, Isa 29[10]: עליכמה = 1QIsa[a]. MT has עליכם.
L. 2: ראשיכמה. MT has ראשיכם.
v. 11: לכמה. MT has לכם.
L. 3: אותו = 1QIsa[a]. MT has אתו.
ספר = MT Qre. Ktb adds the article, as does 1QIsa[a] above the line.

17: Quotation from Isa 29[15–16]

]ר֯אנו ומי [יודענו הפככמה אם כחמר היצר יחשב כיא יאמר

]מ֯עשה[

18–19: Quotation from Isa 29[19–23]

] ◦ ◦ ◦ ◦ ◦ ◦ [

ואב]יוני אדם בקד֯[וש ישראל יגילו כיא אפס עריץ וכלה לץ ונכרתו

כול] שוקדי און מ֯[חטיאי אדם בדבר ולמוכיח בשער יקשון ויטו בתוהו

צדיק] לכן כוה א[מר יהוה אל בית יעקוב אשר פדה את אברהם לוא

עתה יבו]ש֯ יעקוב [ולוא עתה פניו יחורו כיא בראתו ילדיו מעשה

ידי בקרבו] יקדיש֯[ו ש]מי וה[קדישו

L. 3, Isa 29[20]: שוקדי = 1QIsa[a]. MT has שקדי.
L. 4, v. 22: כוה. MT has כה.
L. 5: יעקוב = 1QIsa[a]. MT has יעקב.

20:

]◦[

פשרו] ע֯ל מ֯ל֯[א]כיו ו֯[

]◦ המ֯ה֯ אש֯[ר

]הוא ב֯י֯[

This fragment is placed by Dr. Barnes 'almost certainly' on a line with f. 16 which would put it into the following column and thus part of a *pešer* on Isa 30[1–5] (f. 21): note מלאכיו in l. 2 and in Isa 30[4].

21: Quotations from Zech 11^{11} Isa 30^{1-5} and *pešer*

]◦[
]יחשׄב הלׄ[ב]נון ◦[
]ל לכרמל ושׄבו הׄ[
[◦בחׄרׄבׄ ואשרׄ[
]צׄ◦ם ◦[
[◦◦[...]מׄורהׄ[
ותפר ביום ההואה וידעו]כן ענׄיׄיׄ הצואן הׄ[שמרים
אותי כיא דבר יהוה] הואה]
הוי בנים סוררים נאם] יהוה לעשות עצׄ[ה ולוא
מני ולנסך מסכה ו]לוא רוחי למען סׄ[פות חטאת
על חטאת ההלכים לר]דת מצרים [ופי לוא שאלו לעוז
במעוז פרעוה ולחסו]ת בצל מצׄ[רים והיה לכם מעוז
פרעוה לבשת וההסו]תׄ בצל מצרי[ם לכלמה כיא היו בצען
שריו ומלאכיו] חנס יגיעו כׄ[ול הבאיש על עם לוא יועילו
למו לוא לעזר] ולׄוׄאׄ [להועיל

Ll. 2–3: cf. Isa 29^{17}.
L. 7, Zech 11^{11}: **הצואן**. MT has **הצאן**.
L. 8: **הואה**. MT has **הוא**.
L. 10, Isa 30^{1}: **לוא** = 1QIsa[a]. MT has **לא**.
L. 15, v. 5: **ולוא** = 1QIsa[a]. MT has **ולא**.

22

]פשר הדבר[
]ם אשר דרשׄ[
]בני צדוק[
אש]ר אמר להם ת◦[
]◦אם ההואה[
◦[בׄל[

[1] . . .] The interpretation of the passage [. . . [2] . . .] who sought [. . . [3] . . .] the Sons of Zadok [. . . [4] . . . *whi*]*ch* he said to them [. . . [5] . . .] that [. . .

The placing of this fragment has been suggested by Dr. Barnes who thinks it 'almost certainly' lies on a horizontal plane with f. 23 as indicated in the plate, but 'not near'.

23

Col. I

◦[

בעצ]

◦◦[

L. 17: An *ʿayin* has been inserted above the line between *bēth* and *ṣādē*.

Col. II: Quotations from Isa 30^{15-18} Hos 6^{9} Isa 30^{19-21} and *pešer*

]ם והמה ◦[ ]ה כול ◦[ ]ם ה ◦[

יש]ראל

כיא] כ[ו]ה אמר [יה]וה קדוש [י]שראל בשובה ונ[חת תושעון

בהש]קט ובטח תהיה גבורתכמה ולוא אביתמה ות[אמרו

לוא כיא על סוס ננוס על כן תנוסון ועל קל נרכב על כן

יקלו רודפיכמה אלף אחד [מפ]ני גערת אחד מפני גערת

חמשה תנוסון עד אם נותרתמה כתרן על רואש הר

וכנס על גבעה ולכן יחכה אדוני לחנ[נכ]מה ולכן ירום

לרחמכמה כיא אלוהי משפט יהוה אשרי כול חוכי לו

פשר הדבר לאחרית הימים על עדת ד[ורשי] החלקות

אשר בירושלים [◦◦]◦ה ה◦[ ]◦◦[

בתורה ולוא יה[ ]◦◦[

לב כיא לדרש [

כיחכה איש גדוד[ים חבר כהנים

התורה מאסו

כ]יא עם בציון [ישב בירושלם בכו לוא תבכה חנון יחנכה לקול

זועקכה כשמ[עתו ענך ונתן לכמה אדוני לחם צר ומים לחץ

ולוא יכניף ע[וד מוריכה והיו עיניכה ראות את מוריכה

ואוזניכה תש[מענה דבר מאחריכה לאמור זה הדרך לכו בו

כיא תימ[ינו וכיא תשמאילו

על עון ע[

L. 3, Isa 30^{15}: כוה. MT has כה.
יהוה. MT adds (as 1QIsa^{a} above the line) אדני.
L. 4: ובטח. MT has ובבטחה.
גבורתכמה. MT has גבורתכם.
ולוא = 1QIsa^{a}. MT has ולא.
אביתמה. MT has אביתם.
L. 5, v. 16: לוא = 1QIsa^{a}. MT has לא.
כיא. MT has כי.
L. 6: רודפיכמה. MT has רדפיכם (1QIsa^{a} רודפיכם).

L. 7, v. 17: תנוסון. MT has תנסו (1QIsa^{a} תנוסו).
נותרתמה. MT has נותרתם.
רואש. MT has ראש (1QIsa^{a} adds *wāw* above the line between *'āleph* and *šīn*.
הר = 1QIsa^{a} (cf. LXX ἐπ' ὄρους). MT adds the article.
L. 8: גבעה. Cf. LXX (ἐπὶ βουνοῦ). MT (and 1QIsa^{a}) adds the article.
v. 18: אדוני. MT has יהוה.
לחננכמה. The reconstruction follows MT (לחננכם), but in fact there is hardly room for the second *nūn* (cf. 1QIsa^{a} לחונכם).
L. 9: לרחמכמה. MT has לרחמכם.
כיא = 1QIsa^{a}. MT has כי.
אלוהי . . . כול = 1QIsa^{a}; MT defectively written.
Ll. 10–13: 'The interpretation of the passage: at the Last Days, concerning the congregation of the S[eekers-after-] Smooth Things ^{11} who are in Jerusalem [. . .] ^{12} by the Law and not [. . .] ^{13} a heart for to seek [. . .'
L. 10: דורשי החלקות. Cf. 4QpNahum (**169**) ff. 3–4 i 2 and note.
L. 14a has been inserted above l. 14 by the same hand.
Hos 6^{9}: כיחכה (MT כחכי) perhaps indicating a singular reading (or interpretation) of the following גדודים (cf. LXX's πειρατοῦ). LXX apparently found our text but misread the *yōdh* as *wāw* (ἡ ἰσχύς σου = כוחכה).
L. 15, Isa 30^{19}: כיא. MT has כי.
L. 16: זועקכה. MT has זעקך.
L. 17, v. 20: ולוא = 1QIsa^{a}. MT has ולא.
יכניף. MT has יכנף (1QIsa^{a} יכנפו).
L. 18, v. 21: ואוזניכה. MT has ואזניך (1QIsa^{a} ואוזניך).
L. 19: כיא. MT has כי.
תימינו = LXX Targ Syr. MT has תאמינו (1QIsa^{a} תיאמינו).

Col. III

7 ע]
8 ל]
9 י ◦]

24

]בהר י]הוה
]אשר אמ[ר

L. 1: cf. Isa 30^{29}, which may suggest that this fragment should be placed immediately before f. 25.

25: Quotation from Isa 31^{1} and *pešer*

]מלך בבל ◦[
]בתופים ובכנו[רות
נפץ ו]זרם כלי מלחמה המה[

5 הוי היורדים] מצרים על סוסים [ישענו ויבטחו על רכב
כ]יא רב ועל פרשים כיא עצמ[ו מאד ולוא שעו על
ק]דוש ישראל ואת יה[וה לוא דרשו
פשרו] על העם אשר יב[טחו

Ll. 1–3: '. . .] *the king of Babylon* [. . . [2] . . .] 'with timbrels and ly[res' . . .[3] . . . 'cloudburst and] tempest' are weapons of war [. . .'

L. 5, Isa 31^{1}: MT adds לעזרה after מצרים.
L. 6: כיא . . . כיא. MT has כי in both places.
L. 8: 'Its interpretation] concerns the people who *tr*[*ust* . . .'

26: Quotation from Isa 32^{5-6}

לוא] יקר[א עוד לנבל נדיב ולכילי לוא יאמר שוע כיא
נבל] נבלותׄ[ידבר ולבו יעשה און לעשות חנף ולדבר אל
יהוה תו]עׄהׄ[

L. 2, Isa 32^{6}: נבלות. MT has נבלה.

27

]העתים הא֯[
]ך העם וא[
]◦◦ ח֯סנכ֯ה[

L. 1: cf. Isa 33^{6}: אמונת עתיך.
L. 3: cf. 33^{6}: חסן ישועת.

28

]מ֯צרים[
פש]רו אשר י[
]◦ ◦[

29

]◦ו ב֯כ֯ה֯[
]ל֯ה היא[
]מ֯ה פשר֯ו֯[

30

]◦ א֯ת֯[
]ה֯ בכא ל֯[
הכ]ו֯ה֯ן֯ הרשע[
]הואה[
ב֯◦ מ[ל]כ֯י[

31

] י֯ח֯יה[
]אדם[
]י֯ם עש◦[
]ו מוריש֯[
א]ר֯ץ [

32

]מ֯חמד[
]◦דתׄ ה֯א֯[
]א֯[

33

]ת[
]ר֯ם[

34

]◦ם[
] ל◦[
] ופׄ[

35

]ב הזׄוׄא[ת

36

]ם [
]ת֯עו[
]מים[
הבׄאה ◦[
] אליה[

37

]◦ ר [
]◦ מׄ ◦[
]לו◦[
]ש◦[

38

]אׄם ◦[
]◦ ד ◦[

39
]◦מחׄםׄ[
]שׁלׄשתׄ[

40
]אשור[
]רׄ להזׄעׄ◦[

41
]תׄ ה[
]◦ול[

42
]◦ ה ◦[
]◦דה [

43
]◦ ◦[
]סׄה[
]בב◦[

44
]◦ ◦ ◦[
]◦א א[
]◦◦ תשׄ[
]בכל[

45
]◦ מ[
]נׄח◦[
]ש◦[

46
]חׄר מ[
]מרה[
]ההמׄ[
]בא ◦[
]שבתׄ[

47
[ ]שׁברׄ[
כא]שר כתו[ב

48
]◦ ◦ ◦[
]עׄתׄ[

49
]◦ ◦ ◦ ◦[
]ימים בׄ[

50
]◦ ◦ ◦[
]אׄ לאומי[ם

51
]◦[
]◦ ◦[
]סׄנׄ ◦[

52
]◦צׄחׄ [
]◦ ◦ קי[

53
]כׄהו[

54
]של[

55
]כׄנׄסׄ◦[

56
]רעב נחרו[

Ff. 46, 56, and 57 are but dubiously part of this document. F. 57 consists of two pieces uncertainly joined.

57
]הור ההר ◦ ◦ אוכל[

164. COMMENTARY ON ISAIAH (D)

(PL. IX)

(Already partly published in *JBL* lxxvii (1958) 215–21)

1: Quotations from Isa $54^{11,\ 12}$ and *pešer*

]ך כול ישראל כפיך בעוך ויׄסדתיך בספי[רים . . . פשרו
אש]ר יסדו את עצת היחד [ה]כוהנים והע[ם
עדת בחירו כאבן הספיר בתוך האבנים] . . . ושמתי כדכד

כול שממשותיך פשרו על שנים עשר[
מאירים כמשפט האורים והתומים[
הנעדרות מהמה כשמש בכול אורו וכ.[
פשרו על ראשי שבטי ישראל לא̊[חרית הימים
ג̊ורלו מעמדי[

[1] . . .] all Israel sought thee according to thy word. 'And I shall lay your foundations in lapis [lazuli.' . . . *Its interpretation* is [2] th]at they have founded the Council of the Community, [the] priests and the peo[ple. . .] [3] a congregation of his elect, like a stone of lapis lazuli among the stones [. . . 'And I will make as agate] [4] all thy pinnacles.' Its interpretation concerns the twelve [. . .] [5] giving light in accordance with the Urim and Thummim [. . .] [6] that are lacking from them, like the sun in all its light. And ['. . .]' [7] Its interpretation concerns the heads of the tribes of Israel at the [*end of days* . . .] [8] his lot, the offices of [. . .

L. 1: presumably a *pešer* on Isa 54^{11b}.
L. 2: יסדו, despite the 1st person singular verb of the text. Note, however, that 1QIsa^{a} reads ויסודו with the variant (?) ending תיך written above the line.
L. 3: עדת בחירו. Cf. 4QpPss^{a} (**171**) ff. 1–2 ii 5; ff. 1, 3–4 iii 5.
L. 4: כול additional to MT of Isa 54^{12}.
שמשותיך = 1QIsa^{a}. MT has שמשתיך.
שנים עשר. Cf. 4Q Ordinances (**159**) ff. 2–4, l. 4.
L. 6: כשמש. A *lāmedh* written after this word has been only partly erased.
L. 7: The *pešer* seems to be relevant to the 'gates' of v. 12^{b} named after the Twelve Tribes (cf. Ezek 48^{30-35} Rev 21^{10-21}).

2

]◦ וכולם ה̇ לוא
]◦עמ̊וד כיא אל כול [
]ל[

Ll. 1–2: '. . .] and all of them, is it not [. . . ? [2] . . .] *stand*, for to all [. . .'

3

]לם[
]עת̊[

165. COMMENTARY ON ISAIAH (E)

(PL. IX)

1–2: Quotations from Isa $1^{1(?)}$ 40^{12} and *pešer*

הנ[ב]ו̊אות̊[ ]ש̊ י̊[אשר חזה על יהודה
וירושלם[ ]ד ואשר כתוב[
פשר הדבר[ ] גלה את תורת הצ[דק ואשר כתוב מי מדד בשעלו מים
ושמים ב[זרת תכן וכל בשלש עפר] ה̊א̊ר̊ץ̊ שק̊ל [בפלס הרים וגבעות במאזנים

L. 1: **הנבואות** 'The prophecies [. . .', presumably the title of the document.
L. 3: 'The interpretation of the passage [. . . .] revealed the ri[ghteous] teaching [. . .'
L. 4, Isa 40^{12}: **שקל**. MT has **ושקל**.

3: Quotation from Isa 14^{19}

יורדי אל אבני] בור כפגר [מובס

4: Quotation from Isa 15^{4-6}

י]ריעו ו[נפשו ירעה לו לבי למואב יזעק בריחה עד צער עגלת שלשיה כי מעלה הלוחית
ב]בכי יעלה ב[ו כי דרך חורנים זעקת שבר יעערו כי מי נמרים משמות יהיו כי יבש חציר
כלה דשא] ירק לו[א היה

L. 1, Isa 15^4: **ונפשו**. MT has **נפשו**.

5: Quotations from Isa $21^{2(?), 11-15}$ and *pešer*

]אר ◦[
]ה פשר הדבר ע[ל
קר]א משעיר שומר מה מל[ילה שומר מה מליל אמר שומר אתה בקר וגם לילה
אם תבעיון בעיו שבו אתיו משא
בערב] ביער בערב תלינו א[רחות דדנים לקראת צמא התיו מים יושבי ארץ תימא
בלחמו
כי מפ[ני חרבות נדד מפני]
קדמו נדד] חרב נטושה מפ[ני קשת דרוכה
מדבר] העמים והלחם[
והשודד] שודד ע[לי עילם

L. 3, Isa 21^{11}: **שומר**. MT has **שמר**. This line as reconstructed on the basis of MT seems unnaturally long, probably indicating that not all of it was included in our text.
L. 5*a*: the scribe's eye jumped from **נדד** of v. 14*d* to the **נדד** of his textual tradition (= 1QIsa^a; MT has **נדדו**) in v. 15*a*. He later inserted v. 15*a* above the line.
L. 5, v. 15: **מפני** = 1QIsa^a; MT has **ומפני**.
L. 6: **מדבר העמים**. If the reconstruction is correct, cf. 1QM i 2–3 4QpIsa^a (**161**) ff. 5–6, l. 2.
L. 7: cf. Isa 21^2 and **ממדבר בא** of v. 1 for a possible point of contact with the preceding line of our text.

6: Quotations from Isa 32^{5-7} and *pešer*

ב]חירי ישראל א[
]עולם ואשר כ[תוב לא יקרא עוד לנבל נדיב ולכילי
]לא יאמר שוע כי נ[בל נבלה ידבר ולבו יעשה און לעשות חנף ולדבר

א]ל   תועה ולהמ̊[ית] נ̊[פש רעב ומשקה צמא יחסיר וכלי כליו

רעים] ה̇ואה זמות יעץ [לחבל ענוים באמרי שקר ובדבר אביון

מ]שפט פשרו על] [–◦]

[◦ את ה̇ת̇ור̇ה̊]   [שׄר◦]

Ll. 1–2: '. . .] the chosen ones of Israel [. . . ² . . .] ever. And as it is *wr[itten*. . .'
L. 4, Isa 32⁶: the tetragrammaton after אל has been omitted.
ולהמית, an uncertain restoration but in any case not להריק of MT.
L. 5, v. 7: הואה. MT הוא.
L. 6: after the introduction of the *pešer* there is a break followed by a dash before the beginning of the next word.
L. 7]. ◦שר[. The *rēsh* has been inserted above the line.

7

[ת̊ ידב̇]

[ענוי]

[ב̊ילו]

This fragment is possibly from the *pešer* begun in l. 6 of f. 6; cf. ענוים in Isa 32⁷ᶜ.

8

מל]ך בבל אשר י[

וא]שר כ̊[תוב

Ll. 1–2: . . . kin]g of Babylon who will [. . . ² . . . a]s it is *wr[itten* . . .

9

[◦ותי תחלת̊]

[אשר מלך ב◦]

[אנשי היח̊]ד

[◦ יא ◦]

[◦ כ̊]

Ll. 1–3: . . .] I [. . .] the beginning of [. . . ² . . .] who ruled in [. . . ³ . . .] the men of the Commun[ity . . .

10

נוי◦]

תב]

שמ]

166. COMMENTARY ON HOSEA (A)

(PL. X)

(Already published in *JBL* lxxviii (1959) 142–7)

Col. I: Quotations from Hos $2^{8,\ 9}$ and *pešer*

]יׄצור
]וירצו
]וילוזו

]◦ בסירים ונתיבותיה
]ובעורון ובתמהון
]רׄ וקץ מועלם לוא
]הם דור הפקודה
]מן מׄ[ ]◦ר[ ]רית
]אׄסׄף בקצי חרון כיא

vacat

vacat

ואמרה אלכה ואשובה אל אישי הרא]ישׄון כיא
טוב לי אז מעתה פשרו]בשוב שבי
]◦פר◦[ ]טׄוׄ

Ll. 3–5: '[3] . . .] he will *vex* [4] . . . and they were pleased [5 . . .] and they turned aside [. . .'

L. 7: '. . .] with thorns, and her paths [. . .'; cf. Hos 2^8, the MT of which adds **וגדרתי את גדרה** between these two words.

L. 8: '. . .] and in blindness and bewilderment [. . .'

L. 9: '. . .] and the period of their treachery [. . .'. Cf. **קץ מעל ישראל** CD xx 23.

L. 10: '. . .] the generation of visitation [. . .'. Cf. **מועד פקודתו** 1QS iii 18; **מועד פקודה** 1QS iv 18–19; **קץ הפקודה** CD xix 10.

L. 12: '. . .] *gather* in the times of wrath [. . .'. Cf. 1QH f. 1, l. 5; singular: CD i 5; 1QH iii 28.

L. 15, Hos 2^{9b}: **הראישון כיא**. MT has **הראשון כי**. V. 9*a* appears to have been omitted.

L. 16: '. . .] in the turning of the captivity of [. . .'

Col. II: Quotations from Hos 2^{10-14} and *pešer*

והיא לוא ידעה כיא] אנוכי נתתי לה הדגן [והתירוש
והיצהר וכסף] הׄרביתי וזהב /// עשוׄ[לבעל פשרו
אשרׄ ◦◦[וי]שבעו וישכחו את אל המ◦[
מׄצייתיו השליׄכו אחרי גום אשר שלח אליהםׄ [בפי
עבדיו הנביאים ולמתעיהם שמעו ויכבדום

וכאלים יפחדו מהם בעורונם

לכן אשוב ולקחתי דגני בעתו ותירושי [במועדו
והצלתי צמרי ופישתי מלכסות את̇[ערותה
ועתה אגלה את נבלותה לעיני מאה̇[ביה ואיש
לוא יצילנה מידי
פשרו אשר הכם ברעב ובערום להיות לקלו̊[ן
וחרפה לעיני הגואים אשר נשענו עליהם והמה
לוא יושיעום מצרותיהם והשבתי כו̊ל̊ משושה
ח̊[גה חד]שה ושבתה וכול מועדיה פשרו אשר̊
]ע̇דות יוליכו במועדי הגואים ו◦[
]נהפכה להם לאבל והשמותי [גפנה
ותאנתה] אשר אמרה אתנם הם לי [אשר נתנו
לי מאהב]י ושמתים ליער ואכלתם ח̊[ית השדה

L. 1, Hos 2[10]: אנוכי. MT has אנכי.
L. 2: הרביתי. MT adds לה.
וזהב followed by an erased word, the last letter of which was *hē*. There is room in this line for a word or two additional to MT.
Ll. 2–6: '*Its interpretation is* [3] that [. . .] and they were satisfied and they forgot God who [. . .] [4] his commandments they cast behind them, which he had sent to them [*by the mouth of*] [5] his servants the prophets, yet they listened to those that misled them, and honoured them, [6] and in their blindness feared them like gods.'
L. 9, v. 11: ופישתי. MT has ופשתי.
מלכסות. Cf. LXX (τοῦ μὴ καλύπτειν). MT has לכסות.
L. 10, v. 12: נבלותה. MT has נבלתה.
L. 11: לוא. MT has לא.
Ll. 12–14: 'Its interpretation is that he smote them with hunger and nakedness to be a sha[me][13] and ignominy in the sight of the Gentiles upon whom they relied, but they [14] will not save them from their torments.'
L. 12: רעב. Cf. 4QpIsa[b] (**162**) ii 1; 4QpPss[a] (**171**) f. 1, ii 1; ff. 1, 3–4 iii 3, 4; 4Q **172** f. 1, l. 2.
L. 14, v. 13: כול. MT has כל.
L. 15: וכול מועדיה. MT has וכל מועדה.
Ll. 15–17: 'Its interpretation is that [16] [. . .] they will bring into the Gentile festivals. And [. . . [17] . . .] has been turned for them into mourning.'
L. 17, v. 14: והשמותי. MT has והשמתי.
L. 18: אתנם. MT has אתנה.
הם. MT has המה.

167. COMMENTARY ON HOSEA (B)

(PL. X)

(Already partly published in *JBL* lxxv (1956) 89–95)

1

]ע̇מק[
]נגד[

L. 1: possibly from ע״ יזרעאל (Hos 1[5]) or ע״ עכור (2[17]).

2: Quotations from Hos 5^{13-15} and *pešer*

ולוא יגהה מכ]ם מזור פ[שרו
]◦ כפיר החרון כי אנוכי כשחל [לא]פ[רי]ם [וככפיר לבית
יהודה פשרו ע]ל כוהן האחרון אשר ישלח ידו להכות באפרים
]דו
אלך אשובה אל מקומי ע]ד אשר [י]אשמו ובקשו פני בצר
להם ישחרנני פשרו אשר יסתי]ר אל את פניו מ◦[ ]◦[
]הו ולוא שמעו[

L. 2: כפיר החרון, 'the Lion of Wrath'. Cf. 4QpNah (**169**) ff. 3–4, i 5, 6.
Hos 5^{14}: אנוכי. MT has אנכי.
L. 3: '*Its interpretation con*]*cerns* the Last Priest who will send forth his hand against Ephraim [. . .'. Cf. CD vii 12, 13; xiv 1; 4Q Testimonia (**175**) l. 27. In 4QpPss[a] (**171**) ff. 1–2, ii 17–19, Ephraim will attack the Priest 'in the time of trial that is coming'. For Ephraim as the Jewish renegades of Jerusalem, cf. 4QpNah (**169**) ff. 3–4, i 12; ii 2 (= דורשי החלקות), are led astray (ii 8) but will eventually flee from their false teachers (iii 5).
L. 6: '*Its interpretation is that*] God [*will hid*]*e* his face from [. . . [7] . . .] and they did not listen [. . .'

3

]בה ע[
]לילה לשח[ר
]מסך בטרפו[
]לגרנו[ת

L. 2: '. . .] night to *seek* [*out* . . .'. Cf. ישחרנני (Hos 5^{15}).
L. 3: '. . .] a covering with *his* prey [. . .'. Cf. אטרף (5^{14}) and טרף (6^{1}).
L. 4: '. . .] to the threshing floor[s. . .'

4

]ביום
]ם לנו
vacat
]שר

Ll. 1–2: possibly a statement of Hos 6^{2-3} although there is hardly enough room for the whole of MT.

5–6: Quotation from Hos 6^{4} and *pešer*

]אנשי[
]◦ מוריהם[ ]על[
א]עשה לכה[אפרים] מה [אעשה לכה יהודה

L. 2: מוריהם, presumably a *pešer* on יורה of 6^{3}; cf. Joel 2^{23}.

7–9: Quotation from Hos 6[7] and *pešer*

והמה כאדם ע]ברו ברית פשר[ו

]עֹ֯זבו את אל ו[י]לכו בחוקות[...]לים [א]ו֯תם בכול֯[...] את יש[

L. 2: '. . .] they forsook God and followed the customs of [. . .] them in all [. . .'

10: Quotation from Hos 6[9–10] and *pešer*

ו֯אשר זמה [עשו בבית ישראל ראיתי שעריריה שם זנות לאפרים נטמא

ישראל פש֯]רו

ר]שעי הגואי[ם

Ll. 2–3: '. . . Its] interpretation [. . . [3] wi]cked ones of the Gentiles [. . .'

11–13: Quotations from Hos 8[6–7] and *pešer*

]חת לס◦[

]בן ◦ ◦ [

ישראל והוא] חרש עשה[ו ולוא אלהים הוא

פ]שר[ו א]שר היו בעמי֯ם֯[

כי שי[בבי]ם֯ היה ע֯[גל שמרון

]א֯ל [כי] ר֯וח יזרעו סופו֯ת [יקצרו קמה אין לו צמח בלי יעשה קמח

אול֯י יעש]ה זרים יבלעוה֯[ו נבלע ישראל עתה היו בגואים ככלי אין

חפץ בו[

פש֯ר[ו ...]הס֯[ופות

הב[

Ff. 11 and 12 are uncertainly placed.
L. 4: 'Its in]terpretation is that they were among the peoples [. . .'
L. 5, Hos 8[6]: שיבבים היה (or שובבים). MT has שבבים יהיה.
L. 6, v. 7: סופות. MT has וסופתה.
L. 7: יבלעוהו. MT has יבלעהו.

14

]◦ ◦ ◦[

נ]חשב[ו

Possibly from Hos 8[12].

15: Quotation from Hos 8[13–14]

ישו]בו וישכ[ח ישראל את עשהו ויבן היכלות ויהודה

ה֯רבה ערי֯[ם

16

פ]שרו אשר[
]יתפושו איש[
]אׄל ל[וא] רׄצה[

Ll. 1–3: '. . .] Its [in]terpretation is that [. . . [2] . . .] each man shall take hold [. . . [3] . . .] God has no delight [. . .'
L. 3: רצה. Cf Hos 8[13]: יהוה לא רצם.

17

פשר]ו על מצריםׄ[
]ל[ ]◦ ◦ ◦[

18

]תו ואמׄרׄ[
]אׄשר ישובׄ[
]ל[

19

]פׄשר ה ◦[
]וח את יׄ[
]◦נים י ◦[
]◦ אשר[
]סר ◦[
]◦דה ה◦[
]יׄוׄסׄ◦[
]ל ◦[

20

]םׄ במקדש י◦[
]בנם יבעׄ[

21

]הנה
]וכול

22 Col. I

אלׄ[
◦[

Col. II

]◦
]◦ו
]לם

23

]מצוות[

24

]ים והתׄ◦[

25

י]הודה[
]ל יום[

26

]כול מכ◦[
]לׄ[

27

]ם
]ה

28

]לוא מׄ◦[

29

]ת
]◦

30

]◦ ◦ ◦ ◦ם[
]◦ ◦ ◦[

31

]יׄם
]הׄ

32

]את[
]◦[

33

]להיו[ת
]לפׄנׄ[י

34

]םׄ ורא ◦[

35

]מׄעש[

36

]יׄש[

37

[א ◦]

38

א ◦]

עׄ]

יהׄ]

מ ◦]

ג ◦]

המי ◦]

טרף]

מש ◦]

אׄ ◦]

168. COMMENTARY ON MICAH (?)

(PL. XII)

The script of these fragments is very similar to that of 4QpHos[b] (**167**). It is possible that they originally formed part of a *pešer* of the whole of the Minor Prophets.

1: Quotation from Mic 4^{8-12}

לבת ירוש]לםׄ [עתה למה תריעי רע המלך אין בך אם יועצך אבד כיא

החז]יקכה[חיל כיולדה חולי וגחי בת ציון כיולדה כיא

עׄתׄהׄ תצאי מקרׄ[יה ושכנת בשדה ובאת עד בבל שם תנצלי שם

יגא]לךׄ [י]הוה מ[כף איביך ועתה נאספו עליך גוים רבים

הא]מרים תׄ[חנף ותחז בציון עינינו והמה לוא ידעו מחשבות יהוה ולוא

הבינו] עׄצׄתו[

L. 2, Mic 4^9: החזיקכה. MT has החזיקך.

Ll. 5–6: there are more words in MT of v. 12 than can be conveniently fitted into these lines.

2

[תׄירו

3

◦] [ה]

4

[נים

169. COMMENTARY ON NAHUM

(PL. XII–XIV)

(Already partly published in *JBL* lxxv (1956) 89–95, and *Journal of Semitic Studies* vii (1962) 304–8)

1–2: Quotations from Nah i^{3-6} and *pešer*

בסופה ובשערה דרכו ו]עׄנׄן אׄ[בק רגליו פשרו
הׄ[סופות והשערו]ת ר[קי]עי שמיו וארצו אשר בר֯[אם
גועׄ[ר] בים ויוב[ישהו פ]שרו הים הם כל הכׄ[תיים
לעש[ות] בׄהם משפט ולכלותם מעל פני [הארץ
5a עם [מוש]ליהם אשר תתם ממשלתם
אמלל בשן ו]כרמל ופרח לבנן אמלל [פשרו
יאב]דׄו֯ בו רבים רום רשעה כי הב[
כר]מׄל ולמושליו לבנון ופרח֯ לבנון היא[
אנשי עצ]תם ואבדו מלפני[...] בחיר[י
]◦ל יושבי תבל הׄר֯[ים רעשו ממנו פשרו
]הארץ ממנו ומלפני֯[ ]ל[פני זעמו מי יעמוד ומי
יקום]בׄחרון אפו פׄ[שרו

[1] . . . '*In the tempest and the storm wind is his way and*] a cloud is the d[ust *of his feet.' Its interpretation*:] [2] 'the [*tempests and the storm wind*]*s*' are the *f*[*irma*]*ments* of his heavens and his earth which he *cr*[*eated.*] [3] 'He rebu[kes] the sea and dr[ies it up.'] Its [in]terpretation: 'the sea' is all the *Ki*[*ttim* . . .] [4] to exe[cute] against them judgement and to exterminate them from the face of [*the earth*] [5a] with their [rul]ers whose dominion will be brought to an end. [[5] '*Bashan is withered and*] Carmel and the bloom of Lebanon is faded.' [*Its interpretation* . . . [6] and] many [shall per]ish by it at the height of wickedness for the [. . . [7] 'Car]mel' and to his rulers; 'Lebanon' and 'the bloom of Lebanon' is [. . . [8] the men of] their [coun]sel, and they shall perish from before [. . .] the chosen ones of [. . . [9] . . .] 'the inhabitants of the world.' 'The *moun*[*tains quake before him.' Its interpretation*: . . . [10]] the earth from him and from before [. . .] 'B[efore his indignation who can stand, and who [11] can endure] the heat of his anger?' [Its] in[terpretation: . . .

The preceding column presumably stated Nah i^{2-6}, the relevant phrases of which being repeated here and commented upon.

L. 3, Nah i^{4}: ויובישהו. MT has ויבשהו.

L. 5*a* has been inserted between the lines by the same hand. If מושליהם was intended to follow directly after עם, the apparent gap between them is probably due to the scribe's avoidance of the upright strokes of the *lamedh*s of אמלל, as in his splitting of ממשלתם at the end of this insertion.

L. 6: רום רשעה. Cf. 1QH f. 5, l. 7.

L. 7: לבנון = Kittim in 4QpIsa[a] (**161**) ff. 8–10, ll. 7–8.

3–4

Col. I: Quotations from Nah 2^{12-14} and *pešer*

]מדור לרשעי גוים אשר הלך ארי לביא שם גור ארי
ואין מחריד פשרו על דמי]טרוס מלך יון אשר בקש לבוא ירושלים בעצת דורשי החלקות
]◦יד מלכי יון מאנתיכוס עד עמוד מושלי כתיים ואחר תרמס
] ארי טורף בדי גוריו מחנק ללביותיו טרף
פשרו]על כפיר החרון אשר יכה בגדוליו ואנשי עצתו
וימלא טרף] חׄירה ומעונתו טרפה פשרו על כפיר החרון
נק]מות בדורשי החלקות אשר יתלה אנשים חיים
]בישראל מלפנים כי לתלוי חי עׄל העׄץׄ [יק]רא הנני אלי[כה
נאׄ[ם יהוה צבאות והבערתי בעשן רובכ]הׄ וכפיריכה תאכל חרב והכר[תי מארץ ט]רפה
ולא י[שמע עוד קול מלאככה פש]רׄו רובכה הם גדודי חילו אׄ[שר בירושלי]םׄ
וכפיריו הם
גדוליו[ ]וטׄרׄפו הוא ההׄוׄן אשר קבׄ[צו כוה]נׄי ירושלים אשר
י]תנוהו ע[א]פרים ינתן ישראל לׄ[

Col. II: Quotations from Nah 3^{1-5} and *pešer*

ומלאכיו הם צירו אשר לא ישמע קולם עוד בגוים הוי עיר הדמים כולה [כחש פר]קׄ מלׄאה
פשרו היא עיר אפרים דורשי החלקות לאחרית הימים אשר בכחש ושקׄר[ים י]תהלכו
לא ימוש טרף וקול שוט וקול רעש אופן וסוס דהר ומרכבה מרקדה פרׄשׄ מׄעלה להוב
וברק חנית ורוב חלל וכבוד פגר ואין קץ לגויה וכשלו וגויתם פשרו על ממשלת דורשי החלקות
אשר לא ימוש מקרב עדתם חרב גוים שבי ובז והרחור בינותם וגלות מפחד אויב ורוב
פגרי אשמה יפולו בימיהםׄ ואין קץ לכלל חלליהם ואף בגוית בשרם יכשולו בעצת אשמתם
מרוב זנוני זונה טובת חן בעלת כשפים הממכרת גוים בזנותה ומשפחות ב[כש]פיה
פשר[ו ע]ל מתעי אפרים אשר בתלמוד שקרם ולשון כזביהם ושפת מרמה יתעו רבים
מלכיםׄ שרים כוהנים ועם עם גר נלוה ערים ומשפחות יובדו בעצתם נ[כ]בׄדים ומוש[לים
יפולו [מ]עם לשונם הנני אליך נאם יהוה צ[באו]ת וגלית
שולי[ך] על פניך והראתׄ גׄוים מערׄ[ך] וממׄלכות /// קלונךׄ פשרו ◦[...]הׄ ◦◦[
...]ערי המזרח כי השולׄ[י]םׄ[

Col. III: Quotations from Nah 3^{6-9} and *pešer*

הגוים בנותם[ש]קׄוצי תועבותיהם והשלכתי עליך שקוצים [ונ]בלתיך ושמתיך
כאורה והיה כול רואיך ידודו ממך
פשרו על דורשי החלקות אשר באחרית הקץ יגלו מעשיהם הרעים לכול ישראל

ורבים יבינו בעוונם ושנאום וכארום על זדון אשמתם ובה[ג]לו֯ת֯ כבוד יהודה
ידודו פתאי אפרים מתוך קהלם ועזבו את מתעיהם ונלוו על ישראל ואמרו
שודדה נינוה מי ינוד לה מאין אבקשה מנחמים לך   פ֯ש֯ר֯ו֯ [על] ד֯ו֯ר֯שי
החלקות אשר תובד עצתם ונפרדה כנסתם ולא יוסיפ֯ו֯ עוד לתעות [ה]קהל ופת[אים
לא יחזקו עוד את עצתם   התיטיבי מני א֯מ֯[ון הישבה ב]יארים
פשרו אמון הם מנשה והיארים הם גד[ו]לי מנשה נכבדי ה[...]◦ים את מ[
מים סביב לה אשר חילה ים ומים ח[ו]מותיה
פ]ש֯ר֯ו֯ הם אנשי [ח]י֯לה גבור[י מ]לחמתה /// כ֯ו֯ש עוצמ֯ה֯[ומצרים וא֯י֯ן קצה
]◦◦◦[ ]◦◦[ ]◦ ה֯מ֯ד֯◦[...]◦מ֯[... פוט ולובים היו בעזרתך [

Col. IV: Quotations from Nah 3^{10-12} and *pešer*

פשרו הם רשע֯[י חיל]ה֯ בית פלג הנלוים על מנשה גם היא בגולה ה[לכה בשבי גם
עילוליה ירוטשו בראש כל חוצות ועל נכבדיה יורו גורל וכול ג[דו]ל֯[יה רותקו
בזקים פשר׳ על מנשה לקץ האחרון אשר תשפל מלכותו ביש֯[ראל ...
נשיו עילוליו וטפו ילכו בשבי גבוריו ונכבדיו בחרב֯[...   גם את תשכרי
ותהי נעלמה   פשרו על רשעי א֯[פרים ...
אשר תבוא כוסם אחר מנשה[...]ל[...   גם את תבקשו
מעוז בעיר מאויב פש[רו ע]ל[...
אויביהם בעיר֯[...   כול מבצריך
ת֯א֯נ֯י֯ם֯ עם[בכורים
]◦

Col. I. [1] . . .] a dwelling for the wicked ones of the Gentiles. 'Whither the lion, the lioness went, the lion's cub [[2] and none to terrify.' *Its interpretation* concerns Deme]trius, king of Greece, who sought to enter Jerusalem by the counsel of the Seekers-after-Smooth-Things [. . . [3] . . .] the kings of Greece from Antiochus until the appearance of the rulers of the Kittim and afterwards she will be trodden down [. . . [4] . . .] 'The lion tears sufficient for his cubs, (and) strangles for his lionesses prey.' [[5] . . . Its interpretation] concerns the Lion of Wrath who will smite by his nobles and the men of his counsel [[6] . . . 'And he filled with prey] *his cave* and his den with torn flesh.' Its interpretation concerns the Lion of Wrath [[7] . . . *ven*]*geance* on the Seekers-after-Smooth-Things when he hangs men up alive [[8] . . .] in Israel beforetime, for of the man hanged alive upon a tree it [re]ads: 'Behold I am against [thee] [9] say[s Yahweh of hosts, and I will burn in smoke thine abundance,] and thy young lions the sword shall devour. And I will cut [off from the land] *his* [p]rey.' [10] 'And [the voice of thy messengers] shall no [more be heard.'] Its [interpre]tation: 'thine abundance'—they are his warrior bands *w*[*ho are in Jerusal*]*em*; and 'his young lions'—they are [11] his nobles [. . .] and 'his prey'—it is the wealth which the [*prie*]*sts* of Jerusalem *amas*[*sed*] which [12] they will give [. . . E]phraim, Israel will be given for [. . .]

Col. II. [1] and 'his messengers'—they are his envoys whose voice will no longer be heard among the nations. 'Woe city of blood, all full of [lies and rap]ine.' [2] Its interpretation: it is the city of Ephraim, the Seekers-after-Smooth-Things at the end of days, who in 'lies' and falsehood[s] conduct themselves. [3] 'Prey departeth not and the sound of the whip and the sound of the rattling of wheels, and galloping horses and bounding chariots, the horseman charging, a blade [4] and flashing spear and a multitude of slain and a great heap of carcases: and there is no end to the corpses and they shall stumble *over* their bodies.' Its interpretation concerns the rule of the Seekers-after-Smooth-Things [5] when there shall not depart from the midst of their congregation the Gentile sword, captivity, and plunder, and heated strife among themselves, and exile from fear of the enemy, and a multitude of [6] guilty corpses shall fall in their days, and there shall be no end to the total of their slain, and furthermore, in their body of flesh they shall stumble over their own guilty counsel. [7] 'Because of the multitude of the whoredoms of the well-favoured harlot, the mistress of witchcrafts, that selleth nations through her whoredom and families through her witchcrafts.' [8] [Its] interpretation [con]cerns those who lead Ephraim astray, who, by their false teaching and their lying tongue and lip of deceit, will lead many astray, [9] kings, princes, priests, and people together with the resident alien. Cities and families will perish through their counsel, n[ob]les and rul[ers] [10] will fall because of what they say. 'Behold I am against thee, says Yahweh of hosts, and thou shalt lift up [11] [thy] skirts over thy face and show nations thy nakedness and kingdoms thy shame.' Its interpretation [. . . [12] . . .] cities of the east, for the 'skirts' [. . .]

Col. III. [1] the nations between them [. . . the dete]sted things of their abominations. 'And I will cast upon thee detested things, and I will treat thee with contempt and make thee [2] *repulsive* and all who look on thee will flee from thee.' [3] Its interpretation concerns the Seekers-after-Smooth-Things whose evil deeds will be revealed at the end of time to all Israel, [4] and many will discern their iniquity and hate them and *consider* them *repulsive* because of their guilty insolence. And when Judah's glory is revealed, [5] the simple ones of Ephraim will flee from the midst of their assembly and forsake those who mislead them and join themselves to Israel. 'And they shall say, [6] Nineveh is laid waste; who will mourn for her? Whence shall I seek comforters for thee?' Its interpretation [concerns] the Seekers-after- [7] Smooth-Things whose counsel will perish and their gathering be broken up and they will not again mislead [the] assembly and the simple [ones] [8] will no more sustain their counsel. 'Art thou better than Am[on that dwelt by] the rivers?' [9] Its interpretation: 'Amon' is Manasseh, and 'the rivers' are the nobles of Manasseh, the honoured ones of the [. . .] [10] 'Waters are around her, whose rampart is the sea and waters her walls.' [11] Its [inter]pretation: they are her warriors, mighty men of [w]ar. 'Ethiopia is her strength [and Egypt too, without limit.' . . . [12] . . . 'Put and the Libyans are thy helpers . . .']

Col. IV. [1] Its interpretation: they are the wicked ones of its [army], the House of Peleg who have joined themselves to Manasseh. 'Yet she was carried away, [she went into captivity: even] [2] her young children will be dashed in pieces at the top of all the streets; and they will cast lots for her honourable men and all [her no]bles [were bound] [3] in chains.' Its interpretation concerns Manasseh at the end of the age when his rule over *Is[rael]* will fall [. . .] [4] his wives, his infants, and his children will go into captivity, his warriors and his nobles by the sword [. . . 'Thou also shalt be drunken] [5] and shalt be dazed.' Its interpretation concerns the wicked ones of *E[phraim . . .]* 6 whose cup will come after Manasseh [. . . 'Thou also shalt seek] 7 a stronghold in the city from the enemy.' Its inter[pretation con]cerns [. . .] 8 their enemies in the city [. . . 'All their fortresses shall be] 9 (like) fig-trees with [their first-ripe figs. . .']

Col. I. L. 1: מדור וג״: presumably a *pešer* on Nah $2^{12\,a,\,b}$.

L. 2: לבוא. The *pešer* follows the variant tradition shared by the versions against its own and MT's לביא.

דורשי החלקות. Cf. l. 7; cols. ii 2, 4; iii 3, 6–7; CD i 18; 1QH ii 15, 32; 4Qpap pIsa^{c} (**163**) f. 23, ii 10.

L. 4, Nah 2^{13}: ארי. MT has אריה.

טורף. MT has טרף.

גוריו. MT has גרותיו.

ללביותיו. MT has ללבאתיו.

טרף. Additional to MT.

L. 5: כפיר החרון. Cf. l. 6 and 4QpHos^{b} (**167**) f. 2, l. 2.

L. 6, v. 13: חירה. MT has חריו. For the *hē* as the sign of the 3rd p.s. masc. suffix, cf. טרפה in l. 9 and its *pešer* טרפו in l. 11.

ומעונתו. MT has ומענתיו.

L. 8, v. 14: אליכה, suffix reconstructed thus after וכפיריכה (l. 9) and רובכה (l. 10). MT has אליך.

L. 9: רובכה, reconstructed from the *pešer* in l. 10; cf. LXX Syr. MT has רכבה.

וכפיריכה. MT has וכפיריך.

טרפה. MT has טרפך.

L. 11: ההון. Cf. 1QpHab ix 5.

Col. II. L. 1, Nah 3^{1}: הדמים = Heb MS. MT omits article.

כולה. MT has כלה.

L. 2: אפרים. Cf. 4QpHos^{b} (**167**) f. 2, l. 3 and note.

L. 3, v. 1: ימוש. MT has ימיש.

v. 2: וקול. MT omits conjunction.

v. 3: להוב. MT has ולהב חרב.

L. 4: ורוב. MT has ורב.

וכבוד. MT has וכֹבֶד.

קץ. MT has קצה.

וכשלו = Heb MS and MT Qre. MT Ktb has יכשלו.

וגויתם, an error for בג״, as MT; cf. a similar error corrected in 4QpPss^{a} (**171**) ff. 3–10, iv 7.

L. 6: פגרי אשמה. Cf. 1QM xiv 3 and חללי אשמתה (vi 17).

L. 7, v. 4: מרוב. MT has מרב.

הממכרת. MT has המֹכרת.

בזנותה. MT has בזנוניה.

L. 10, v. 5: וגלית. MT has וגליתי.

L. 11: והראת. MT has והראתי.

וממלכות, followed by an erasure.

Col. III. L. 1, Nah 3^{6}: שקוצים. MT has שקצים.

L. 2: כאורה, apparently a *qal* part. pass. fem. of כאר (a weakened form of כער?). Cf. l. 4 for the *piʿēl* of the verb. MT has כראי.

v. 7: כול רואיך. MT has כל ראיך.

ידודו. MT has ידוד.

L. 4: ובה[ג]לות. Reconstruction suggested privately by K. G. Kuhn.

L. 5: ואמרו. MT has ואמר.

L. 6: שודדה. MT has שדדה.

אבקשה. MT has אבקש.

L. 8, v. 8: התיטיבי. MT has התיטְבי.

מני. MT has מנא (LXX has *μερίδα* = מני?).

L. 9: מנשה Cf. col. iv 3, 6; 4QpPss^{a} (**171**) ff. 1–2, ii 17.

L. 10: חילה. MT has חיל.
ומים = LXX (*καὶ ὕδωρ*). MT has מַיִם.
חומותיה. MT has חומתה.
L. 11, v. 9: כוש, preceded by a semi-erased *ʿayin*.
עוצמה. Cf. LXX (*ἡ ἰσχὺς αὐτῆς*); MT has עָצְמָה.

Col. IV. L. 1: בית פלג. Cf. CD xx 22, being those who 'went out from the holy city' but later caused dissension among the people and apostatized, joining the party of the ruling house ('Manasseh') apparently as warriors, רשעי חילה; cf. אנשי מלחמה, who 'returned (to be) with the Man of Lies' (CD xx 14–15; cf. i 13–21).
Nah 3^{10}: בגולה. MT has לגלה.
L. 2: עילוליה. MT has עֹלליה.
ירוטשו. MT has ירטשו.
יורו. MT has ידו.
וכול. MT has וכל.
L. 3: פשרו. The *wāw* at first omitted and later inserted above the line.
L. 5, v. 11: ותהי. MT omits conjunction.
L. 7: בעיר, additional to MT and possibly inserted the better to conform with the *pešer* (l. 8).

5: Quotation from Nah 3^{14} and *pešer*

]◦ ים ◦[
]כ̊ול גבול ישרא[ל] ל̊י̊ם[
חזקי מבצ]ר̊י̊ך̊ ב̊ו̊א̊י בט̊י̊[ט

L. 2: '. . .] all the territory of Isra[el] to the sea [. . .'; presumably a *pešer* on Nah 3^{13b}.
L. 3, v. 14: בואי. MT has באי.

170. COMMENTARY ON ZEPHANIAH

(PL. XIV)

1–2: Quotation from Zeph 1^{12-13} and *pešer*

לוא ייט̊י̊]ב יהוה ול̊[ו]א ירע והיה̊]חילם למ[שיסה ו̊]בתיהם לשממה
]◦◦[   ] לוא יוכל̊[   ]פשרו[

L. 1, Zeph 1^{13}: למשיסה. MT has למשסה.
L. 2: '. . .] will not be able [. . .': apparently a quotation but not MT.

171. COMMENTARY ON PSALMS (A)

(PL. XIV–XVII)

(Already partly published in *Palestine Exploration Quarterly* lxxxvi (1954) 69–75 and *JBL* lxxv (1956) 89–95)

1–2
Col. I: Quotation from Ps 37^{7} and *pešer*

]ה̊

]י̊ר

5

]◦ב֯
]◦ר
]ת֯
]י֯ת
]◦
]צ֯ה֯רים
]◦ת רצון
]ת הוללים בחרי
]א֯והבי פרע ומתעים
]ר֯שעה ביד א֯ל֯[והי]ם֯
דו]ם֯ ל[יהוה ו]ה֯תחולל לו ואל תחר֯ במצליח דרכו באיש
עוש]ה֯ מזמות [פשר]ו על איש הכזב אשר התעה רבים באמרי
שקר כיא בחרו בקלות ולוא שמ֯[עו] למליץ דעת למען

Col. II: Quotations from Ps 37^{8-19a} and *pešer*

יובדו בחרב וברעב ובדבר הרף מאף ועזוב ח֯מ֯ה ואל
תחר אך להרע כיא מרעים יכרתו פשרו על כול השבים
לתורה אשר לוא ימאנו לשוב מרעתם כיא כול הממרים
לשוב מעוונם יכרתו וקואי יהוה המה ירשו ארץ פשרו
המה עדת בחירו עושי רצונו ועוד מעט ואין רשע
ואתבוננה על מקומו ואיננו פשרו על כול הרשעה לסוף
ארבעים השנה אשר יתמו ולוא ימצא בארץ כול איש
ר]שע וענוים ירשו ארץ והתענגו על רוב שלום פשרו על
עדת האביונים אשר יקבלו את מועד התעות ונצלו מכול פחי
בליעל ואחר יתענגו כול ב֯[...]י הארץ והתדשנו בכול תענ֯ו֯ג֯
בשר
זומם רשע לצדיק וחורק ע֯[ליו שניו יה]ו֯ה֯ ישחק לו כיא ראה
כיא בא יומו פשרו על עריצי הברית א֯ש֯ר בבית י֯ה֯ודה אשר
יזומו לכלות את עושי התורה אשר בעצת היחד ואל לוא יעזבם
בידם חרב פתחו רשעים וידרוכו קשתם לפיל עני ואביון
ולטבוח ישרי דרך חרבם תבוא בלבם וקשתותיהם תשברנה
פשרו על רשעי אפרים ומנשה אשר יבקשו לשלוח יד

בכוהן ובאנשי עצתו בעת המצרף הבאה עליהם ואל יפדם
מידם ואחר[י] כן ינתנו ביד עריצי גואים למשפט

vacat

טוב מעט לצדיק מהמון רשעים רבי[ם ... פשרו על]
עושה התורה אשר לוא י[...]◦ה
לרעות כיא אזרוע[ות רשעים תשברנה וסומך צדיקים]
יה[וה יודע יהוה ימי תמימים ונחלתם לעולם תהיה פשרו על אנשי]
רצונ[ו ...]◦[
ל[וא י]בושו ב[עת רעה ... פשרו על]

1, 3–4
Col. III: Quotation from Ps 37^{19b-26} and *pešer*

שבי המדבר אשר יחיו אלף דור בישרה ולהם כול נחלת
אדם ולזרעם עד עולם ובימי רעב יש[בע]ו כיא רשעים
יובדו פשרו א[שר] יחים ברעב במועד ה[תע]ות ורבים
יובדו ברעב ובדבר כול אשר לוא יצא[ו ...]להיות ע[ם
ואוהבי יהוה כיקר כורים פשר[ו
עדת בחירו אשר יהיו רשים ושרים ◦[
צון בתוך עדריהם
כלו כעשן כולו פשר[ו] על שרי ה[רש]עה אשר הונו את עם
קודשו אשר יובדו כעשן האוד [בר]וח לוה רשע ולוא ישלם
וצדיק חונן ונותן כיא מבורכ[ו יר]שו ארץ ומק[ל]ל[ו יכר]תו
פשרו על עדת האביונים ה[...]ם נחלת כול ה[◦]◦ל[
ירשו את הר מרום ישר[אל וב]קודשו יתענגו ו[מקול]לו
יכרתו המה עריצי הב[רית ר]שעי ישראל אשר יכרתו ונשמד[ו
לעולם
כיא מיהו[ה מצעדי גבר כונ]נו בכול דרכו יחפץ כיא יפ[ול] ל[וא
יוטל כיא יה[וה סומך ידו] פשרו על הכוהן מורה ה[צדק אשר
ד]בר בו אל לעמוד ו[אשר] הכינו לבנות לו עדת[
ודר]כו ישר לאמתו[נער היי]תי וגם זקנתי ולוא[ראיתי צדיק
נעזב וזרעו מבקש לחם[כול היום] חונן ומלוה וזר[עו לברכה פשר
הדבר על מור[ה הצדק ...]אל מ[...
ואת[...

3–10

Col. IV: Quotations from Ps 37^{28c-40} and Ps 45^{1-2} and *pešer*

משׁ[פט עולים לעו]לם נשמדו וזרע ר[שעים נכרת] המה עריצי
[...]התורה צדיקי[ם ירשו ארץ וישכנו ל]עד עליה
[פשרו ...]באלף[דור פי צדיק יהגה] חכמה ולשונו תדבר
[משפט תורת אלהיו בלבו לוא תמעד אשריו פשרו על] האמת אשר דבר
[...]∘∘ אליהם הגיד

vacat

צופה רשע לצדיק ומבקש[להמיתו 𐤉𐤄]𐤅𐤄 [לוא יעזבנו בידו ולוא י]רשיענו בהשפטו
פשרו על [הכו]הן הרשע אשר צ[ופ]ה הצד[יק ומבקש] להמיתו[...]ת והתורה
אשר שלח אליו ואל לוא יע[זבנו] ולוא[ירשיענו ב]השפטו ול[ו י]שלם[אל ג]מולו לתתו
ביד עריצ[י] גואים לעשות בו[משפט קוה אל 𐤉]𐤄𐤅𐤄 ושמור דרכו וי[]רוממכה לרשת
ארץ בהכרת רשעים תר[אה פשרו על ...] אשר יראו במשפט רשעה ועם
בחירו ישמחו בנחלת אמת
ראי]תי רשע עריץ מתע[רה כאזרח רענן] אעבור על פ[ניו והנה אינ]נו וא[בקשהו] ולוא
נמצא פשרו] על א[י]ש הכזב[אשר ...]∘ ל ∘[...]על בח[יר]י אל[ויב]קש לשבית את
[...]∘מ∘[...]לעשות[...]∘עי משפט[...]הזיד ביד רמה
[...]∘ל∘ל∘[... שמור תם וראה] ישר[כיא אח]ר[ית לאי]ש שלום פשרו ע[ל
[...]∘[...]∘∘דם הא[...]∘[...]ת שלו[ם] ופושעים
נשמדו יחד ואחר[ית רשעים נכרתה פשרו ...]יובדו ונכרתו
מתוך עדת היחד ות[שוע]ת[צדיקים מ𐤉𐤄𐤅𐤄 מעוזם בעת צרה ויעזרם 𐤉𐤄𐤅𐤄]
וימלטם ויפלטם מרשעים[ויושיעם כיא חסו בו פשרו ...]
יושיעם אל ו[י]צילם מיד ר[שעי ...]

vacat

למנצח על [שושנ]ים[לבני קרח משכיל שיר ידידות ... ה]מה שבע מחלקות
שבי יש[ראל ... רח]ש ל[ב]י דבר טוב
[אומר אני מעשי למלך פשרו ... רו]ח קודש כיא
[...]ספרי[...] ולשוני עט
[סופר מהיר פשרו] על מורה[הצדק ...]∘∘ו אל במעני לשון

Col. I. [12] . . .] '*noonday*' [[13] . . .] favour [[14] . . .] boasting in the *burning of* [[15] . . .] lovers of (long) locks, and seducers [[16] . . .] wickedness by the hand of *G*[*o*]*d*.

[[17] 'Be sti]ll before [Yahweh, and] wait patiently for him, and do not fret thyself over him who prospers in his way, over the man [[18] who work]s evil designs.' Its [interpretation] concerns the Man of Lies who has led many astray with words of [19] falsehood, for they chose worthless things and did not lis[ten] to the Mediator of Knowledge, so that

Col. II. [1] they will perish by the sword and by hunger and by plague. 'Cease from anger and forsake wrath and be not [2] fretful, tending only to evil; for the wicked shall be cut off.' Its interpretation concerns all who turn back [3] to the Law, who refuse not to repent from their wickedness, for all those who rebel [4] from repenting of their iniquity will be cut off. 'But those who wait for Yahweh will possess the earth.' Its interpretation: [5] they are the congregation of His Elect who do His will. 'And in a little while the wicked will be no more, [6] and I shall look carefully for his place and it will be gone.' Its interpretation concerns all the wickedness at the end of [7] the completion of forty years when they will be consumed and there will not be found on earth any [wi]cked [8] man. 'And the humble shall possess the earth and they shall delight in the abundance of peace.' Its interpretation concerns [9] the congregation of the Poor Ones who will accept the season of error and will be delivered from all the snares of [10] Belial, and afterwards all the [. . .] of the earth will delight and will luxuriate in all the delights of [11] the flesh.

[12] 'The wicked plots against the righteous and gnashes [his teeth at him. Yah]weh laughs at him for he sees [13] that his day is coming.' Its interpretation concerns the ruthless ones of the covenant in the House of Judah who [14] will plot to obliterate those in the Council of the Community who carry out the Law. But God will not leave them [15] in their power. 'The wicked have drawn the sword and bent their bow to cast down the poor and needy [16] and to slay the upright of way. Their sword shall penetrate their own heart and their bows shall be broken.' [17] Its interpretation concerns the wicked ones of Ephraim and Manasseh who will seek to put forth a hand [18] against the Priest and the men of his counsel in the time of trial that is coming upon them. But God will redeem them [19] from their hand and afterwards they will be given into the hand of the ruthless Gentiles for judgement. [21] 'Better is the little that the righteous has than the abundance of ma[ny] wicked.' [. . . *Its interpretation concerns*] [22] those who carry out the Law, who will not [. . .] [23] *for evil things*. 'The arm[s of the wicked shall be broken, but] Yah[weh upholds the righteous. [24] Yahweh knows the days of the perfect, and their heritage will abide for ever.' *Its interpretation concerns the men of* [25] his] favour [. . . [26] 'They will] n[ot] be put to shame in [evil times.' *Its interpretation concerns* . . .]

Col. III. [1] the penitents of the desert who will live a thousand generations in uprightness; and to them will be all Man's [2] inheritance, and to their seed for ever. 'And in the days of famine they will be satisfied, but the wicked [3] will perish.' Its interpretation is that he will keep them alive in famine, in the season of error, whilst many [4] shall perish by famine and plague, all who did not go out [. . .] to be with[5] the Congregation of his Elect. [5a] 'And those who love Yahweh are like the preciousness of lambs.' [Its] interpretation: [5] they will be chiefs and princes [. . .] [6] sheep in the midst of their pastures. [7] 'All of them are consumed like smoke.' [*Its*] interpretation concerns the princes of [*wick*]*edness* who have oppressed his holy [8] people, who will perish like the smoke of a *firebrand* [in the w]ind. 'The wicked man borrows and does not repay, [9] but the righteous is gracious and generous. For those who are blessed [of him will in]herit the earth, and those who are accursed [of him will be c]ut off.' [10] Its interpretation concerns the congregation of the Poor Ones who [. . .] the inheritance of all the [. . .] [11] will possess the mount of the height of Isra[el and on his] holy place luxuriate, whilst [those who are accursed] of him [12] will be cut off: they are the violators of the [*covenant*, the wi]cked ones of Israel who will be cut off and destroyed [13] for ever.

[14] For 'by Yahwe[h are Man's steps secur]ed, *in all* his ways does he delight; *for though he f*[*all* he will not] [15] be hurled headlong, for Ya[hweh supports his hand.'] Its interpretation

concerns the Priest, the Teacher of [*Righteousness* whom [16] God [*com*]*manded* to arise and [*whom*] he established to build for him a congregation [. . . [17] and] his [wa]ys he directed towards *his* truth. ['A lad was] I and now I am old, yet [I have] not [seen a righteous man] [18] forsaken, nor his seed seeking food. [All the day] he is gracious and lending and [his] se[ed is a blessing.' The interpretation of] [19] the passage concerns the *Teach*[*er of Righteousness* . . .

Col. IV. [1] *jud*[*gement*. '*The unjust* for ev]er will be destroyed and the seed of the wi[cked is cut off.'] They are the violators of [2] [. . .] the Law. 'The righteou[s shall possess the earth and dwell for] ever upon it.' [3] [*Its interpretation* . . .] in a thousand [*generations*. 'The mouth of the righteous utters] wisdom and his tongue speaks [4] [justice. The law of his God is in his mouth, his steps will not slip.' *Its interpretation concerns*] the truth which [. . .] spoke [5] [. . .] *to* them he related. [7] 'The wicked watches for the righteous and seeks [to slay him. Yah]weh [will not abandon him in his hand and will not] condemn him when he is judged.'[8] Its interpretation concerns the Wicked [Pri]est who *wa*[*tche*]*s* the *Righteous* [*One and seeks*] to slay him [. . .] and the Law [9] which he sent to him. But God will not *ab*[*andon him*] and will not [*condemn him* when] he is judged. But [God will] pay [him] his recompense by giving him [10] into the hands of the terrible Gentiles to carry out [*judgement*] on him. ['Wait for Ya]hweh and keep his way, and [he] will exalt thee to possess [11] the land; thou shalt lo[ok] upon the destruction of the wicked.' [*Its interpretation concerns* . . .] who will look upon the judgement of wickedness and with [12] his Elect they will rejoice in the inheritance of truth. [13] 'I [have seen] a ruthless wicked person [. . . like a cedar of Lebanon.] I pass by before [him, and, lo,] he is [no more;] though I [seek him] he is not [14] [to be found.' Its interpretation] concerns the Man of Lies [*who* . . .] against the El[ect] of God; [and he so]ught to bring to an end [15] [. . .] to carry out [. . .] judgement [. . .] behave with presumptuous arrogance. [16] [. . . 'Mark the blameless man and see] the upright [for there is posterity for the ma]n of peace.' Its interpretation con[cerns [17] . . .] peac[e.] 'But the rebellious [18] shall be destroyed together, and the poster[ity of the wicked shall be cut off.' *Its interpretation* . . .] will perish and be cut off [19] from the midst of the Congregation of the Community. 'And the sa[lvation of the righteous is from Yahweh; he is their refuge in time of trouble. And Yahweh has helped them [20] and delivered them and rescued them from the wicked, [and saved them because they took refuge in him.' *Its interpretation* . . .] [21] God will save them and deliver them from the hand of the *wi*[*cked ones of* . . .] [23] To the choirmaster: according to [Lil]ies. [A maskîl of the Sons of Korah; a song of *lots*.'] They are the seven divisions [24] of the penitents of Is[rael . . .] 'My hea[rt is asti]r with a good thing [25] [I address my verses to the king.' *Its interpretation* . . .] holy [spir]it for [26] [. . .] books of [. . .] 'and my tongue is the pen of [27] [a ready scribe.' *Its interpretation*] concerns the Teacher *of* [*Righteousness* . . .] God [. . .] him with an eloquent tongue [. . .

Col. I. L. 15: 'lovers of (long) locks'. Cf. Ezek 44[20], where the opposite is said of the 'sons of Zadok' (ופרע לא ישלחו).

L. 17, Ps 37[7]: ואל תחר. MT has אל תתחר.

L. 19: מליץ דעת. Cf. Isa 43[27]; Job 33[23]; 1QH ii 13; f. 2, l. 6 (= Teacher of Righteousness?).

Col. II. L. 1: בחרב. Cf. 4QpIsa^{b} (**162**) ii 1.

ברעב. Cf. iii 3, 4; 4QpIsa^{b} (**162**) ii 1; 4QpHos^{a} (**166**) ii 12; 4QpUnid. (**172**) f. 1, l. 2.

בדבר. Cf. iii 4.

Ps 37[8]: ועזוב. MT has ועזב.

ואל. MT omits conjunction.

L. 2: תחר. MT has תתחר.

v. 9: כיא. MT has כי.
יכרתו. MT has יכרתון.
Ll. 2–3: השבים לתורה. Cf. iii 1: שבי המדבר.
L. 4: וקואי. MT has וקוי.
ירשו. MT has יירשו.
L. 5: עדת בחירו. Cf. iii 5; 4QpIsa^{d} (**164**) f. 1, l. 3.
עושי רצונו. Cf. 1QS ix 13.
L. 6, v. 10: ואתבוננה. MT has והתבוננת.
Ll. 6–7: הרשעה . . . יתמו. Cf. iii 7; iv 11; 4QpNah (**169**) ff. 1–2, i 6 and n.
L. 7: ארבעים השנה. Cf. CD xx 15; 1QS iv 18, 23 (קץ להיות עולה).
L. 8, v. 11: ירשו. MT has יירשו.
רוב. MT has רב.
L. 9: עדת האביונים. Cf. iii 10.
מועד התעות. Cf. iii 3.
L. 10: תענוג. Cf. 1Q28^{b} iv 2.
L. 12, v. 12: זוממ . . . וחורק. MT has זמם . . . וחרק.
𐤉𐤄𐤅𐤄. MT has אדני.
Ll. 12–13, v. 13: כיא (twice). MT has כי.
L. 13: בא = Ken. MT has יבוא.
עריצי הברית. Cf. iii 12; 1QpHab ii 6.
L. 15, v. 14: וידרוכו. MT has ודרכו.
לפיל. MT has להפיל.
L. 16: ולטבוח. MT omits conjunction.
v. 15: וקשתותיהם. MT has וקשתותם.
L. 17: אפרים ומנשה. Cf. 4QpHos^{b} (**167**) f. 2, l. 3 and n.
L. 18: בכוהן. Cf. iii 15.
עת המצרף הבאה. Cf. 4QFlor (**174**) ff. 1, 3, ii 1; 4QCatena (**177**) ff. 5–6, l. 3.
L. 19: עריצי גואים. Cf. iv 10.
L. 23, v. 17: כיא אזרועות. MT has כי זרועות.
L. 26, v. 19: יבושו. MT has יבשו, but the placing of f. 2 here is uncertain.

Col. III. L. 1: שבי המדבר. Cf. השבים לתורה (ii 2–3); שבי פשע (1QS x 20; 1QH ii 9, vi 6, xiv 24; CD ii 5, xx 17); שבי ישראל (CD iv 2, vi 5, viii 16).
אלף דור. Cf. iv 3; CD vii 6, xix 1, 2, xx 22.
L. 2, Ps 37^{19}: רעב. MT has רעבון.
v. 20: כיא. MT has כי.
L. 3: יובדו. MT has יאבדו.
רעב. Cf. l. 4 and ii 1 and n.
מועד התעות. Cf. ii 9 and n.
L. 5: עדת בחירו. Cf. ii 5.
שרים. Cf. CD vi 6.
L. 5*a*, v. 20*b*: ואוהבי. MT has ואיבי. The insertion, in a different hand (note the tetragrammaton in the normal square script) is intended to be read after בחירו in l. 5.
כורים. MT has כרים.
L. 7, v. 20*c*: כעשן = Ken LXX Vulg Syr; MT has בעשן.
כולו. MT has כלו.
הרשעה. Cf. ii 6; iv 11.
L. 8, v. 21: ולוא. MT has ולא.
L. 9, v. 22: כיא. MT has כי.
מבורכ[ו יר]שו . . . ומקׄלל[ו: MT has מברכיו יירשו . . . ומקלליו.
L. 10: עדת האביונים. Cf. ii 9.
L. 11: הר מרום ישראל. Cf. Ezek 17^{23}, 20^{40}, 34^{14}.
L. 12: עריצי הברית. Cf. ii 13.
L. 14, v. 23: בכול דרכו. MT has ודרכו.
כיא מ𐤉״. MT omits introductory כיא.
v. 24: כיא. MT has כי.

L. 15: כיא. MT has כי.
הכוהן: Cf. ii 18.
L. 16: דבר בו אל לעמוד. Cf. CD i 11: ויקם להם מורה הצדק בדרך לבו.
L. 17, v. 25: וגם. MT omits conjunction.
ולוא. MT has ולא.

Col. IV. L. 1, Ps 37^{28c}: עולים, restored with LXX.
נשמדו = LXX. MT has נשמרו.
L. 3: באלף דוד. Cf. iii 1.
L. 7, v. 33: בהשפטו. A partly erased *wāw* stands before this word, possibly through a misreading of the initial *bēth*. For a similar confusion, see 4QpNah (**169**) ff. 3–4, ii 4 and n.
L. 8: the placing of f. 6, although lacking a direct join, seems probable.
הצדיק. Cf. CD i 20.
L. 10: עריצי גואים. Cf. ii 19.
v. 34: ושמור. MT has ושמר.
וירוממכה. MT has וירוממך.
L. 11: רשעה. Cf. ii 6 and n., iii 7.
L. 13, v. 35: . . .]◦ מת. MT has ומתערה.
אעבור = LXX Vulg Syr. MT has ויעבר.
על פניו is omitted by MT.
ולוא. MT has ולא.
L. 14: לשבית: for להשבית.
L. 17, v. 38: ופושעים. MT has ופשעים.
L. 18: יחד. MT has יחדו.
L. 20, v. 40: וימלטם ויפלטם. MT has ויפלטם יפלטם.
L. 26, Ps 45^{2c}: ולשוני. MT omits conjunction.
L. 27:]על מורה[. F. 9 is, however, uncertainly placed.
]ו אל במעני לשון[: of the author of 1QH ii 7, xi 34, xvi 6, xvii 17.

11

לשוב יחד לתורה בֹּ[
בחירْ[י] ישראْל[· · ·]◦א◦[

L. 1: 'to turn together to the Law *in* [. . .' Cf. ii 2–3; 1QS v 8; CD xv 9, 12; xvi 1–2, 4–5.

12

בשפת ע[

'with the lip of [. . .'. The fragment comes from the top of a column and the hand and skin seem to connect it closely with f. 11.

13: Quotation from Ps 60^{8-9} (108^{8-9}) and *pešer*

]◦[

אלו]הْים דבר [בקדשו אעלזה אחלקה שכם
ועמק סכ]וֹת אמדדה לי[גלעד ולי מנשה ואפרים מעוז ראשי
פשרו על גלע]ד וחצי שבט[מנשה
]וْנקבצוْ[

L. 4. MT has **אמדד**.
L. 5: '*Its interpretation concerns Gilea*]*d* and half the tribe of [*Manasseh*. . .'
חצי שבט מנשה. Cf. Jos 4^{12} 13^{7} 18^{7}, etc.
L. 6: '. . .] and they shall be gathered together [. . .'
More fragments similar in hand to 4QpPss[a] may be found in 4QpUnid (**172**).

172. COMMENTARIES ON UNIDENTIFIED TEXTS

(PL. XVIII)

Here are grouped fragments whose script is reminiscent of pIsa[a] (**161**), pHos[a, b] (**166, 167**) and pPss[a] (**171**).

1

א[מ̊ר כול]
[ב̊עת רעב̇ ואשר̊] אמר
פש[ר̊ו היא̊ה ה̊צ̊◦◦]
יא[ס̊פו את צ◦]
[◦◦]

L. 2: 'in the time of famine'. Cf. 4QIsa[b] (**162**) ii 1; 4QpHos[a] (**166**) ii 12; 4QpPss[a] (**171**) f. 1, ii 1; iii 3, 4.
L. 3: '. . .] Its [inter]pretation: it is the [. . .'
L. 4: '. . . and *they shall gat*]*her together* [. . .'

2

[◦◦◦ אשר האו◦]
[ת̊ו̊כ̇ן כבגד על הא]
[◦ ו]

L. 2: '. . .] *fastened* like a garment upon the [. . .'. Cf. 4QpIsa[a] (**161**) ff. 8–10, l. 24. This fragment possibly comes from the top of the following column.

3

[כ̊ות ביד̊]
[ת̊ר̊בות מלכותו]

L. 2: '. . .] the increase of his kingdom [. . .'. Cf. Isa 9^{6} and 4QpIsa[a] (**161**) ff. 8–10 and f. 2, above, which is of similar skin texture.

4

[ב̇ה̊יותו̊ ע̇מם]
[העול ברחו]
[פחז עמורה̊]
[בוערת וגם כ̇◦]
[לבבם
[◦◦יתי ב◦]

Ll. 1–5: '. . .] when he is with them [. . . [2] . . .] iniquity have *fled* [. . . [3] . . .] lasciviousness of Gomorrah[. . . [4] . . .] burning, and also [. . . [5] . . .] their heart.'

5

]◦נ֯ימים א֯[
]ה בה הבש֯[
]כול מה֯[

6

]י֯ם֯[
]שקר ומ[
]◦[

F. 6, l. 2: cf. Ps 38^{20-21}.

7

]מורה ה[
]ש֯ כול[

Ll. 1–2: '◦. . .] Teacher of [. . . [2] . . .] all [. . .'

8

]להושי֯[ע
]ד֯[

9

]שובם֯[
]שואגים֯[
]ד◦[

10

]מ֯הותלות[

F. 10. Cf. Isa 30^{10}: מַהֲתַלּוֹת 'deceit' (|| חלקות).

11

]את[

12

]כ֯ול[

13

]ד֯עה[

14

] פשר֯[
]על[

F. 14. This fragment is but doubtfully placed in this group.

173. COMMENTARY ON PSALMS (B)

(PL. XVIII)

1: Quotations from Ps 127^{2-3} and *pešer*

]◦[
שו]א לכם֯[משכימי קום מאחרי שבת אוכלי לחם העצבים כן
יתן לידידו שנא פשרו א]שר יבקשו[
ע]תרות מורה הצדק֯[
כו]הן לאחרית הק[ץ֯

הנה נחלת יהוה בנים פשרו על י]ורשי הנחלה֯[

[2] . . . It is va]in for you [to rise early, to go late to rest, eating the bread of anxious toil; thus [3] he gives to his beloved sleep.' *Its interpretation is* th]at they seek [. . . [4] . . . *sup*]*plications* of the Teacher of Righteousness [. . . [5] . . . pri]est at the end of ti[me . . .[7] '*Lo, sons are a heritage from Yahweh.' Its interpretation concerns*] those who take possession of the inheritance[. . .

L. 4: עתרות. Cf. NH עתירה 'entreaty, prayer'. Another possible reading is סתרות 'hiding-places, secrets'.
L. 5: 'priest at the end of time': cf. כוהן האחרון of 4QpHos[b] (**167**) f. 2, l. 3.

2: Possibly a quotation from Ps 127^{3b} and *pešer*

שכר פרי הבטן] פשרוׄ הפר֯[י
מ]וׄרה הצד֯[ק

[1] . . . 'a reward is the fruit of the womb']. Its interpretation: 'the fruit [. . .' [2] . . . the Te]acher of Righteous[ness . . .

3: Quotation from Ps 127^{5} and *pešer*

א]שׄר֯יׄ הגבר[אשר מלא את אשפתו מהם
פשרו] אשר יהיו ק[הל
]לוׄאׄ יבושו כׄ[י ידברו את אויבים בשער

[1]'H]appy is the man [who has a quiver full of them!' [[2] *Its interpretation is*] that they will be a *con*[*gregation* . . . [3] . . .] 'They will not be ashamed wh[en they speak with enemies in the gate. . .'

L. 3: MT has לא יבשו.

4: Quotation from Ps 129^{7-8} and *pešer* (?)

שלא] מׄלא כפו קוצׄר ו[חצנו מעמר ולוא אמרו העברים
ברכת י]הוהׄ עׄל[יכ]םׄ בר֯[כנו אתכם בשם יהוה
]ר֯שׄעׄ[

'with which] the reaper does [not] fill his hand or [the binder of sheaves his bosom, while those who pass by do not say, [2] The blessing of Ya]hweh be upo[n yo]u! [We] ble[ss you in the name of Yahweh!' . . . [3] . . .] *wicked* [. . .

L. 2, Ps 129^{8}: עליכם. MT has אליכם.

5: Quotations from Ps 118 and *pešer*

ע]ב֯רו מ֯◦◦[
]ב֯ית מכשול[
עד קרנ]ות המזבח יב֯[או

זה] השער לאל צדי֯[קים יבאו בו
מר]ח֯יבי שמות וחריב֯[ות
]ל ליעקו֯ב֯[

[1] . . . *pass*] *over from* [. . . [2] . . .] House of Stumbling [. . . [3] . . . unto the hor]ns of the altar they will *co*[*me* . . . [4] . . . 'This is] the gate of God; the righ[teous shall enter through it . . .' [5] . . . those who wi]den the waste places and the desol[ate places . . . [6] . . .] to Jacob [. . .

L. 2 'House of Stumbling': cf. צור מכשול of Isa 8^{14}; here a reference to בית יהוה of Ps 118^{26}.
L. 3: cf. v. 27.
L. 4, v. 20: לאל. The script is presumably some cryptic form used for the divine name. The *'āleph* is in the form of a reversed Greek minuscule alpha. MT has ליהוה.

174. FLORILEGIUM

(PL. XIX–XX)

(Already partly published in *JBL* lxxv (1956) 176–7; lxxvii (1958) 350–4.)

1–2

Col. I: Quotations from II Sam 7^{10-14} (I Chr 17^{9-13}) Ex 15^{17-18} Amos 9^{11} Ps 1^{1} Isa 8^{11} Ezek 37^{23} (?) Ps 2^{1} with *pešer*

[···]◦ד אויב֯[···ולוא יוסי]ף בן עולה֯[לענות]ו֯ כאשר בראישונה ולמן היום אשר
[צויתי שפטים] על עמי ישראל הואה הבית אשר[···]ל[···ב]א֯חרית הימים כאשר כתוב בספר
[··· מקדש אדני כ]ו֯ננו ידיכה יהוה ימלוך עולם ועד הואה הבית אשר לוא֯ יבוא שמה
[··· עד]ע֯ולם ועמ֯וני ומואבי וממזר ובן נכר וגר עד עולם כיא קדושי שם
י◦[◦]ה֯[···]עולם תמיד עליו יראה ולוא ישמוהו עוד זרים כאשר השמו בראישונה
את מקד֯[ש י]שראל בחטאתמה ויואמר לבנות לוא מקדש אדם להיות מקטירים בוא לוא
לפניו מעשי תורה ואשר אמר לדויד ו[הניחו]תי לכה מכול אויביכה אשר יניח להמה מכ[ול
בני בליעל ה֯מכשילים אותמה לכלותמ֯[ה···]מה כאשר באו במחשבת[ב]ל[י]על להכשיל ב֯[ני
או֯[ר] ו֯לחשוב עליהמה מחשבות און למ֯[···נ]פשו לבליעל במשגת א֯[···]◦מה
וה]ג֯יד֯ לכ֯ה יהוה כיא בית יבנה לכה והקימותי את זרעכה אחריכה והכינותי את כסא ממלכתו
[לעו]ל֯ם֯ אני א֯ה֯י֯ה֯ לוא לאב והוא יהיה לי לבן הואה צמח דויד העומד עם דורש התורה אשר
[···]בצי֯[ון בא]חרית הימים כאשר כתוב והקימותי את סוכת דויד הנופלת היאה סוכת
דויד הנופל֯[ת א]שר יעמוד להושיע את ישראל
מ֯ד֯רש מאשרי [ה]איש אשר לוא הלך בעצת רשעים פשר הדב[ר···]סרי מדרך֯[···]
אשר כתוב בספר֯ ישעיה הנביא לאחרית [ה]ימים ויהי כחזקת֯[היד ויסרני מלכת בדרך]
הע֯ם הזה והמה אשר כתוב עליהמ֯ה בספר יחזקאל הנביא אשר לו[א יטמאו עוד]
[בג]ל[ו]ליהמה המה בני צדוק ו֯א֯[נ]שי עצ֯ת֯[מ]ה רו◦[···]י◦ א֯ח֯ריהמ֯ה֯ ל֯ע֯צ֯ת֯ ה֯יחד
[למה רגש]ו גויים ולאומים יהג֯[ו ריק ית]י֯צבו[מלכי ארץ ור]וזנים נוסדו יחד על יהוה ועל
[משיחו פ]שר הדבר[··· גו]יים וה֯[···]בחירי ישראל באחרית הימים

1–3

Col. II: Quotations from Dan 12[10] 11[32] and *pešer*

היאה עת המצרף הב[אה ··· י]הודה להתם[

בליעל ונשאר ש[···]ם ◦[ג]ורל ועשו את כול התורה[

מושה היאה ה[··· אש]ר כתוב בספר דניאל הנביא להרשי[ע רשעים ···

וצדיקים [··· יתלב]נו ויצטרפו ועם יודעי אלוה יחזיקו המ[4a

◦◦◦◦[···]אחרי ה[···]אשר אליהמה יו◦[4

···]ה ברדתו מ[

]ל◦◦◦◦◦[

Col. I. ‘[1] . . .] enemy [. . . ‘And] the son of wickedness [shall no more afflict] him as at first, and as from the day that [[2] I commanded judges] (to be) over my people Israel’—that is the house which [. . . in] the end of days, as it is written in the book of [[3] . . . ‘The sanctuary, O Lord, which] thy hands have [es]tablished. Yahweh will rule for ever and ever.’ That is the house ‘where there shall never more enter [[4] . . .] and ‘the Ammonite and the Moabite’ and ‘bastard’ and ‘alien’ and sojourner ‘for ever’, for my holy ones are there. [[5] . . .]ever, he shall be seen continually upon it, and strangers shall not again make it desolate as they desolated formerly [6] the sanc[tuary of I]srael because of their sin. And he purposes to build for him a man-made sanctuary in which sacrifices may be made to him; [7] (that there may be) before him works of the Law. And as he said to David, ‘And I shall [give] thee [rest] from all thine enemies’—(meaning) that he will give rest to them from a[ll] [8] the sons of Belial who made them stumble to destroy them [. . .] when they came with the device of [Be]lial to make the s[ons of] [9] Li[ght] stumble and to devise against them wicked imaginations, to [. . .] his [l]ife to Belial through their [. . .] error.

[10] [‘And] Yahweh tells you that he will build a house for you, and I shall set up your seed after you, and I shall establish his royal throne [11] [for eve]r. I shall be to him as a father, and he will be to me as a son.’ He is ‘the Shoot of David’ who will arise with the Interpreter of the Law, who, [12] [. . .] in *Zi*[*on* in the l]ast days; as it is written, ‘And I shall raise up the tabernacle of David that is fallen.’ That is ‘the tabernacle of [13] David that is fal][len’ is he] who will arise to save Israel.

[14] Midrash of ‘Happy is the man that walketh not in the counsel of the wicked’. The interpretation of the passa[ge . . .] those who turn aside from the way of [. . .] [15] As it is written in the book of Isaiah the prophet concerning the last days, ‘And it was as with a strong [hand that he turned me aside from walking in the way of][16] this people.’ And they are the ones of whom it is written in the book of Ezekiel the prophet, [‘*They shall*] *no*[*t defile themselves any more* [17] *with*] their [*i*]*do*[*l*]*s*’—they are the Sons of Zadok and the m[e]n of the[ir] community [. . .] *after them to the counsel of* the community.

[18] [‘Why do] the nations [rag]e and the peoples imag[ine a vain thing? The kings of the earth set] themselves, [and the ru]lers take counsel together against Yahweh and against [19] [his anointed.’ The in]terpretation of the passage [. . . *na*]*tions* and [. . .] the Elect of Israel in the last days:

Col. II. [1] that is the time of trial that is co[ming . . . J]udah to complete [. . .] [2] Belial, and there shall remain [. . . l]ot, and they shall carry out the whole of the Law [. . .] [3] Moses. That is the [. . . a]s it is written in the book of Daniel the prophet, ‘For [*the wicked*] *to act* [*wickedly*

. . .] ^{4a} and righteous [. . . 'shall make themselves wh]ite and purify themselves', and 'a people knowing God will seize' the [. . . ^{4} . . .] *after* the [. . .] which is to them [. . . ^{5} . . .] when he goes down *from* [. . .'

Col I. L. 1, II Sam 7^{10} I Chr 17^{9}: יוסיף בן עולה = LXX and Ps 89^{23}. MT has plural verb and subject.
בראישונה. MT has בראשונה.
L. 2: הבית. If a comment on מקום of MT, an uninterrupted statement of the biblical text probably preceded, in which case the first visible letters of line 1 are the remnants of עוד and the following אויב is a non-massoretic intrusion, the subject of ירגז.
L. 3, Ex 15^{17}: ידיכה. MT has ידיך.
v. 18: ימלוך עולם. MT has ימלך לעלם.
לוא יבוא שמה. Cf. Deut 23^{3-4} Ezek 44^{9}.
L. 6: בוא לוא . . . לוא = בו לו . . . לו. Cf. לוא = לו in l. 11, בוא = בו in l. 2 of 4QpGen ('Patriarchal Blessings': *JBL* lxxv (1956) pp. 174–6).
L. 7, II Sam 7^{11}: לכה מכול אויביכה. MT has לך מכל אויביך.
L. 9: משגת. Cf. CD iii 5; 1QH ii 19.
L. 10, II Sam 7^{11}: לכה . . . כיא. MT has לך . . . כי.
בית יבנה = I Chr 17^{10}; LXX II Sam. MT of II Sam has יעשה (but cf. v. 13 יבנה בית).
לכה. MT II Sam and I Chr has לך.
II Sam 7^{12} I Chr 17^{11}: והקימותי = I Chr; MT II Sam has והקימתי.
זרעכה אחריכה. MT II Sam and I Chr has זרעך אחריך.
והכינותי = MT I Chr; MT II Sam has והכינתי.
כסא omitted from MT II Sam and I Chr, but cf. II Sam 7^{13}.
L. 11, II Sam 7^{14} I Chr 17^{13}: לוא = לו of MT; cf. l. 6.
צמח דויד. Cf. Jer 23^{5} etc.; 4QpIsa^{a} (**161**) ff. 8–10, l. 17; 4QpGen ('Patriarchal Blessings': *JBL* lxxv (1956) 174–6) ll. 3–4.
L. 11: דורש התורה. Cf. 1QS vi 6 (בת"); viii 15 (מדרש הת"); CD vi 7; vii 18 (= הכוכב).
L. 12, Amos 9^{11}: והקימותי = CD vii 16 (cf. Acts 15^{16}). MT has אקים את סכת דויד הנפלת.
L. 14, Ps 1^{1}: לוא. MT has לא.
סרי מדרך. Cf. CD i 13; ii 6; viii 4, 16; xix 17, 29; 1QS ix 20; x 21.
L. 15, Isa 8^{11}: ויהי omitted by MT.
כחוקת = 1QIsa^{a} and other MSS. MT has בח".
Ll. 16–17: לוא . . . בגלוליהמה. If the reconstruction at the beginning of l. 17 is correct, the quotation may be from Ezek 37^{23} (MT: ולא . . . בגלוליהם); otherwise possibly a paraphrase of Ezek 44^{10}.
L. 18, Ps 2^{1}: גויים ולאומים. MT has גוים ולאמים.

Col. II. The positioning of f. 3 on the horizontal plane is uncertain.
L. 1: עת המצרף הבאה. Cf. 4QpPss (**171**) ff. 1–2, ii 18; 4Q Catena^{a} (**177**), ff. 5–6, l. 3.
L. 3: להרשיע. Cf. Dan 12^{10}.
L. 4^{a} was inserted by the same hand above l. 4.
ויצטרפו. MT of Dan 12^{10} has ויצרפו (Palest. ויתצרפו).
יודעי אלוה יחזיקו. Cf. Dan 11^{32}: ידעי אלהיו יחזקו.

4

]ה̊מבלעים את צאצאי̊
נ]וטרים להמה בקנאתמה
]היאה העת אשר יפתח בליעל
]לבית יהודה קשות לשוטמם
]ו̊בקש בכול כוחו לבזרמה
]ר̊ הביאמה להיות
יה]ו̊דה ואל י̊[שר]א̊ל י◦[

[1] . . .] those who consume the offspring of [[2] . . . an]gry towards them in their zeal [[3] . . .] that is the time when Belial shall open [[4] . . .] to the house of Judah severe things to cherish enmity against them [[5] . . .] and shall seek with all his strength to scatter them [[6] . . .] brought them to be [[7] . . . Ju]dah and to I[sr]ael [. . .

5

]◦ה כאשר ה◦[
י]שׂראל ואהרון[
י]דׂע כיא הואה מ◦[
]ה בכול החוזים[
]ל ◦[

[1] . . .] when [. . . [2] . . . I]srael and Aaron [. . . [3] . . . k]now that he [. . . [4] . . .] among all the seers [. . .

6–7: Quotation from Deut 33^{8-11} and *pešer*

]ל להאביד את קרן [

ולוי אמר תמיכה ואוריכה לאיש חסידכה אשר נס]יתו[במסה תרי]בׂהו על מי מריבה הא[מר
לאביו ולאמו לוא ראיתיו ואת אחיו לוא הכיר ואת בנו לוא יד]ע כיא [שמרו אמרתכה] ובריׂתׂ[כה ינצרו
יורו משפטיכה ליעקב ותורתכה לישראל ישימו קטורה] באפכה וכליל על מזבחכה[ברך יהוה חילו ופעל
ידיו תרצה מחץ מתנים קמיו ומשנאיו מן י]קומון
א]וׂרים והתומים לאיש[
]לׂ[

L. 1: '. . .] to destroy the horn of [. . .'
L. 4, Deut 33^{9}: כיא. MT has כי.
L. 5, v. 10: באפכה . . . מזבחכה. MT has באפך . . . מזבחך.

8: Quotation from Deut 33^{12}(?) and *pešer*

]אשר ◦[
]אׂרץ כיא ה[
לבנימן אמ]ר ידׂיד יׂ[הוה

9–10: Quotation from Deut 33^{19-21} and *pešer*

וההיד]ד . . .   ]◦ה זבח הצדׂ[ק
טוב הא[רץ . . .
ולגד א]מר ברוך מרחיב גד כלביא שכן וטרף זרוע אף קדקד וירא ראשית לו כי שם חלקת[
מחקקׂ[ספון ויתא ראשי עם צדקת יהוה עשה ומשפטיו עם ישראל   פשרו]
על שבׂיׂ[
להצׂיׂל[

L. 1: 'And the shou[t . . .] "right sacrif[ice". . .] ^{2} good of the la[nd . . .'. זבח הצדק. Cf. Deut 33^{19}: זבחי צדק.
Ll. 3–4: vv. 20–21.
L. 5: 'concerning the penitents of [. . .'
L. 6: 'to deliver [. . .'

11

]הספון עْ[
]כול אשר צונו עשו את כולْ[

Ll. 1–2: '. . .] hidden [. . . ^{2} . . .] all that he commanded us, they have done all [. . .'. הספון. Cf. Deut $33^{19, 21}$.

12

◦
]כול[
]אמםْ[
]לוא[
]בק◦[

13

]◦רו◦◦◦◦[
הקש[
הדבר[

14

]◦בْה לק◦[
]לאْחרית ה[
]כْיא המה[

15

]◦יה הנ◦[
]◦ומי ה̶עמי[
]הْ כיא זרע[

F. 15, l. 2: the remains of an erased *hē* before]עמי are just visible.

16

]אْ[
]◦יקים[
]וْברקי[
]אْ◦[

17

]גْורלْ[
]מה את פ[
]בתו עליהْ[
]ל[

18

]נْ[
]ה א[
]בט◦[

19

]רْו ל◦[
]המה◦[

20

]◦את כל[

21

]יהוה ב[
]◦[

22

]ם
]◦ה יחד

23

]◦ דורש[

24

]◦[
]מْצרף[

25

]ש[
]לשמוْ[
]שْ[

26

]◦◦[
]◦ צ◦[

175. TESTIMONIA

(PL. XXI)

(Already published in *JBL* lxxv (1956) 182–7)

Quotations from Deut 5^{28-29} 18^{18-19} (SAM Ex 20^{21}) Nu 24^{15-17} Deut 33^{8-11} Jos 6^{26} (4Q Pss of Joshua)

וידבר •••• אל מושה לאמור שמעת את קול דברי
העם הזה אשר דברו אליכה היטיבו כול אשר דברו
מי ינתן ויהיה לבבם ^זה^ להם לירא אותי ולשמור את כול

מצותי כול היומים למעאן יטב להמ ולבניהם לעולם
נבי אקים לאהמה מקרב אחיהמה כמוכה ונתתי דברי
בפיהו וידבר אליהמה את כול אשר אצונו והיה ˹ה˺איש
אשר לוא ישמע אל דברי אשר ידבר הנבי בשמי אנוכי
אדרוש מעמו
וישא משלו ויאמר נאום בלעם בנבעור ונאם הגבר
שהתם העין נואם שומע אמרי אל וידע דעת עליון אשר
מחזה שדי יחזה נופל וגלו עין אראנו ולוא עתהא
אשורנו ולוא קרוב דרך כוכב מיעקוב ˹ויקומ˺ שבט מישראל ומחץ
פאתי מואב וקרקר את כול בני שית
וללוי אמר הבו ללוי תמיך ואורך לאיש חסידך אשר
נסיתו במסה ותרבהו על מי מריבה˹ה˺ אמר לאביו ///
/// ולאמו לידˈ˹ע˺תיכהו ואת אחיו לוא הכיר ואת בנו לוא
ידע כי שמר אמרתכה ובריתך ינצר ˹ויאירו˺ משפטיך ליעקוב
תורתכה לישראל ישם(ו) קטורה באפך וכליל על מזבחך
ברך •••• חילו ופעל ידו תרצה מחץ ˹מתנים˺ קמו ומשנאו
בל יקומו
בעת אשר כלה ישוע להלל ולהודות בתהלותיהו
ויאמר ארור היש אשר יבנה את העיר הזות בבכורו
ייסדנה ובצעירו יציב דלתיה ואנה ˹איש˺ ארור אחד בליעל
עומד להיות פ[ח י]קוש לעמו ומחתה לכול שכניו ועמד
◦◦[◦מ◦] ••• לה]יות שניהמה כלי חמס ושבו ובנו את
העיר הזות ויצ]יבו לה חומה ומגדלים לעשות לעוז רשע
ורעה גדלה]בישראל ושערוריה באפרים וביהודה
••• וע]שו חנופה בארץ ונצה גדולה בבני
יעקוב ושפכו ד]ם כמים על חל בת ציון ובחוק
ירושלמ

L. 1, Deut 5^{28}/SAM Ex 20^{21}: MT Deut has: **ויאמר יהוה אלי**. The use of four dots to represent the tetragrammaton is found elsewhere in l. 19, 1QS viii 14 (written by the same scribe) and 4Q *Tanḥūmîm* (**176**) ff. 1–2, i 6, 7, 9, etc.

שמעת. MT has **שמעתי**.

L. 2: **אליכה**. MT has **אליך**. The *lāmedh* has been written over a previous *wāw* and *tāw*, the beginning perhaps of an intended **אותם**.

כול. MT has **כל**.

L. 3, v. 29: **ינתן**. MT has **יתן**.

ויהיה. MT has **והיה**.

זה, inserted above the line by the same hand.
לירא. MT has ליראה.
כול . . . אותי ולשמור. MT has *scr. def.* in each case.
L. 4: כול היומים. MT has כל הימים.
למעאן. MT has למען; cf. לאהםה in the next line.
יטב. MT has ייטב.
להמ, with medial *mēm* in the final position; cf. ירושלמ in l. 30.
לעולם. MT has לעלם.
L. 5, Deut 18 18/SAM Ex 20[21]: נבי. MT has נביא.
לאהמה. cf. אחיהמה following, and אליהמה in l. 6.
מקרב, written over a previous מתוך.
אחיהמה. MT has אחיהם.
כמוכה. MT has כמוך.
L. 6: בפיהו. MT has בפיו.
וידבר. MT has ודבר.
אליהמה. MT has אליהם.
כול. MT has כל.
v. 19: האיש. The *hē* was inserted above the line by the same hand.
L. 7: לוא. MT has לא.
אל. The *'āleph* was written over a previous *'ayin*.
הנבי = LXX, but omitted by MT.
אנוכי. MT has אנכי.
L. 8: אדרוש. MT has אדרש. Between the lines 8 and 9, 13 and 14, 20 and 21 are marginal signs reminiscent of those in 1QS (e.g. ii 18–19; iii 12–13, 18–19, etc.).
L. 9, Nu 24[15]: וישא. The *'āleph* has been written over a previous *hē*.
נאום. MT has נאם (cf. following נאם, and נואם in l. 10). The *'āleph* has been written over a previous *hē*.
בנבעור. MT has בנו בער.
L. 10: שהתם. MT has שתם. Cf. T° דשפיר חזי, LXX ὁ ἀληθινῶς ὁρῶν.
v. 16: נואם. MT has נאם.
שומע. MT has שמע.
אשר, omitted by MT.
L. 11: נופל. MT has נפל.
וגלו. MT has וגלוי.
עין. MT has עינים.
v. 17: ולוא עתהא. MT has ולא עתה.
L. 12: ולוא. MT has ולא.
דרך וג׳׳. Cf. CD vii 19–20; 1QM xi 6.
מיעקוב. MT has מיעקב.
ויקומ was inserted above the line by the same hand. MT has וקם.
ומחץ. The final letter was written over another, possibly a *kaph*, and then repeated above.
L. 13: את, omitted by MT.
כול. MT has כל.
שית. MT has שת.
L. 14, Deut 33[8]: הבו ללוי = LXX, but omitted from MT.
ואורך. MT has ואוריך.
L. 15: ותרבהו. MT has תריבהו (SAM ותריבהו).
v. 9: האמר. The article was inserted above the line by the same hand.
לאביו. After this word there follows an erasure of an original לוא and another indecipherable word at the beginning of the next line.
L. 16: לידעתיכהו. The first *yōdh* was written over a previous *'āleph*, and the *'ayin* inserted above the line by the same hand. MT has לא ראיתיו (SAM לא ראיתי; LXX οὐχ ἑόρακά σε).
לוא . . . לוא. MT has לא . . . לא.
L. 17: שמר, sing. as LXX; MT has שמרו.

אמרתכה. MT has אמרתך.
ינצר, sing. as LXX; MT has ינצרו.
v. 10: ויאירו was inserted above the line by the same hand. MT has יורו, cf. מאירים in 4QpIsa[d] (**164**) f. 1, l. 5.
ליעקוב. MT has ליעקב.
L. 18: תורתכה. MT has ותורתך.
ישים(ו). The second *yōdh* was inserted above the line, and the final *mēm* written over a previous medial *mēm*.
וכליל. The *kaph* was written over a previous letter, and the *yōdh* inserted above the line.
L. 19, v. 11: ופעל. A *tāw* at the end of the word has been blocked out.
ידו = SAM; MT has ידיו.
מתנים was inserted above the line by the same hand.
משנאו . . . קמו. MT has משנאיו . . . קמיו.
L. 20: בל יקומו. MT has מן יקומון.

Ll. 21–30: [21] 'At the time when Joshua finished praising and giving thanks with his praises, [22] he said, "Cursed be the man who builds this city; with his firstborn [23] shall he lay its foundation, and with his last-born shall he set up its gates". And behold, a man accursed, the one of Belial,[24] shall arise to be a fowl[er's sn]are to his people, and destruction to all his neighbours. And he shall arise[25] [. . .] that the two of them may be instruments of violence. And they shall return and build[26] [this city and will es]tablish for it a wall and towers, to create a refuge of wickedness [27][and a great evil] in Israel, and a horrible thing in Ephraim, and in Judah [28] [. . . and they] shall cause pollution in the land, and great contempt among the sons of [29] [Jacob, and they shall pour out bl]ood like water on the rampart of the daughter of Zion, and in the boundary of [30] Jerusalem.'

L. 21: בעת . . . בתהלותיהו. MT Jos 6^{26} begins: וישבע יהושע בעת ההיא לאמר.
L. 22, Jos 6^{26}: היש. MT has האיש לפני יהוה.
יבנה = LXX[B] and 4QPssJos (. . .] אשר יב[נ]ה֯ את[). MT has יקום ובנה.
הזות. MT has הזאת and adds את יריחו.
בבכורו. MT has בבכרו.
L. 23: ואנה = והנה?
איש was inserted above the line in the same hand.
אחד was written over a previous word, probably איש.
L. 24: פח יקוש, restored after 4QPssJos.
לכול. 4QPssJos has לכל.
L. 25: להיות, restored with 4QPssJos.
שניהמה. 4QPssJos has שניהם.
L. 26: העיר . . . ויציבו, restoration based partly on 4QPssJos which has זאת ויציבו [. . .
L. 27: ורעה גדלה, restored with 4QPssJos.
L. 28: ונצה גדולה. 4QPssJos has ונאצה גדלה.
L. 29: יעקוב ושפכו דם, a restoration based partly on 4QPssJos which has]בבני יעקב ושפ֯ .

176. *TANḤÛMÎM*

(PL. XXII–XXIII)

1–2

Col. I: Quotations from Ps 79 $^{2-3}$ Isa 40^{1-5} 41^{8-9} and *pešer*

ועשה פלאכה והצדק בעמכה והי֯ו֯[
מקדשכה וריבה עם ממלכות על ד֯ם֯[
ירושלים וראה נבלת כ֯ה֯ניכה[
ואין קובר ומן ספר ישעיה תנ֯ח֯ומי֯ם֯[נחמו נחמו עמי]
יומר אלוהיכם דברו על לב ירושלים וק֯[ראו אליה כיא מלאה צבא]ה֯ כיא
נרצה עוונה כיא לקחה מיד • • • • כפלים בכול ח֯ט֯ותיהא קול קורה

במדבר פנו דרך •••• ישר ב[ערבה] מסלה לאלוהינ[ו] כול גיא ינשא
[וכול הר וגב]עה ישפלו והיה העקוב ל[מי]שור[והרכסים לב]קעה
ונגלה כ]בוד •••• ואתה ישראל עב[די י]עק[ו]ב [אשר ב]חרת[י]כה
[זרע אבר]הם אהבי אשר החזקתיכה[ ]י ה[א]רץ ומאצילהא
[קראתיכה ואמר] לכה עבדי אתה[בחרתיכה ולוא מאסת]יך

Ll. 1–4: '[1] and perform thy wonder and righteousness among thy people, and [. . .] [2] thy sanctuary, and contend with kingdoms over the blood of [. . .] [3] Jerusalem, and see the "bodies of" thy priests [. . .] [4] and "none to bury (them)".'

Ll. 3–4: נבלת . . . ואין קובר. Cf. Ps 79^{2-3} of which this passage is probably the *pešer*.

L. 5, Isa 40^{1}: יומר. MT has יאמר.

אלוהיכם. MT has אלהיכם.

v. 2: ירושלים. MT has ירושלם.

כיא. MT has כי.

L. 6: עוונה. MT has עונה.

כיא. MT has כי.

• • • • representing the tetragrammaton as in ll. 7, 9 and elsewhere; see 4Q Testimonia (**175**) ll. 1, 19 and note.

בכול. MT has בכל.

חטותיהא. MT has חטאתיה.

v. 3: קורה. MT has קורא.

L. 7: ישר. MT has ישרו.

לאלוהינו. MT has לאלהינו.

v. 4: כול. MT has כל.

L. 8: העקוב. MT has העקב.

L. 9, Isa 41^{8}: בחרתיכה. MT has בחרתיך.

L. 10, v. 9: החזקתיכה. The initial *hē* was inserted above the line. MT has החזקתיך.

]י הארץ. MT has מקצות הא״. Possibly we should restore ירכתי.

ומאצילהא. The last two letters were inserted above the line for lack of space. MT has ומאציליה.

L. 11: לכה. MT has לך.

Col. II: Quotations from Isa $49^{7,\ 13-17}$

•••• אשר נ]אמן קדוש יש[ראל ויבחרכה
פצחו הרים כיא נחם אלה[ים עמו ועניו ירחם ותאמר ציון]
עזבני •••• [ואדני שכחני התשכח אשה עולה מרחם בן בטנה]
גם אלה תשכח[נה ואנכי לוא אשכחך הן על כפים חקותיך]
וחומותיך נג[די תמיד מהרו בניך מהרסיך ומחרביך]
ממך יצ[או

L. 1, Isa 49^{7}: קדוש. MT has קדש.

L. 2, v. 13: פצחו. MT (Ktb) has יפצחו; Qre and MSS ופצחו.

הרים. MT adds רנה.

כיא. MT has כי.

אלהים. MT has יהוה.

L. 5, v. 16: וחומותיך. MT has חומתיך.

3: Quotation from Isa 43^{1-2}

ועתה כ]וֺא אמר יה[וה בראך יעקב ויצרך ישראל
אל תיר]אֺ כיא גאלתיך [קראתי בשמך לי אתה כיא תעבר
במים] אֺתך אני ובנ[הה]ר[ות לוא ישטפוך

L. 1, Isa 43^{1}: כוא for כה of MT, unless כיא is intended.
יהוה apparently written fully instead of the four dots found elsewhere.
L. 2: כיא. MT has כי.

4–5: Quotation from Isa 43^{4-6}

וא]תֺןֺ אדם תֺח[תיך ולאמים תחת נפשך
אל ת]ירא [כיא אתך א]נֺיֺ ממזרח אבי[א זרעך וממערב אקבצך
אמ]רֺ לצפון [תני ולתימן] אל תכלאי הבֺ[יאי בני מרחוק ובנותי מקצה
הא]רץ
]כיא[

6–7: Quotation from Isa 51^{22-23}

כה אמר אדונ]יֺךֺ [····· א[לו]היך[יריב עמו הנה לקחתי מידך את
כוס התר]עלה[את קבע]תֺ כוס ח[מתי לוא תוסיפי לשתותה עוד
ושמתיה] ביד מוגיך[ ]◦יֺמֺיֺ ◦◦[

L. 1, Isa 51^{22}: אלוהיך. MT adds a conjunction.
L. 3: the remains of the word beginning the third line of f. 7, excised by the scribe with dots above the letters, may indicate an original ותשימי, perhaps a false start with v. 23^{d}, omitting v. $23^{b, c}$.

8–11: Quotation from Isa 52 $^{1-3}$ 54^{4-10} and *pešer*

]מֺ[ ]כאר[ץ]◦ירים
עוריֺ[עורי לבשי עוזך] צֺיון לב[שי בגדי תפארתך י]רֺושלים עֺיר הקודש כיא
[לוא יוסיף יבוא בך עוד ערל וטמא התנערי מעפר קומ]י שובי ירושלם התפתחי
מוסרי צוארך ש]בֺיֺהֺ[בת ציון כיא כה]אמר[···· חנם נמכרתם ולוא] בֺכסף תגאלו
]אל תירֺ[אי כיא] לוא /// תבושי[ואל תכלמי כי]א לא תחפירי כיא בשת
עלומי]כי תשכחיֺ[וח]רֺפת ארמלותך לוא[תזכרי עוד]כבעלך עושיך ····
צבאות] שמו וגאליכי קדוש יש[ראל א]ל[והי כו]ל [הא]רץֺ יֺקרא כיא כאשה עזוֺבה
ועצובת] רֺוֺח קראך ···· ואשת נעורים כיא[ת]מֺאס אמר ···· אלוהיךֺ
ברגע] קטנה עזבתיך וברחמים גדולים אקבֺצך בשצף קצף ◦◦[ ]
רגע מ]מֺךֺ ובחסדי עולמ רחמתיכה אמר גואלֺךֺ ···· כימי נוח זות לי אשר
נשבעתי מ]עבֺ[ור מי] נוח אל ארץ כֺן נשבעתי מֺקצוף עליך עד ו̊געור בך
כיא ההר]ים ימושו והגבעות תתמוטטנה וחסֺדי מאתיכי לוא ימושֺ[

נ]ואש עד דברי תנחומ֯י֯ם֯ וכבוד רב כתוב ב֯[

]ב֯אוה֯ב֯[י]אין עוד מעת[

בלי]ע֯ל לענות את עב֯ד֯יו בו[ ]◦ת י◦[

]י ישמח֯ [ ]ו֯[ ] ארים֯[ ]יושבת[

]◦בת[ ]תמ֯ע◦[

L. 1: כאר]ץ. Cf. Isa 51^{23}.
L. 2, Isa 52^{1}: הקודש. MT has הקדש.
כיא. MT has כי.
L. 3, v. 2: שובי. MT has שבי.
ירושלים. MT has ירושלם.
התפתחי. As Qre; MT Ktb has חו″.
L. 5, Isa 54^{4}: לוא. MT has לא. 4Q is followed by a semi-obliterated letter, possibly *pē*.
כיא. MT has כי.
L. 6: עלומיכי. MT has יך″.
ארמלותך. MT has אלמנותיך.
לוא. MT has לא.
v. 5: כבעלך. MT has כי בעליך.
L. 7: וגאליכי. MT has וגאלך.
v. 6: כיא. MT has כי.
L. 8: כיא. MT has כי.
אלוהיך . . . . . MT has אלהיך.
L. 9, v. 7: קטנה. MT has קטן.
גדולים. MT has גדלים.
v. 8: קצף. The remains of the next two letters look quite unlike the *hē* and *sāmekh* of MT's הסתרתי.
L. 10: ובחסדי. MT has ובחסד.
רחמתיכה. MT has תיך″.
גואלך. MT has גאלך.
v. 9: נוח. MT has נח.
זות. MT has זאת.
L. 11: נוח אל ארץ. MT has נח עוד על הארץ.
מקצוף. MT has מקצף.
עד ומגעור. MT has ומגער. The *mēm* of ומגעור was first omitted and inserted later above the line.
L. 12, v. 10: [כיא]. F. 41 possibly belongs here.
תתמוטטנה. MT has תמוטנה.
מאתיכי. MT has מאתך.
לוא. MT has לא.
L. 13: '. . . *w*]*eary* unto the words of comfort; and great glory is written *in* [. . . [14] . . .] *among lovers of* [. . .] no more from the time of [. . . [15] . . . *Beli*]*al* to oppress *his servants* by it [. . . [16] . . .] will rejoice [. . .] *I will raise up her who sits* [. . .'.
תנחומים. Cf. ff. 1–2, col. i, l. 4.
יושבת. F. 11 is placed here only because the skin, script and spacing conform well to ll. 16–17.

12–13: Quotation from Isa 52^{1-2}

]◦[

]כי לוא[יוסי]ף֯ יבוא[בך עוד ערל וטמא התנערי

מע]פר ק[ו]מי

Possibly a restatement of the biblical text at the end of the *pešer* of ff. 8–11, at the foot of the same column.
לוא . . . יבוא. MT has לא . . . יבא.

14

]בכׄשו[
]◦ם שנאׄיׄתׄ ◦[
]שוׄנאנו שברנו[
]אׄ הבטתה אוׄלׄינו[
]כׄהׄ על מׄכה בו[
]אין לוא דורש[
]◦אׄבׄדׄה ◦ל[

Possibly part of the prayer at the beginning of ff. 1–2.

L. 3: שונאנו. The dots above and beneath the *wāw* are indication of erasure, as with אולינו in the following line where also a *yōdh* has been inserted above *nūn*.

L. 6: 'he has no interpreter', i.e. לוא = לו.

15: Quotation from Zech 13[9]

]◦[
והב[אית]י[
את השלשית באש וצרפתים כצרף את הכסף ובחנתים[כבחון את
הזהב הואה יקרא בשמי ואני אענה אתו אמרתי[עמי והואה
]◦ר ואמר
]לׄ[

L. 2: והבאיתי. MT has והבאתי.
L. 3: כבחון. MT has כבחן.
L. 4: עמי והואה. MT has עמי הוא.

16

]◦◦◦◦[
]רזי הפיל גורל[ ]◦ ◦◦◦[
ב[ית קודש ולתת מילת איש ל[
]◦ר על אוהבו ועל שומרי מצ]ותו
]שׄ◦א◦ת בריתו ול◦[
]לׄ[ ]ל[

[2]. . .] *secrets* of casting the lot [. . . [3] . . .] holy [h]ouse, and to give man's speech to [. . . [4] . . .] upon those who love him and those who keep [his] command[ments . . . [5] . . .] his covenant. And to [. . .

L. 5:]שׄ◦א◦ת. The letter after '*āleph* has possibly been erased.

17

]◦[

דור]ות עולמים ◦[

]◦ על כול א[יש

]במלאך פ◦[

] שמונה ש[

]יֹפע לנו ממ[

ע]שׂו התורה ו[

]התורה[

L. 1: cf. Isa 51[9].

18

]נֹחלת ידו כי לוא יצדק[

]לֹטֹו דרֹכי כול◦◦◦◦◦◦[

19

]א בחֹ[

]ם בחרב ולמשפט ◦[

]שׂים עֹליהמה י[

20

לוא בא]מֹתֹ ולוא בצדקה

]ויהי קצף גדול על מעשי הדור

]ולב◦[ ] ולאיבו להֹבֹער עליהים

]◦ובֹלֹ[ ]לֹ[ ]שאוֹ[ ]ליאי

[1]. . . *not in tru*]*th* and not in righteousness [. . . [2] . . .] and there was great wrath upon the works of the generation [. . .[3] . . .] and to his enemies to *kindle against them* [. . .

L. 1: cf. Isa 48[1].

21

]ו◦ ◦◦[

]בכול קללתֹ[

]ורוחותיהם ◦[

]יש אל עושה◦[

]לֹ[ ]◦[ ]הֹלר[

L. 4: יש אל; or perhaps יש(ר)אל. The parchment is badly rubbed at this point and the missing letter could have been rubbed away.

22

]וגם אף בׄקדוש [
]כיא הוא ברא את כול[
]◦נו טרם הייתם ובע[
]לׄ[ ]ול אמרׄ[
]◦ ◦[

23

]◦[
]שמׄתׄיׄה להיותׄ[
]◦[ ]ל[ ]כלותם[
]◦[

24

]מ◦ ◦ ◦[
]◦ עׄ עיצים ◦[
]ציון ◦◦[

25

]ה ◦◦[
]◦תיו[
]◦ות[
]מארץ[
]◦ו בת[
]◦ אש[

26

]◦[
]לאר[
]באש[
]◦אאׄ פת[
]לטמׄ ◦[
]הל◦[
]◦ ◦ ◦[

F. 26, l. 4: the second *'āleph* erased by dots placed above and beneath the letter. The scribe absent-mindedly took the left-hand leg of the first *'āleph* as the right-hand tick of another.

27

]שפטו[
]◦ורם[
]תׄוכהׄ[
]ל◦ו[

28

]◦[
לי בעבור ה[
]◦◦]ל[

29

]ואו ◦[
]או ◦[

30

]כפ◦[
]◦◦ל[
]ה ומׄרפה[
]◦◦◦[

31

]◦מה [
]◦ [
א]לוהים [

32

]שט◦ וא◦[
]אׄות כי[
]◦[

33

]ירׄ[
]ל[

34

]כׄאפס[
]יונים[

35

]◦ת◦[
]◦הולל[

36

]◦מימׄ[
]◦לד◦[

37

]◦[
]◦לש◦◦ ◦[
]ל[

38

]ישר[

39

]רי[
]◦ף ק[
]◦ו ◦◦[

40

]◦שנׄא[
]אדם [
]◦[

41

]כיא[
]ל[

42

]וחי[
]רׄי ע◦[
]◦◦ה◦[

43
]ים ה[
]◦יאים[

44
]◦תם֯[
]ל[

45
]ם֯[
]◦סו◦[

46
]◦ו֯ל֯י֯[

47
]ע א[

48
]וי◦[
]ו֯ל[

49
]◦ד֯◦[

50
]מ֯ל֯ח֯מ֯כי[
]הן֯ ◦◦◦[

51
]◦[
]בר֯◦[
]ל֯[

52
]◦[
]אין יב֯[

53
]◦◦◦[
]ל֯◦יש[

54
]כ֯ו֯ל֯[
]◦[

55
]◦◦[
]הן֯ ◦[

56
]◦[
]שב[
]ל֯[

57
]◦[
]◦א֯[

177. CATENA (A)

(PL. XXIV–XXV[a])

1–4

]לדבריהם֯[
והסיר יהוה] מ֯מ֯כ֯ה כול חלי [
]◦ נהיה כמש[פחות הארצות
]◦◦ד[ ]◦[ ]ל֯◦תמה שמה֯[
]ו֯ באחרית הימים בע֯ת אשר יבקש ◦[
]◦פשר הדבר אשר י֯עמוד איש מב◦[ ]בה ממנו ו◦[
ו]היו כ֯אש לכול תבל והמה֯ אשר כתוב עליהם באחרית [הימים ···]◦◦ה פוח֯[זים ··· הת]ע֯וללו ברוחי֯[
]מ ◦◦[ג]ורל אור אש֯ר הי֯ה מתאבל בממשלת בל[יעל ···]אשר היה מתאבל֯[···]ב֯מספר שמות֯[
]לר֯אשי אבל שוב ת֯◦[··· א]ל֯והי הרחמים וא֯ל ישרא[ל··· ג]מול נ֯ב֯י֯אי יהודה֯[
]א֯שר ה[···ב]ל֯יעל ונסלו֯ להם לעולם וברכם֯[···ה]ג֯י֯ד כיא לעולם יברכם[··· ימ]ל֯או קצים֯[
]◦ת אבותם[···]מפורשים ב֯שמות לאיש ואיש ◦[····ש]נ֯ותיהם וקץ מעמדם י[···]ו לשונם[
]א֯ את צאצ֯[אי···]ע֯תה הנה הכול כתוב בלוחות אשר[···]א֯ל וידי֯עהו את מס֯פר ◦[···]ת וינח[ילהו

]°°[···]ל̊[ו] ולזרׄעו [עד] עולם ויקום משמה ללכׄת[···]תקׄעׄו שופר בגבעה השופר הואה ספר[

]°[הו]אה ספר התורה שנית אשרׄ[··· א]נשׄי עצתו וידברו עליו סרה ויש°°[

או]תותׄ גדולות על ה[···]° ויעקוב עומד על הגתות ושמח על רׄדׄתׄ[

]תׄ בחׄרב איׄבׄ[יהם ···] לאנשי עצתו המה החרב ואשר אמר[

[1] . . .] to their words [. . . [2] . . . 'And Yahweh will take] from thee all sickness' [. . . [3] . . .] 'let us be like the tr[ibes of the countries' . . . [4] . . .] thence [. . . [5] . . .] in the end of days, in the time when he shall seek [. . . [6] . . .] The interpretation of the passage is that there shall arise a man from [. . .]from him [. . . [7] . . . *and*] they shall be like a fire to all the world; and they are those about whom it is written in the end of [days . . .] *wan*[*ton men . . . have* dealt] ruthlessly in the spirits of [. . . [8] . . . the l]ot of light which was in mourning during the dominion of Bel[ial . . .] which was in mourning [. . .] by the number of names [. . . [9] . . .] to the *heads* of mourning return [. . . G]od of mercy, and to Israe[l . . . *re*]*compense* of the *prophets* of Judah [. . . [10] . . .] who [. . . Be]lial and they shall be exalted by them for ever, and he shall bless them [. . . *t*]*old* that for ever he would bless them [. . .] epochs be [*ful*]*filled* [. . . [11] . . .] their fathers [. . .] clearly set out by name, man by man [. . .] their [y]ears and the epoch of their existence [. . .] their tongues [. . . [12] . . .] offsp[ring of . . .] Now, behold, everything is written on the tablets which [. . .] and he taught him the number of [. . .] and caused [him] to *inher*[*it* . . .[13]. . .] to [him] and to his seed [for] ever. And he arose from thence to go [. . .] 'Blow the horn in Gibeah': 'the horn' is the book of [. . .[14] . . . *i*]*t* is the book of the Second Law which [. . . m]en of his counsel, but they spoke rebelliously against him and [. . . [15] . . .] great [*si*]*gns* upon [. . .] and Jacob shall stand upon the winepresses and rejoice over the *flowing down* [. . . [16] . . .] by the sword of [their] enemies [. . .] to the men of his counsel: they are 'the sword'; and as it says [. . .

L. 2: cf. Deut. 7^{15}.
L. 3: cf. Ezek 20^{32}, where MT adds כגוים.
L. 6:]בה ממנו[. . . . The positioning of f. 4 is only very tentative.
L. 7: פוחזים. Cf. Zeph 3^{4}. The lateral placing of ff. 3 and 4 can only be conjectural.
L. 8: גורל אור. Cf. 1QM xiii 9 and, by restoration, CD xiii 12.
L. 10: כיא. A large and crudely drawn *kaph* has been written over the original initial letter, possibly *mēm*.
L. 11: מפורשים וג״. Cf. CD ii 13 and iv 4–5.
שנותיהם וקץ מעמדם. Cf. CD ii 9 and iv 5.
L. 13: תקעו וג״. Cf. Hos 5^{8}.
L. 15: אותותת. Dots above and below the last *tāw* indicate erasure.
L. 16: בחרב. The second *bēth* has been written over another letter.

5–6

]ה ההוללים אשר יׄ[··]בׄא על אנשי היׄ[חד
הנ]ביא אכול השנה שפ[יח פשר הדב]ר השפיח הו[אה
]רׄה עד עת המצ[רף הבאה ו]אחרי כן יעמודׄ[
]כׄיא כולם ילדים[···]אׄמרו ההולליׄ[ם

אשר כתוב] עליהם בספר י[··· הנב]יא תורת ההו֯[
]קרא להם כאשר [אמר הוא ז]מות יעץ לח[בל ענוים באמרי שקר
ל]ה֯לעין את ישרא[ל למנצח] לדויד ביהו֯ה[חסיתי איך תאמרו לנפשי נודו
הרכם צפור כיא הנה הרשעים ידרכון
קשת]ויכינו חצי֯ם עׄ[ל יתר פשרו א]שׄר ינודו אנ[שי
כצ]פור ממקומו וגלׄ[ה ··· עליה]ם בספר ה[
]ץ לה איש ו֯ילך ד֯◦[···]◦◦ם היא֯[
]אׄשר כתוב עליהם בספר[
]ך רׄ֯אׄו למנצח על ה[שמינית
]המה העונה השמינית[
א]ין שלום אשר המה ד◦[
]ה֯רוג בקר ושחוט צואן א[כול בשר
]◦ת התורה עושי היחד ס◦[

[1] . . .] the boasters who [. . .] against the men of the *co*[*mmunity* . . . [2] . . . *the* pr]ophet, 'This year eat what gr[ows of itself.' *The interpretation of the phra*]se 'what grows of itself' is [. . . [3] . . .] until the time of tri[al *that is coming*, and] afterwards there shall arise [. . . [4] . . .] for all of them are children [. . .] the boaster[s] say [. . . [5] . . . *as it is written*] concerning them in the book of [. . . *the proph*]*et*, the law of the [. . . [6] . . .] called to them when [he said, 'He] counsels evil [de]vices to ru[in the poor with lying words' . . . [7] . . . *to*] curse Israe[l. 'To the director;] of David. In Yahweh [I take refuge; how can ye say] to me, [*Flee to your mountain, O bird: for lo, the wicked bend* [8] *the bow*] and they have fitted arrows t[o *the string*.' *Its interpretation is* th]at the me[n of . . .] will flee [. . . [9] . . . *like* a sp]arrow from his place and shall depa[rt. *And that which concerns th*]*em* in the book of the [. . . [10] . . .] a man to her and he went [. . . [11] . . .] as it is written concerning them in the book of [. . . [12] . . .] 'To the director; according to the [*Sheminith* . . .' [13] . . .] they are the eighth period ('*Onah*) [. . . [14] . . . *There*] *is no* peace, that they are [. . . [15] . . .] 'slaying oxen and killing sheep, ea[ting flesh' . . . [16] . . .] the Law, those who institute the community [. . .

L. 2: שפיח. Cf. Isa 37^{30}; MT has ספיח.
L. 3: עת המצרף הבאה. Cf. 4QpPss[a] (**171**) ff. 1–2, ii 18; and 4QFlorilegium (**174**) ff. 1, 3, ii 1.
L. 6: cf. Isa 32^{7}.
L. 7: הלעין. Cf. Arab, Nab.
דויד. Cf. Ps 11^{1}; MT has דוד.
L. 8, v. 2: ויכינו. MT has כוננו.
חצים = LXX; MT has חצם.
L. 12: ראו. Dots above and below the first and above the last letter mark the word's deletion.
למנצח וג״. Cf. Ps 12^{1}.
L. 15: הרוג . . . ושחוט צואן. Cf. Isa 22^{13}; MT *scr. def.*

7

]מ̇ר̇נ̇ן[ ]◦◦[

]ד אשר יבקשו לחבל[

אש]ר̇ כ̇ת̇וב בספר יחזקאל הנ[ביא

]הימים אשר יקבצו עליה[ם

]ע̇י האנשים אשר עבדו אל̇[הים אחרים

]◦◦[ ]◦[ ]לאשר לה̇מה ט̇מא ול◦[

[2] . . .] that they seek to ruin [. . . [3] . . . a]s it is written in the book of Ezekiel the pr[ophet . . . [4] . . .] the days when there will be gathered against th[em . . . [5] . . .] of men who have served [*other*]*go*[*ds* . . . [6] . . .] to those who are *unclean* and to [. . .

8

]◦◦[

]ח̇ד ערומי ◦[

] כיא לוא עם מ̇[

]סף ההר ספ◦[

9

]◦◦◦◦◦[

עליה]מ̇ה ב̇אחרי[ת הימים

]י̇הם ברוב̇ ה̇ברורי̇[ם

]המה ע̇דת דורשי ה[חלקות

]ב̇קנאתמ̇ה ובמ̇שטמ[תמה

]מ̇יהודה̇ בכול העמ[י]ם

]עם צדיק̇ ורשע אויל ופת[י

]◦רי ערלות ל̇ישרם בדור הא[חרון

[2] . . . concerning th]em in the las[t *days* . . . [3] . . .] them in the multitude of the purified one[s . . . [4] . . .] they are the congregation of Seekers after [Smooth Things . . . [5] . . .] in their zeal and in [their] hostility [. . . [6] . . .] *from* Judah amongst all the peoples [. . . [7] . . .] *a people* righteous and wicked, foolish and *simp*[*le* . . . [8] . . .] of foreskins to lead them aright in the *L*[*ast*] Generation [. . .

10–11

אמרות יהוה אמרות טהרות כסף צרוף בעליל לארץ מזק]ק שבעתים כאשר כתוב

···כי הנה האבן אשר נתתי לפני יהושע על אבן אחת שבעה עינים···מפ]ת̇חת

פתוחה נואם יהוה אשר

א]ש̇ר עליהם כתוב ורפאתי את

]◦ל אנשי בליעל וכול האספסוף

]המה דורש התורה כיא אין
]איש על מצורו בעומדם
]המכשילים את בני האור
... עד אנה יהו]ה תשכח[ני נצח עד אנה תסת]יר פניכה ממני עד אנה אשיתה
עצות בנפשי יגון בלבבי יומם] עד אנה[ירום איבי עלי פ]שר הדבר לנצח לב אנשי
]◦ה◦מי[ ]לבוחנם ולצורפם
]◦◦◦[ ]ואמר אויב

[1] . . . 'The promises of Yahweh are promises that are pure, silver refined in a furnace on the ground, purif]ied seven times.' As it is written [. . . [2] . . . 'For behold, upon the stone which I have set before Joshua, upon a single stone with seven facets,] its inscription [*is engrav*]*ed*, says Yahweh', as [. . . [3] . . . *whi*]*ch* is written concerning them, 'And I shall heal [. . .' [4] . . .] the men of Belial and all the rabble [. . . [5] . . .] them the Interpreter of the Law, for there is no [. . . [6] . . .] each man upon his rampart when they stand [. . . [7] . . .] those who cause the Sons of Light to stumble [. . . [8] . . . 'How long, O Yahw]eh? Wilt thou forget [me for ever? How long wilt thou] hide thy face from me? How long must I bear [[9] *pain* in my soul, (and) sorrow in my heart by day? How long [shall my enemy be exalted over me?' The inter]pretation of the phrase 'for ever': the hearts of men of [. . . [10] . . .] at their testing and trying [. . . [11] . . .] and 'the enemy said . . .'

L. 1: cf. Ps 12[7].
L. 2: cf. Zech 3[9]; MT has הנני מפתח פתחה נאם.
יהוה. MT adds צבאות.
L. 6: איש על מצורו. Cf. CD iv 11–12. The last letter is presumably intended for a *wāw* although clearly written here as *yōdh*; cf. 1QpHab vi 13 (MT Hab 2[1] מצור).
L. 8: cf. Ps 13[2–3]. פניכה: MT has את פניך.
v. 3: אשיתה. MT has אשית.
L. 11: cf. Ex 15[9] (MT אמר).

12–13
Col. I

]לאה◦[ ]◦[ ]תורה מכ[והן ועצה מחכם ודבר] מנביא
]לאחרית ה[י]מים אשר אמר דויד יה[ו]ה אל באפכה תו[כיחני···כי]א אמלל אני
]ונפשי נבהלה מאדה ועתה יהוה עד מתי חונני חלצה נפ[שי ...]למים על
ב]ליעל להאבידמה בחרונו אשר לוא יותיר ל[...]◦◦ח לבליעל
]◦הם עד עשרה צדיקים בעיר כיא רוח אמת ה◦[... כי]א אין
]◦מה ואחיהמה במחשבל בליעל ויחזק עליו[...]◦◦◦ל◦◦◦[
]מלאך אמתו יעזור לכול בני אור מיד בליעל[
]◦◦◦[ ]ולפזר[ם] בארץ ציה ושממה היא עת ענות המ◦[
]תמד ידוד הצ[די]ק ויד אל הגדולה עמהמה לעוזרם מכול רוחו[ת
]◦או אל וקדושו שמו ובאו ציון בשמחה וירושלים[
ב]ל[יע]ל וכול אנשי גורלו ו◦[ ] לעד ונאספו כול בני א[ור

[1]'. . .] law from the pri[est nor counsel from the wise, nor word] from the prophet' [. . . [2] . . .] at the end of days as David said, 'O Yahweh, re[buke me] not in thine anger [. . . fo]r I am languishing; [. . . [3] . . .] and my soul is sorely troubled. And now, O Yahweh, how long? Be gracious unto me, save [my] li[fe . . .' . . .] upon [. . . [4] . . . Be]lial to destroy them in his anger, whom he will not leave to [. . .] to Belial [. . . [5] . . .] them unto ten righteous men in the city, for the spirit of truth [. . . f]or there is no [. . . [6] . . .] and their brothers by the device of Belial that he might prevail over *him* [. . . [7] . . .] his angel of truth will help all the Children of Light from the power of Belial [. . . [8] . . .] and to scatter [them] in 'a dry and desolate land'. That is the time of affliction that [. . . [9] . . .] *continually* the *ri*[*ghte*]*ous man* will flee, and the great hand of God will be with them to help them from all the spirit[s of . . . [10] . . .] God, and his holy ones they have appointed and they shall enter Zion with gladness and to Jerusalem [. . . [11] . . . Be]l[ia]l and all the men of his lot, and [. . .] for ever, and all the Children of L[ight] shall be gathered together [. . .

L. 1: cf. Jer 18^{18}.
L. 2: cf. Ps 6^{2-3}. For כיא . . . באפכה MT has כי . . . באפך.
L. 3, v. 4: מאדה ועתה. MT has מאד ואת.
v. 5: חונני. MT has שובה יהוה.
L. 6: במחשבל, presumably an error for במחשבת; cf. following בל״.
L. 7: cf. 1QS iii 24–25.
L. 8: ארץ ציה וג״. Cf. Joel 2^{20}. A supralinear cross precedes the *pešer*, cf. Col. II, l. 9 and f. 29, l 2.
L. 9: תמד, *scr. def.* for תמיד?
L. 10: ציון. From this word the script deteriorates to the end of the column.

Col. II

הׄעׄ◦[ ]םׄ[
בליעל י[
לאׄחרית[
שׁוׄפר ב◦[
אמׄרׄתי[
אׄלׄ את◦[
בליע[ל
אנשי[
×◦[

L. 6: a *wāw* (or *yōdh*) has been inserted after *'āleph* supralinearly.
L. 9: a cross sign, cf. i 8, f. 29, l. 2.

14

]ובחרׄ[]הכבׄוׄדׄ אשר יואמׄ[ר
לקדושים אשר]בא[רץ ה]מה ואדיׄ[ר]יׄ כול חפציׄ[בם
ו]פׄיק[ב]רכים וחלחלה בכול מתׄנ[ים
]הקשׁיבה רנתי האזינה ל[תפלתי
]ר את עצת היחד וׄהואה[
] הרי ◦◦◦◦◦[ ]ל[

1 . . .] the *glorious* [. . .] as it will *sa*[*y* . . . 2 . . . 'to the holy ones who are] in the la[nd, th]ey and the nobles [in whom] is all my delight' [. . . 3 . . . 'and] tottering of [kn]ees and anguish is in all loi[ns' . . . 4 . . .] 'attend to my cry, give ear to [my prayer' . . . 5 . . .] the council of the community, and it [. . .

L. 2: cf. Ps 16^{3}. כול: MT has כל.
L. 3: cf. Nah 2^{11}. כול . . . פיק: MT has כל . . . פק.
L. 4: cf. Ps 17^{1}. ל[תפלתי: MT omits preposition.

15

ידיהם̊[
כיא ה[
◦◦[

16

]וילם[
]לעצ[
]ם[
]ה◦[

17

]במ[
]◦ב◦[
]א̊ותות[

18

]מ◦◦[
]ספר[
]בב◦[
]◦רא◦[
]◦[

19

]◦◦[
]ש̊י נ◦ה ב◦◦◦ א̊לי ה◦[
]◦התלוננו יחד ול◦[
]◦יתגוללו ה◦[
]◦דריו אקבוץ חרון̊[
]י̊שובון וב◦◦[

20

]◦[
]ם כיא[
]מזוקק̊[
]◦ות המ◦[
]◦ל ב[

21

]◦◦[
]אשר יבקש◦[
ב]ק̊ש ל[

22

]מה[
]◦נו[
]בח◦[

23

]◦יא[
]אסף̊[
]◦◦[

24

]◦[
]לקח̊[
]ה◦[

25

]◦◦◦[
]◦ב̊[

26

]◦נפשי̊[
]ה̊[ ]◦ת̊[

F. 26. This f. should perhaps be placed in l. 7 of ff. 5–6, or in l. 9 of ff. 10–11.

27

[ש◦]
[ב֯חירי]

28

[ת◦]
[שר א◦]
[לה◦]

29

[ר֯עיכה]
[×ת◦]
[י֯דח◦]

F. 29, l. 2: for the cross sign, cf. ff. 12–13, i 8, ii 9.

30

[◦◦◦◦◦◦◦]
[ס֯פסוף◦◦]
[ים לשל֯]

178.

(PL. XXV)

1

[◦◦◦ם֯ ו֯לע]מ[וד לפני◦]
[אשר֯ צוה בצר למו בא]
[◦דת הארץ י◦]
[בקש הי◦]
[ה֯שלום ו]
[ה֯רוח]

2

[◦◦ם וי]
[דבר בש◦]
[ת הימים]
[ת֯ורה ינדפ]
[ובמחשבו֯]ת
[◦◦◦]

3

[ש֯או] [◦]
[◦כאשר כתוב]
[ל֯ם ושבי י◦]
אחר[ית הימי]ם
[◦דם]

4

[◦הל◦]
[◦לאדם]
[צ֯דקה ול◦◦]
[צאצאי◦]

5

ויב]
פיתאו]ם
בא◦]

6

הו֯]
למעשי]
וענות]

F. 5, l. 2: cf. 1QH viii 18.

7
]◦האשה֯ וש◦[
]◦ת ◦ ◦ ◦[

8
]◦ותיה֯ם◦[
]ושו להשמ[
] ◦[ ]◦ים |

9
]◦[
]ה֯ימים ולוא[
]◦ו֯ הטוב[
]ל֯[

10
]בליעל[
]◦ע֯ו[

11
]◦[
] ולענוי
]ל[

12
]דניא[ל
] הנות◦[

13
]בו יש[
]◦[

179. LAMENTATIONS

(PL. XXVI)

1
Col. I

]◦[
]ש֯ר כ֯ל עוונותינו ואין לאל ידנו כי לוא שמענ֯[ו
]◦י֯ה֯ודה לקרותנו כל אלה ברוע [ ]
]◦את בריתו אוי לנו[ ]
]היה לשרפת אש והפכה [ ]
]◦תפ֯א֯ר֯ת֯נו וניחוח אין בו במ◦[ ]
]ח֯צרות קודשנו היו
]◦כ֯◦[ ]◦◦תים ירושלים עיר
]◦לחיה ואין ◦[ ]ורחובותיה
]◦הו֯י֯ כל ארמונותיה שממו
]◦ובאי מועד אין בם כ֯ל ערי
]נ֯חלתנו היתה כמדבר ארץ לוא
]שמ[ח]ה֯ לוא נשמ֯עה בה ודורש
]ל איש ל֯מכאו֯ב֯נ֯ו֯[ ]כול איבינו
פ]ש֯עינו י◦[ ]ח֯טאותינו

Col. II

אוי לנ֯ו֯ כי אף אל עלה[
ונגוללה עם המתים ◦[
כמשונאה יש◦[

לעוליהן ובת עמי אכזריה]
עלומיה שוממו בני ◦]
מלפני חורף בדל ידיהן]
אשפותות מדור בית ◦]
שאלו מים ואין̊ מגיר̊]
המסלאים̇ [ ]◦◦ת̊◦◦]
וחפץ אין בו ˹ה˺אמונים עלי תול̊[ע
וכתם טוב עדים נושאים̇ הלבו[שים
ימשו תכלת ידי קמה מפ̊[ני
בנו˹ת˺ ציון ה̇י̇ק̇ר̇י̇ם̇ הרכות ע̊מ̊ם̊ ◦◦]

Col. I. [2]. . .] all our iniquities and we served not God for *w*[*e*] did not obey [. . . [3] . . .] *Judah* that all these things befall us in the *evil* [. . . [4] . . .] his covenant. Woe to us [. . . [5] . . .] has been burned with fire and overturned [. . . [6] . . .] our glory and there is no soothing savour in it [. . . [7] . . .] our holy courts were [[8] . . .] Jerusalem, city of [[9] . . .] *to wild beasts* and none [. . .] and her broad places [[10] . . .] *Alas!* All her palaces are desolate [[11] . . .] and those who attend the appointed assembly are not in them; *all* the cities of [[12] . . .] our inheritance has become like a desert, a land not [[13] . . .] rejoicing is no longer heard in her, and the seeker after [[14] . . .] man for our wounds, [. . .] all our enemies [[15] . . .] our [*trans*]*gressions* [. . .] our sins

Col. II. [1]Woe to us for the wrath of God has gone up [. . .] [2] and *we are defiled* with the dead [. . .] [3] like a hated (wife) [. . .] [4] for their sucklings, and the daughter of my people is cruel [. . .] [5] her youth; the children of [. . .] are desolate [. . .] [6] because of the winter when their hands are feeble [. . .] [7] dunghills *than dwelling* (in) [. . .] house [. . .][8] they asked for water and there was none to pour out [. . .] [9] weighed [. . .] [10] and there is no delight in him; those who were brought up in purp[le. . .] [11] and pure gold their adornment, the wearers of *garm*[*ents* . . .] [12] they *depart*. The perfection of my hands has arisen from *be*[*fore* . . .] [13] the tender daughters of Zion *with them* [. . .

Col. I. L. 2: שמענו, inserted at the end of the line, overrunning the left-hand margin.
L. 5: היה לשרפת אש. Cf. Isa 64[10]. The *tāw* of שרפת seems to have been altered from an original *hē*.
L. 9: לחיה, or perhaps 'her cheek', cf. Lam 1[2].
L. 12: cf. Isa 64[9].
L. 13: נשמשעה. A point of erasure has been placed above the intrusive *shīn*.
L. 14: מכתינו, as emended from an originally written למכאובנו (cf. Isa 53[3]), the *lāmedh* being given a point of erasure above the letter, and 'אוב' being scratched through and replaced above the line with 'תי'.

Col. II. L. 4: אכזריה. Cf. Lam 4[3].
L. 7: אשפותות. Cf. Lam 4[5] (MT: אשפתות).
L. 8: cf. Lam 4[4].
L. 9: cf. Lam 4[2].
L. 10: האמונים. Cf. Lam 4[5] (MT: האמנים); the article has been inserted above the line.
L. 11: נושאי: the scribe has erased a final *mēm* by a supralinear point.
L. 12: בנות ציון, originally written as MT of Lam 4[2]: בני צ״, but emended by inserting a *tāw* above the line (leaving the *wāw*/*yōdh* unaltered!) and erasing היקרים by supralinear points.

2

]ך[

]◦[ ]◦◦נו֯[

]◦ ◦◦[ ]ע באה֯לך[

איכה ישבה] בדד העיר[ ]◦ו◦[ ]לים ◦[

]◦ים֯ שרתי כל לאומ֯[ים] שוממה כעז֯ו֯ב֯ה֯ וכל [בנ]ו֯תיה ע֯ז֯ו֯ב֯[ות

כ]א֯שה עז֯[ו]ב֯ה כעצובה וכעזובת [בע]ל֯[ה] כל ארמונתיה וחו[מותיה

כ֯ע֯קרה וכמסככה כול אורחו֯[ת]י֯[ה]ה֯ כאשת מרורים

וכל בנותיה כאבלות על על בע֯[לן]◦יה כמשכלות

ליחידיהן בכו תבכה ירו֯[שלים]ו על לחיה על בניה֯

]◦[ ]ל ◦ והגתה

[3] . . .] in *thy tent* [. . . [4] How] lonely [sits] the city [. . . [5] . . .] princess of all nation[s] is desolate like an abandoned woman, and all her [dau]ghters are aband[oned [6] like] a woman forsaken, like a woman grieved and like a wife abandoned by [her hu]s[band.] All her palaces and [her] wal[ls] are [7] like a barren woman and all [her] paths are like a woman shut away [. . .] like an embittered woman, [8] and all her daughters are like women mourning for [their] hus[bands . . .] her [. . .] like women bereaved of [9] their only children. *Jeru*[*salem*] shall surely weep [. . .] upon her cheek over her sons [. . .

L. 3: אהלך. Cf. Isa 54[2].
L. 4: cf. Lam 1[1].
L. 5: שרתי כל לאומים. Cf. Lam 1[1]: ש״ במדינות.
L. 6: כעצובה וג״. Cf. Isa 54[6].
ארמונתיה וחומותיה. Cf. Lam 2[7]: חומת ארמנותיה.
L. 7: כאשת. The preposition was inserted above the line.
L. 8: על written twice in error.
L. 9: cf. Lam 1[2].

3

]◦◦מ ◦[

]חללו[

]ל֯[ ]◦[

4

]◦ של[

]מאנו֯[

5

]אים֯[

180. THE AGES OF CREATION

(PL. XXVII)

(Already partly published in *The Annual of the Leeds University Oriental Society*, vol. iv, 1962–3, Leiden 1964, pp. 3–5)

1

פשר על הקצים אשר עשה אל קץ֯ להתה֯[לך

ונהיה כטרם בראם הכין פעולו֯ת[יהם

קץ֯ לקצו והוא חרות ל֯[

[ל֯[קצ֯י ממשלותם זה סרך ט

[◦הוליד ישחק את עשרים ה֯[

vacat

פ֯שר על עזזאל והמלאכים אש[ר

וי]לדו להם גברים ועל עזזאל[

[עולה ולהנחיל רשעה כל◦[

[◦ משפטים ומשפט סוד֯[ ]◦[

[1] An interpretation concerning the ages which God made: an age for *walk*[*ing* . . .][2] and is to come. Before he created them he ordained [their] works [. . .][3] an age to its age; and it was engraved upon tablets [. . . [4] . . .] the ages of their rule. This is the order of [. . . [5] . . .] Isaac begot twenty [. . . [7] . . .] *interpretation* concerning Azazel and the angels wh[o . . . [8] . . . *and they* b]ore to them giants; and concerning Azazel [. . . [9] . . .] iniquity and to make all [. . .] inherit wickedness [. . . [10] . . .] judgements and the judgement of the *Council* [. . .

L. 2: **כטרם בראם**. Cf. ff. 2–4, ii 10; 1QH i 5, xiii 8, xv 14.
L. 3: cf. Ex 32^{16}.
L. 8: cf. Gen 6^{4}; 4Q**181**. f. 2, l. 2.
L. 9: cf. 4Q**181**. f. 2, l. 4; Enoch 9^{6} 10^{8}.

2–4: fragments 2 and 3 have been particularly badly preserved, and even infra-red photographs make their inscription barely legible.

Col. I

[ד֯ר֯ך֯

[ע֯ל פ֯נ֯י֯ו֯

vacat

[י֯א

[מ֯ה֯

[◦◦ ◦

|א֯מ֯ר֯ נ֯ו֯ח֯

[◦◦ ◦

Col. II

א֯ש֯ר֯ א֯[ ]◦ין֯ הוא אש֯ר֯ שכן֯ ◦[ ]◦[ ]◦ץ֯[

אד֯ע֯ [ ]ת֯ יפה֯ א◦[ ]י֯פ֯◦[ ]◦ש◦[

◦[ ]שלושת האנ֯ש֯י֯[ם

[ם מאלונ֯י֯ ממרה מלאכ֯י֯ם֯ המה֯[

[יעמוד ◦◦◦[ ]חטאתמה ◦[

◦◦ה מא◦◦[ ]ה נא ואדֹ◦ה ◦◦עתֺ◦[
]שה כֺל ◦◦◦◦◦לא אד◦[
ב◦[ ]אש◦◦[ ]אֺ[
דובר[···]ואראה כיא הכול[
◦[···]בטרם בראם ידע מחשבֺ[ותיהם

[1] who [. . .] he it is who dwelt [. . .] [2] I know [. . .] beautiful [. . . [3] . . .] three *men* [. . . [4] . . .] from the oaks of Mamreh angels *they* [. . . [5] . . .] will arise [. . .] their sin [. . .] [9] speaking [. . .] and I saw that all [. . . [10] . . .] before he created them he knew [their] plans . . .

L. 3: cf. Gen 18².
L. 4: ממרה. MT Gen 18¹ has ממרא.
Ll. 8–10: f. 4 placed only very tentatively here, the line of the stitched upper edge corresponding roughly with the lower edge of f. 2.

5–6

]לם [
אשר כ]תֺוב על הארֺ◦[
]דֺרך שני ימֺים ◦[
]אֺ הרֺ ציון ירושליֺ[ם
אש]ר כתוב על פרעהֺ[
]◦◦◦◦[

[2] . . . *as* it is wr]itten concerning [. . . [3] . . .] two days' journey [. . . [4] . . .] Mount Zion, Jerusal [em . . . [5] . . . a]s it is written concerning Pharaoh [. . .

181.

(PL. XVIII)

(Already partly published in *The Annual of Leeds University Oriental Society*, vol. iv (1962–3), Leiden 1964, pp. 3–5)

1

לאשמה ביחד עם ס◦[ ]ע◦[ ]ל ◦◦[ ]ל בחטאת בני אדם ולמשפטים גדולים ומחלים רעים
א
בבשר לפי גבורות אל ולעומתֺ רשעֹם לפי מֺרדֺתם מסוד בני שֺ[מים] וארץ ליחד רשעה עד
קצה לעומת רחמי אל לֹפי טובו והפלא כבודו הגיש מבני תבל להתחשב עמֹו בֺ[סוד
א]לים לעדת קודש במעמד לחיי עולם ובגורל עם קדושיו בֺ[
מ]לאו איש לפי גורלו אשר הפֺ[י]ל[ ]ל[
]לחיי עֺ[ו]ל[ם

[1] for guilt in the community *with* [. . .] in the sin of mankind and for great judgements and grievous ills [2] in the flesh according to God's mighty deeds and corresponding to their wickedness, according to their *rebellion* from the Council of the sons of h[eaven] and earth to the community of wickedness to [3] its end, corresponding to God's mercies, according to his goodness. But wonderfully his glory has brought near some of the children of the world, to be reckoned with him in [*the Council* [4] *of* the g]ods, for a holy congregation in the station to everlasting life and in a lot with his holy ones [. . . [5] . . . est]ablished a man according to his lot which *he had cast for* [. . . [6] . . .] to everlasting life [. . .

L. 2: מרדתם, or possibly שרירתם. Whatever was intended latterly by the scribe, he had written it over a half-obliterated word to which perhaps the supralinear *'āleph* belonged.
L. 4: חיי עולם. Cf. Dan 12^2 Sir 37^{26}; CD iii 20 (ח״ נצח).

2

[◦]   [◦ יׯשחק]
[הׯאדם וילׯד[ו] להמה גבור[ים
א]ת ישראל בשבעים השביע ל[
אוהבׯי עולה ומנחילי אשמה ◦[
לעינׯי כול יודעיו ◦◦שׯ[
ולטובו אין חקׯר[
אלה נפלאי מדעׯ[
תׯכנם באמתו ו[
בכול קצותם[
בריאותיה[

[1] . . .] *Isaac* [. . . [2] . . .] man and there were *born* to them giant[s. . .] [3] Israel he has sated with plenty [. . .] [4] lovers of iniquity and those who cause to inherit guilt [. . .] [5] before the eyes of all who know him [. . .] [6] and his goodness is unsearchable [. . .] [7] these are the wonders of knowledge [. . .] [8] *he has measured them* by his truth and [. . .] [9] in all their ages [. . .] [10] her created things [. . .

L. 2: cf. Gen 6^4; 4Q **180**, f. 1, l. 8.
L. 4: cf. 4Q **180**, f. 1, l. 9.

3

א[

182. CATENA (B)

(PL. XXVII)

1

[אׯחרית הימים על /// [
[ה אשר יקשו את עורפם[
[ויפרעו ביד רמה להחל[
אשר כ]תׯוב עליהם בספר ירמׯ[יה
[◦ הׯ עׯ ◦◦◦◦◦◦[ ]לׯן

¹ . . .] the end of days concerning [. . . ² . . .] who will stiffen their necks [. . . ³ . . .] and they cast off restraint arrogantly to profane [. . . ⁴ . . . as it is wr]itten concerning them in the book of Jerem[iah. . .

L. 1: על is followed by a semi-erased letter, probably ʿ*ayin* with a supralinear point.

2

]מׄיׄא לאחרית הי[מי]םׄ[
]◦ה להכותם ◦[

¹ . . .] at the end of d[ay]s [. . . ² . . .] to smite them [. . .

183.

(PL. XXVI)

1
Col. I

]ם[

Col. II

אויביהם ויטמאו את מקדשם[
מהם ויקומו למלחמות איש[
בבריתו הושיע אל וימלט[
רצון ויתן להם לב אחד ללכ[ת
כול הון רשעה וינזרו מדר[ך
תועי רוח ובלשון האמת ◦[
וירצו את עוונם בנגיעׄ[הם
עוונם]
ואׄשר אמר רדׄ[
]◦◦[ ]◦[ ]◦[

¹ their enemies. And they defiled their sanctuary [. . .] ² from them, and they arose for wars of man [. . .] ³ against his covenant. God has saved and delivered [. . .] ⁴ favour and gave to them a single heart to wal[k . . .] ⁵ all wealth of wickedness, and they separated themselves from the wa[y . . .] ⁶ those who err in spirit and with a truthful tongue [. . .] ⁷ and they expiated their iniquity by [their] afflictions [. . .] ⁸ their iniquity. [. . .] ⁹ and as it says [. . .

L. 1: ויטמאו וג״. Cf. Ezek 23[38]; 1QpHab xii 8–9; CD xx 23 (cf. v 6, xii 1).
L. 4: cf. Ezek 11[19].
L. 5: הון רשעה. Cf. CD vi 15, viii 5, xix 17.
וינזרו. Cf. Lev 22[2]; CD vi 15, vii 1, viii 8, xix 20.
L. 6: תועי רוח. Cf. Isa 29[24]; 1QS xi 1.
L. 7: cf. 1QS viii 3.

2

]יׄהוה ◦[

]יׄם ◦◦◦[

]שמׄ[

3

]יהו [ה

184.

(PL. XXVIII)

(Already partly published in *Palestine Exploration Quarterly* Jan.–June 1964, pp. 53–55)

1

הזונ]ה תוציא הבל וב[ ]א תועות תשחר תמיׄדׄ[ל]שנן דברׄיׄ[ה
וקלס תחלׄ[י]ק ולהליץ יחד בש[וא] עול לבה יכין פחוז וכליותיה מקׄ[
בעול נגעׄלׄי הׄוה תמכו שוח רגליׄהׄ להׄרׄשיע ירדו וללכת באׄשמות[פשע
מוסדי חושך רוב פשעים בכנפיה [ ]ה תועפות לילה ומלבשיה[
מכסיה אפלות נשףׄ ועדיה נגועי שחׄת ערשיה יׄצׄוׄעׄיׄהׄ יצועי שחׄתׄ[
מעמקי בור מלונותיה משכבי חושך ובאישני ליל[ה ממ]שלותיה ממוסדי אפׄלׄוׄתׄ
תאהל שבת ותשׄכון באהלי דומה בתוך מוקדי עולם ואין נחלתה בתוך בכולׄ
מאזרי ///נוגה והׄיאה ראשׄית כׄול דרכׄיׄ עול הוי הוה לכול נוחליה ושדדה לכ[ול]
תוׄמכי בה כיא דרכיה דרכי מות ואורחותיה שבילי חטאת מעגלותיה משגות
עול ונתיבו[תי]הׄ אשמות פשע שׄעריה שׄערי מות בפתח ביתה תצעד שאוׄ[לה]
כׄ[ו]לׄ[ ]ישובון וכול נוחליה ירדו שחת וה[י]אׄ במסתרים תארוב ◦[ ]
כוׄלׄ[ ]בׄרחובות עיר תתעלף ובשערׄיׄ קריות תתיצב ואין להרג[יעה]
מה[ ]תׄ תׄ◦◦◦[ ]עיניה הנה והׄנה ישכילו ועׄפעפיה בפחז תרים לראו[ת לא]יׄשׄ
צדיק ותשיגהו ואישׄ[ע]צׄום ותכשׄילׄהו ישרים להטות דרך ולבחורי צדקׄ
מנצור מצוה סמוכי ◦[ ]◦ להביל בפחז והולכי ישר להשנות ח[וק] להפשיע
ענוים מאל ולהטות פעמיהם מדרכי צדק להביא זדׄ[ו]ן ◦[ ]בׄמה בל עׄרוכי[ם
במעגלי יושׄר להשגות אנוש בדרכי שוחה ולפתות בחלקות בני איש

1 *The har*]*lot* utters vanities,
and [. . .] errors;
She seeks continually [to] sharpen [her] words,
[. . .][2] she mockingly flatters

and with *emp*[*tiness*] to bring altogether into derision.
Her heart's perversion prepares wantonness,
and her emotions [. . .].
3 In perversion they seized the fouled (organs) of passion,
they descended the pit of her legs to act wickedly,
and behave with the guilt of [*transgression* . . .
. . .] 4 the foundations of darkness,
the sins in her skirts are many.
Her [. . .] is the depths of the night,
and her clothes [. . .].
5 Her garments are the shades of twilight,
and her adornments are touched with corruption.
Her beds are couches of *corruption*,
[. . .] 6 depths of the Pit.
Her lodgings are beds of darkness,
and in the depths of the nigh[t] are her [do]minions.
From the foundations of *darkness* 7 she takes her dwelling,
and she resides in the tents of the underworld,
in the midst of everlasting fire,
and she has no inheritance (in the midst of) among all 8 who gird themselves with light.
She is the foremost of all the ways of iniquity;
Alas! ruin shall be to all who possess her,
And desolation to a[ll] 9 who take hold of her.
For her ways are the ways of death,
and her path[s] are the roads to sin;
her tracks lead astray 10 to iniquity,
and her paths are the guilt of transgression.
Her gates are the gates of death,
in the opening of her house it stalks.
To Sheol 11 *a*[*l*]*l* [. . .] will return,
and all who possess her will go down to the Pit.
She lies in wait in secret places,
[. . .] 12 all [. . .].
In the city's broad places she displays herself,
and in the town gates she sets herself,
and there is none to distur[b her] 13 from [. . .].
Her eyes glance keenly hither and thither,
and she wantonly raises her eyelids
to seek out 14 a righteous man and lead him astray,
and a perfect man to make him stumble;
upright men to divert (their) path,
and those chosen for righteousness 15 from keeping the commandment;
those sustained with [. . .] to make fools of them with wantonness,
and those who walk uprightly to change the *st*[*atute*];
to make 16 the humble rebel from God,
and to turn their steps from the ways of righteousness;

to bring *presumptuousness* [. . .],
    those not arraign[ed] 17 in the tracks of uprightness;
to lead mankind astray in the ways of the Pit,
    and to seduce by flatteries the sons of men.

F. 1, composed of some dozens of fragments, is shown in Pl. XXIX in a partly 'exploded' form since warping of the skin prevents the document from lying flat.

The over-all metre of the poem is 3:3, and the translation has been arranged on that basis.

L. 2: תחליק. Cf. Prov. 2^{16} 7^{5}.

יכין. Cf. Job 15^{35}.

L. 3: הוה. Cf. Arab *hawan* 'passion'.

שוח. Cf. שוחה, of the harlot, Prov 23^{27} and l. 17.

אשמות [פשע: restored after l. 10.

L. 5: שחת. Cf. בני שחת in CD vi 15 and similarly Rev 17^{8} (Rabin *Zadokite Documents* 1954 pp. 24 f.).

ערשיה. BH has the plural in ות ״ (Am 6^{4}).

יצועיה apparently an error for the following word and half-erased.

L. 6: אישני לילה. Cf. Prov 7^{9}.

L. 7: אהלי דומה. Cf. Ps 94^{17} 115^{17}.

מוקדי עולם. Cf. Isa 33^{14}.

בתוך, an error for the following בכול?

L. 8: מאירי, or possibly מאזרי; cf. Isa 50^{11} and vrss. for the same confusion.

נוגה is preceded by an erased letter.

הוה 'destruction' with perhaps a play on the alternative meaning 'passion' in l. 3, above.

L. 11: תארוב. Cf. Prov 7^{12}.

L. 12: תתעלף lit. 'enwrapped', probably a euphemism, cf. Gen 38^{14}.

L. 15: מנצור מצוה. Cf. Prov 6^{20} 13^{13}.

L. 17: במעגלי יושר. Cf. Prov 4^{11}.

2

]נפשכה ◦[
]בכה ובתור[ה
]בׄ ◦[ ]גול עליו וה[
]לב נדכׄה התחנן לו[
|ורום עינים לב ערלׄ[
]ם רום לבב ואף אף הׄ[

This fragment is in private hands.

L. 4: לב נדכה. Cf. Ps 51^{19}.

3

]תׄחׄלׄץ ◦[
]תמיד הבר אליו ◦[
פ[רוש אליו כפיכה בתׄפׄ]לה
]הׄרׄ ממכה עול צי◦[
]עם אישוני פחז וׄ◦[

4

]◦[
]◦◦[ע[מוקׄיׄ]
]◦ כמׄים ימלׄאׄ וא[
]בן אדם ורוחו ◦[
]לוא באשמות מע[ל

F. 4, l. 5: אשמות מעל. Cf. 1QH iv 30, xi 11.

5

]∘∘[
]∘ותיה[ ]מע∘[
]לונ∘ אל תלח[
]לׄ בׄאזן ובח[
מש]פׄטׄ וחׄוׄקׄ[

6

]ברחובותי[ה
]אל תבוא בׄ[
]∘∘[

185.

(PL. XXIX–XXX)

1–2
Col. I

]כׄיׄ ∘[
]טׄהור וקדוש[
]מתו ו∘∘∘∘∘[
]ש ועד עשר פעׄמיׄם[
]ואין כח לעמוד לפניה ואׄיׄן מקוה
ל∘∘[ ]ומי יכלכל לעמוד לפני מלאכיו כי כאש
להבה ישפטׄ[ו]י רוחתיו ואתם בני אדם א[ ]כי הנׄה
כח[צ]יר יצמח מארׄצו ופרׄח כציץ חסדו נשבׄ[ה]רוחו
ויבש ∘∘∘ וציצו תשא רוׄח עד איׄקום לע[ ]∘ד
ולא ימצא מׄרוח יׄבקשוהו ולא ימצאהו ואין מקוה
והוא כצל י∘∘∘ על האׄו[ר] ועתה שמעו נא עמי והשכילו
לי פתאום ∘תׄמו מן [ח]בורת אלהים יׄזכרו נפלאים עשה
במצרים ומופתׄיׄו ∘[ ]∘יערץ לבבכם מפני פחדו

Col. II

ועשו רׄ∘[נ]פׄשכם כחסדיו הטבים חקרו לכם דרך
לחיים מסלהׄ[ ]לׄשארית לבניכם אחריכם ולמה תתנו
[ ]כׄם לשאׄ∘[מ]שׄפט שמעתי בני יצׄל תמרו דברי יהוה
אל תצעדׄו[י]עׄקׄב חׄתׄימה חקק לישחק הלוא טׄב יום
אחד[ ]∘∘∘ מעשרׄ[ה]∘יׄרׄאתו ולא לעתת מפחד ומפח יקוש
]∘∘ולהׄ∘∘[ ] מן מלאׄכיו כי אין חשך
י∘∘∘[ ]∘∘הׄ הוא ∘∘[ ]יעי ידעתי ואתׄמׄה
מה ת∘[ ]∘∘[ ]לפניו תצא רעהׄ לכל עם אשרי אדם נתנה לו

מן א◦[ ]◦דם ואל יתהלל[ו] רשעים לאמור לא ימנה
לי ולא[ ]לישראל וממד[ת ט]ב ימדה וכל עמו גאל
והרג ש◦◦◦◦[ ]אב[ ]יאמר המתמ◦◦◦ בה ישאנה[ ]שה
ומצאה ו◦[ ]◦בה יכילה ועמה[ ]מים ורשף עינים ושמחת לבב ע◦[
וחסדיו עלמיה וישועות ◦[ ]◦◦ אשרי אדם יעשנה ולא יאל על[ ]ו[ ]
מרמה לא יבקשנה ובחלקות לא יחזיקנה כן תתן לאבתיו כן ירשנה[ ]◦◦[ ]
בכל עוז כחו ובכל[ ]◦ו לאין חקר ויורישנה לצאצאיו ידעתי לעמ[ש]וב

Col. III

אליה כי פני[
וממאורות ית◦[
ומ◦[
4–6 *vacat*
ה◦◦[
◦◦[
והוא[
ו◦א ע[ ]◦◦ם[
הל◦◦◦[ ]ם עשה לביתו וי◦[
אל כל חדרי בטן ויחפש כלותו[
לשון יודע דברה אלהים עשה ידים[
]טוב ואם ד◦[
]במחש[בות

Col. I. [4] . . .] pure and holy [. . . [6] . . .] unto ten times [. . . [7] . . .] and no strength to stand before her and no hope [8] to [. . .] and who can endure to stand before his angels, for like a flame [9] of fire they will judge [. . .] his spirits; but ye, sons of men, [. . .] *for behold,* [10] like grass it springs from its earth and bears fruit; like a blossom is his mercy: his wind blo[ws] [11] and [. . .] dries up, and the wind whisks its blossom away into oblivion [. . .] [12] and it shall not be found from the wind. They shall seek it but not find it, and there will be no hope. [13] Like a shadow it [. . .] against the *li*[*ght*]. And now listen, my people, pay attention [14] to me: suddenly [. . .] be *destroyed* by the [chast]isement of God, they shall remember the wonders he did [15] in Egypt and his portents [. . .] your hearts [. . .] terrified before his visitation.

Col. II. [1] and they shall do [. . .] your [*sou*]*ls* according to his good mercies, they have sought out for you a way, [2] for life a high road [. . .] for a remnant, for your children after you. And why do you give [3] *your* [. . .] to [. . . *ju*]*dgement.* I have heard, my children, '*Let him deliver!*' Ye rebel against the words of Yahweh; [4] do not *step* [. . . *Ja*]*cob* the formula he inscribed for Isaac: 'is not one [5] day [. . .] better than ten [. . . *to*] fear him, and not for periods from punishment and the fowler's snare [. . . [6] . . .] his angels for there is no darkness

[. . . [7] . . .] I have knowledge; and ye, [8] what [. . .] before him there shall go out evil to all people. Happy is the man to whom is given [9] from [. . .]. And let not the wicked boast, saying, it shall not be accounted [10] to me and not [. . .] to Israel, and with the *meas[ure of good]ness* he will measure her and all *his* people [he will] redeem, [11] but he will slay those [. . .] says: She who [. . .] herself he will lift up [. . .] [12] and will find her [. . .] *by* her *he will sustain her* and with her [. . .] and *sparkling eyes* and joyful heart [. . .] [13] and his mercies her youth and the salvation [. . .]. Happy is the man who does it and is not *willing* [. . .] [14] deceit he does not seek her and with flatteries does not apprehend her: as she is given to his fathers, so shall he inherit her [. . .] [15] with all the power of his strength and with all his immeasurable [. . .], and he shall give her as an inheritance to his offspring. I have knowledge *concerning* [. . .]

Col. III. [1] to her, for *the face of* [. . .] [2] and from the *luminaries* [. . . [11] . . .] he has done to *his* house and [. . .] [12] to all the innermost parts of the body, and he sought his destruction [. . .] [13] the tongue of Him Who Knows has spoken: God made the hands [. . . [14] . . .] good, and if [. . . [15] . . .] *with devi[ces . . .*

Col. I. Ll. 10–11: cf. Isa 40^{6-8}.
L. 11: אייקום 'non-existence'; the second *yōdh* has been inserted supralinearly.

Col. II. Ll. 1–2: דרך לחיים. Cf. 1QH xv 22: דרך כול חי.
L. 3: תמרו is written over a partly erased word.
L. 4: תצעדו or possibly תצערו 'do not treat as insignificant', i.e. hiph. of צער (defect.).
L. 7: ידעתי; as in l. 15 possibly an introductory formula to the following revelation; cf. לשון יודע דברה in iii 13.

3

]◦[ ]ם̊ כ̇◦[

אל]הים יבחן כל◦◦[

]◦עשה דברי ברי[ת

ש]פט במסורת̊[

4

Col. I

]◦ לעול̊[ם

]◦וטי ◦◦◦ ויש◦◦[

]קודש

Col. II

ולע̊מ̊י[

ונריבה ו◦[

5

ו◦[

מיפ[

הד̊◦[

6

]◦מ̊◦[

]וה◦◦אתי א◦[

]ב◦◦[

186.

(PL. XXXI)

(Already partly published in *Journal of Semitic Studies* ix (1964) 291–4)

1
Col. I

◦◦[
ה[
vacat
שיאו רשא היהי קׄ[
[illegible] [illegible][
מעורביםי ולוא שארׄ היׄשׁ[

Decipherment (on the basis of reversing the order of the letters and transliterating the Greek, proto-hebraic, and cryptic alphabets used).

]◦◦
]ה
vacat
ואיש אשר יהיה קׄ]
רחבים וׄגׄלׄגׄלים]
מעורבים ולוא שאר הׄיׄשׁ]

Col. II

אמט ג]   [
אבן צונם]
יע שיא[
×[ו]◦מ/נׄ הׄ[נ]הו ×וׄ◦◦]
וילגר ×ועבצאו ×וקדו ×וכורא ויקושו
ינשה דומעה נמ האוהו ×וכוראו תוקד
יBB שולשו שש [illegible] ×לBB ול חור
וילע דולי האוה ׳שא דלומה האוה הזו כש[illegible]
רוש ותמהב הזו היהי ינע רושה לגרב

Decipherment

]ג טמא

]אבן צונם

]איש עי[

]◦◦ות וה[נ]הֹ נֹצֹי[ו]ת

ושוקיו ארוכות ודקות ואצבעות רגליו
דקות וארוכות והואה מן העמוד השני
רוח לו בבית האור שש ושלוש בבור
החושך וזה הואה המולד אשר הואה ילוד עליו
ברגל השור עני יהיה וזה בהמתו שור

Col. III

]Ab

]ושוארו

ˣועבצאו רבאל ˣומור וינשו[ ]ˣוארימ
תחאל רע[ש] תואלמו תובע ויקושו ˣובעֹ וידי
ˣBḂ ול חורו ˣורצקו תובע וילגר תועבצאו
שיֹאֹו רואה ˣיבמ תחאו הנומֹ[ש כשוחה]

Decipherment

ואס◦ה[

וראושו[

מיראות[ ]ושניו רומות לאבר ואצבעות
ידיו עֹבות ושוקיו עבות ומלאות [ש]ער לאחת
ואצבעות רגליו עבות וקצרות ורוח לו בבית
[החושך ש]מֹונה ואחת מבית האור ואֹיֹש

Col. IV

הלא המש[

כות היהי[

ל[

Decipherment

]שמה אלה

]יהיה תוך

]ל

Col. I. . . .] [4] and a man who will become [. . .] [5] broad and *rounded* [. . .] [6] *pleasing* and not the *flesh* of [. . .

Col. II. [1] . . .] unclean [[2] . . .] granite [[3] . . .] a man of [[4] . . .] [5] and his thighs are long and thin, and his toes [6] are thin and long, and he is of the Second Vault. [7] He has six (parts) spirit in the House of Light, and three in the Pit of [8] Darkness. And this is the time of birth on which he is brought forth— [9] on the festival of Taurus. He will be poor; and this is his beast—Taurus.

Col. III. 2 And his head [. . . 3 . . .] and his teeth are . . . and the fingers of 4 his hands are thick, and his thighs are thick and each covered with [h]air; 5 and his toes are thick and short. He has [ei]ght (parts) spirit in the House of [6 Darkness] and one (part) from the House of Light. And a man . . .

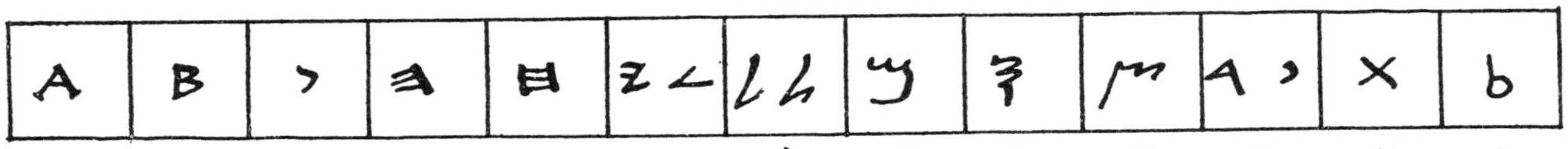

א ב ג ה ח י ל מ ו צ ר ת ?

Greek, proto-hebraic and cryptic scripts used in 4Q186.

Col. I. L. 5: גלגלים: Cf. NH Aram גלגל 'eyeball'?
L. 6: מעורבים, *puʿal* part. of ערב 'be sweet, pleasing'? Cf. f. 2, ii 2.

Col. II. L. 2: אבן צונם (written uncoded): NH Aram 'hard stone'.
L. 3:]איש עי; perhaps to be reconstructed עיש, i.e. the constellation of Jb 38[32] (9[9]).
L. 4: נׄצ◦[ו]ת. The second letter is clearly a proto-hebraic *ṣādē*.
L. 6: העמוד השני. Cf. f. 2, i 7 and עמודי שמים of Jb 26[11], explained as 'vaults' in Enoch 18[3].
L. 7: רוח לו. Cf. iii 7; f. 2, i 6.
בית האור, written less cryptically in iii 6.
בבור. The last letter is a cursive *rēsh* used cryptically.
Ll. 7–8: for the apportionment of the spirits of light and darkness, cf. esp. 1QS iii 19, 25; iv 16.
L. 8: אשר. The *rēsh* was omitted and inserted above the line.

Col. III. L. 3: מיראות, perhaps erroneously for מילאות, cf. l. 4.
רומות לאבר, presumably indicating a meaning opposite to על סרכמה of the teeth of the more favoured individual of f. 2, i 3; so perhaps here = 'lying askew' or the like.

2
Col. I

ונקזו ˣוירמׂגׄהׄ [ני]בו ˣורוחש ניב ויׄנׄיׄ[ע]◦כׂרס
וינשו הינע ולוק תבו לגרת האיהו[ ]◦צׄבׄ
כורא אול האוהו המכרס לע ˣובשויו ˣׄוקד
ˣוקד וידי ˣועבצא[ו] ◦לימממ הׄאוהו רצק אולו
וילגר תופכו ˣוקלח ויקושו ˣו[כ]ורׄאׄו
[ו]ל חורו המכרס לע ˣובשוי[ ]לׄ[ ]
תח]או הנׄומש ינשה דומעׄ[
וילע הא]וׄה דולי ודלוצׄ[
]◦◦◦ ותׄבהב האו[ה
]תוז ינ◦[
]לׄ[]◦◦◦[

Decipherment

סרכ֯◦[ע]י֯נ֯י֯ו בין שחורות וב[ין] ה֯ג֯מריות וזקנו
ממ◦[ ]והיאה תרגל ובת קולו עניה ושניו
דקות ויושבות על סרכמה והואה לוא ארוך
ולוא קצר והואה֯ ממי֯ל◦[ו]אצבעות ידיו דקות
וא֯ר֯ו[כ]ות ושוקיו חלקות וכפות רגליו
[ ]ל֯[ ]יושבות על סרכמה ורוח ל֯[ו
]ע֯מוד השני שמונ֯ה וא[חת
]מולדו ילוד הו[אה עליו
ה]ואה בהבת֯ו ◦◦◦[
]◦ני זות[
]◦◦◦[]ל֯[

Col. II

]אוה
ברוע֯]מ
]גולש

Decipherment

]הוא
מ]ע֯ורב
]שלוג/גולש

[1] . . .] order. His [ey]es are both black and glowing coals, and his beard [2] [. . .] and it is curly. And the pitch of his speech (?) is subdued, and his teeth [3] are fine and well ordered. He is neither tall [4] nor short, and he is [. . . *and*] the fingers of his hands are fine [5] and tapering. His thighs are smooth and the soles of his feet [[6] . . .] arranged in good order. [He] has of spirit [[7] . . .] Second Vault eight (parts) and o[ne [8] . . .] his time of birth [*at which*] he is born [. . . [9] th]at is his beast [. . .

(The straight cut through the centre of the fragment has been made to facilitate arranging the pieces where the skin has warped.)

Col. I. L. 1: הגמריות. Cf. Aram גומרא, but the 'gentilic' form is strange unless it presupposes an adjective *גומרי 'glowing'. Possibly here an error for גומרות.

L. 2: תרגל. Cf. Arab *rajila* 'of a quality between lankness and crispness or curliness'; II 'make curly' or 'comb' (Lane I iii 1043).

L. 9: בהבתו for בהמתו; cf. f. 1, ii 9.

Col. II. L. 2: cf. f. 1, i 6.

L. 3: שלוג/גולש. If to be deciphered in the usual way, the word is presumably connected with שלג 'snow' and indicates 'fairness' of skin, or the like (cf. Lam 4[7]); but more probably to be understood as uncoded like אבן צונם of f. 1, ii 2 and connected with the hair, as in Cant 4[1] 6[5].

3

מבי◦[
]תכב
]◦[ ]י֯פו[

Decipherment

מבי]
]בכת
]◦[ ]ופי֯[

This f. possibly belongs above f. 1, col. iii, l.h. side.

INDEX OF HEBREW WORDS APPEARING IN NON-CANONICAL TEXTS

אבותַי: **158** 3 3
לאבתיו: **185** 1–2 ii 14
אבותם: **177** 1–4 11
ואבדו: **169** 1–2 8
תובד: **169** 3–4 iii 7
יובדו: **169** 3–4 ii 9 **171** 1–2 ii 1 1, 3–4 iii 4, 8 3–10 iv 18
אובדה: **176** 14 7
להאביד: **174** 6–7 1
להאבידמה: **177** 12–13 i 4
אבדן: **163** 14 3
האביונים: **171** 1–2 ii 9 1, 3–4 iii 10
כאבלות: **179** 2 8
מתאבל: **177** 1–4 8 (2x)
אבל: **177** 1–4 9
לאבל: **166** ii 17
אבן: **186** 1 ii 2
האבן: **163** 12 5
כאבן: **164** 1 3
האבנים: **164** 1 3
לאבר: **186** 1 3
אברהם: **158** 4 6
אדם: **163** 31 2 **171** 1, 3–4 iii 2 **174** 1–2 i 6 **176** 40 2 **181** 1 1 **184** 4 4 **185** 1–2 i 9 ii 8, 13
האדם: **163** 4–7 ii 8 **181** 2 2
לאדם: **178** 4 2
אוהבו: **176** 16 4
אוהבֵי: **171** 1–2 i 15 **181** 2 4
ואוהבֵי: **171** 1, 3–4 iii 5a
באוהבֵי: **176** 8–11 14
תאהל: **184** 1 7
באהלך: **179** 2 3
באהלֵי: **184** 1 7
אהרון: **174** 5 2
האוד: **171** 1, 3–4 iii 8
אותות: **177** 1–4 15 17 3
אוי: **179** 1 i 4 ii 1
אויל: **177** 9 7
אול: **177** 12–13 ii 6
אולינו: **176** 14 4
און: **174** 1–2 i 9
ויאירו: **175** 17
אור: **174** 1–2 i 9 **177** 1–4 8 12–13 i 7, 11
האור: **177** 10–11 7 **185** 1–2 i 13 **186** 1 ii 7 iii 6
אורו: **164** 1 6
האורים: **164** 1 5 **174** 6–7 7
וממאורות: **185** 1–2 iii 2
מאירים: **164** 1 5
באזן: **184** 5 4
מאזרֵי: **184** 1 8
ואחיהמה: **177** 12–13 i 6
אחד: **158** 10–12 6 **161** 8–10 24 **163** 4–7 i 5 **175** 23 **183** 1 ii 4 **185** 1–2 ii 5
אחת: **159** 1 ii 7
לאחת: **186** 1 iii 4
ואחת: **186** 1 iii 6 2 i 7
יאחזהו: **158** 1–2 4
אחר: **169** 3–4 iv 6
ואחר: **161** 5–6 3 **169** 3–4 i 3 **171** 1–2 ii 10
אחרֵי: **166** ii 4 **174** 1, 3 ii 4
ואחרֵי: **171** 1–2 ii 19 **177** 5–6 3
אחריכם: **185** 1–2 ii 2
אחריהמה: **174** 1–2 i 17
האחרון: **167** 2 3 **169** 3–4 iv 3
אחרית: **182** 1 1
באחרית: **161** 8–10 17 **169** 3–4 iii 3 **174** 1–2 i 12, 19 **177**, 1–4 5, 7 9 2
לאחרית: **161** 5–6 10 **162** ii 1 **163** 4–7 ii 14 23 ii 10 **169** 3–4 ii 2 **173** 1 5 **174** 1–2 i 2, 15 14 2 **177** 12–13 i 2 ii 3 **182** 2 1
אי(יקום): **185** 1–2 i 11
אויב: **169** 3–4 ii 5 **174** 1–2 i 1 **177** 10–11 11
ולאיבו: **176** 20 3
אויביהם: **169** 3–4 iv 8 **183** 1 ii 1
איביהם: **177** 1–4 16
איבינו: **179** 1 i 14
אין: **159** 1 ii 4 **176** 8–11 14 14 6 52 2 **177** 5–6 14 10–11 5 12–13 i 5 **179** 1 i 6, 11 ii 10 **181** 2 6 **185** 1–2 ii 6
ואין: **161** 5–6 12 **169** 3–4 ii 6 **171** 1–2 ii 5 **176** 1–2 i 4 **179** 1 i 2, 9 ii 8 **184** 1 7, 12 **185** 1–2 i 7(2x), 12
לאין: **185** 1–2 ii 15
האיפה: **159** 1 ii 13
איש: **159** 1 ii 3, 6 2–4 8 **167** 16 2 **171** 1–2 i 18 ii 7 **175** 23 **176** 16 3 **177** 1–4 6 5–6 10 10–11 6 179 1 i 14 **181** 1 5 **183** 1 ii 2 **184** 1 17 **186** 1 ii 3
ואיש: **177** 1–4 11 **184** 1 14 **186** 1 i 4 1 iii 6
היש: **175** 22 **186** 1 i 6

לאיש: **174** 6–7 7 **177** 1–4 11
אנשים: **159** 2–4 3 **169** 3–4 i 7
האנשים: **177** 7 5 **180** 2–4 ii 3
אנשי: **161** 1 3 **162** ii 6, 10 **165** 9 3 **167** 5–6 1 **169** 3–4 i 5 iii 11 **177** 1–4 14 5–6 1 10–11 4, 9 12–13 i 11 ii 8
ואנשי: **174** 1–2 i 17
לאנשי: **177** 1–4 16
ובאנשי: **171** 1–2 ii 18
אישוני: **184** 3 5
ובאישני: **184** 1 6
יאכל: **159** 1 ii 5
יאוכלנה: **159** 1 ii 4
אכול: **177** 5–6 2
אַל: **159** 2–4 6, 7
אֶל: **159** 1 ii 5 **185** 1–2 iii 12
אליו: **171** 3–10 iv 9 **184** 3 2, 3
אליה: **163** 36 5 **185** 1–2 iii 1
אליהם: **166** ii 4 **171** 3–10 iv 5
אליהמה: **174** 1, 3 ii 4
לאל: **179** 1 i 2
אֵל: **159** 5 1 **166** ii 3 **167** 2 6 7–9 2 16 3 **171** 1, 3–4 iii 16 3–10 iv 14, 21, 27 **177** 12–13 i 9, 10 **179** 1 ii 1 **181** 1 2, 3; 𐤀𐤋: **180** 1 1 **183** 1 ii 3
ואל: **161** 8–10 18 **171** 1–2 ii 14, 18 3–10 iv 9
לאל: **173** 5 4
מאל: **184** 1 16
וכאלים: **166** ii 6
אלים: **181** 1 4
אלוה: **174** 1, 3 ii 4a
אלוהים: **158** 1–2 18 **171** 1–2 i 16 **176** 31 3 **185** 1–2 i 14 iii 13 3 2
אלהים: **177** 7 5
האלוהים: **160** 1 5
לאלוהים: **158** 4 7
אלוהֵי: **177** 1–4 9
אלוהַי: **160** 3–4 ii 2
אלה: **162** ii 6 **179** 1 i 3 **181** 2 7 **186** 1 iv 1
האלה: **159** 2–4 4 **162** iii 5
מאלוני: **180** 2–4 ii 4
אלף: **171** 1, 3–4 iii 1
האלף: **159** 1 ii 8
באלף: **171** 3–10 iv 3
אם: **158** 10–12 7 **159** 2–4 1, 8, 9 (2x) **161** 2–4 2 **163** 38 1
ואם: **185** 1–2 iii 14
אמון: **169** 3–4 iii 9
אמונים: **179** 1 ii 10
נאמנות: **159** 2–4 9
אמת: **171** 3–10 iv 12 **177** 12–13 i 5
האמת: **171** 3–10 iv 4 **183** 1 ii 6
באמת: **161** 2–4 5 **176** 20 1
באמתו: **181** 2 8
אמתו: **177** 12–13 i 7
לאמתו: **171** 1, 3–4 iii 17
אמר: **159** 5 3 **161** 2–4 2 8–10 21 **162** i 3 iii 7 **163** 8–10 4 22 4 **174** 1–2 i 7 **176** 22 4 **177** 1–4 16 12–13 i 2 **180** 2–4 i 7 **183** 1 ii 9
ואמר: **167** 18 1 **177** 10–11 11
אמרתי: **177** 12–13 ii 5
אמרו: **177** 5–6 4
יאמר: **185** 1–2 ii 11
ויאמר: **158** 1–2 7, 12 7–8 3 **175** 22
יואמר: **159** 2–4 8 **177** 14 1
ויואמר: **174** 1–2 i 6
אמור: **158** 6 6
לאמור: **158** 1–2 14, 16 **175** 1 **185** 1–2 ii 9
אמרת: **162** ii 7
באמרֵי: **171** 1–2 i 18
אנה: **175** 23
אף: **162** ii 8 **179** ii 1 **184** 2 6 (?)
אנוש: **184** 1 17
מאנתיכוס: **169** 3–4 i 3
אסף: **166** i 12 **177** 23 2
ונאספו: **177** 12–13 i 11
יאספו: **172** 1 4
ואף: **169** 3–4 ii 6 **176** 22 1 **184** 2 6 (2x?)
אפלות: **184** 1 5, 6
כאפס: **176** 34 1
אפרים: **169** 3–4 i 12 ii 2, 8 iii 5 **171** 1–2 ii 17
באפרים: **167** 2 3 **175** 27
ומופתיו: **185** 1–2 i 15
תארוב: **184** 1 11
וארזֵי: **163** 8–10 3
אורחותיה: **179** 2 7
ואורחותיה: **184** 1 9
ארוך: **186** 2 i 3
ארוכות: **186** 1 ii 5
וארוכות: **186** 1 ii 6 2 i 5
ארמונותיה: **179** 1 i 10
ארמונתיה: **179** 2 6
ארץ: **174** 8 2 **179** 1 i 12
הארץ: **162** ii 1, 2 **169** 1–2 10 **171** 1–2 ii 10 **178** 1 3
וארץ: **181** 1 2
בארץ: **158** 3 2 **14** i 4 **161** 2–4 5 **171** 1–2 ii 7 **175** 28 **177** 12–13 i 8
להארץ: **158** 14 i 3
מארץ: **176** 25 4
וארצו: **169** 1–2 2
מארצו: **185** 1–2 i 10
בארצות: **160** 3–4 ii 4
ארצותיכה: **160** 3–4 ii 5
ארור: **175** 22, 23

אש: **176** 25 6 **179** 1 i 5
באש: **176** 26 3
כאש: **177** 1–4 7 **185** 1–2 i 8
אִשָּׁה: **159** 2–4 6, 7 (2x)
האשה: **178** 7 1
כאשה: **179** 2 6
אשת: **158** 7–8 2
כאשת: **179** 2 7
נשיו: **169** 3–4 iv 4
אשור: **163** 40 1
אשמה: **169** 3–4 ii 6 **181** 2 4
לאשמה: **181** 1 1
אשמות: **184** 1 10 4 5
באשמות: **184** 1 3
אשמתם: **169** 3–4 ii 6 iii 4
אשרי: **185** 1–2 ii 8, 13
אותו: **158** 1–2 10
אותה: **159** 2–4 8
אותם: **160** 2 1
אותמה: **174** 1–2 i 8
אתם: **158** 4 7
אַתָּה: **160** 3–4 ii 5 6 2
ואתה: **160** 6 1
ואתם: **185** 1–2 i 9
ואתמה: **185** 1–2 ii 7

בא: **162** ii 6
בו: **169** 1–2 6 **171** 1, 3–4 iii 16 3–10 iv 10 **176** 8–11 15 14 5 **179** 1 i 6 ii 10
בוא: **174** 1–2 i 6
בה: **159** 2–4 9 **172** 5 2 **179** 1 i 13 **184** 1 9
בהם: **169** 1–2 4
בם: **179** 1 i 11
בבל: **163** 4–7 ii 4 8–10 1 25 1 **165** 8 1
לבגוד: **163** 4–7 ii 6
כבגד: **172** 2 2
בגדי: **161** 8–10 24
ובגדֵי: **161** 8–10 19
בגדיהם: **159** 1 ii 16
בהמה: **158** 10–12 14
בהמתו: **186** 1 ii 9 2 i 9
בא: **178** 5 3
באו: **174** 1–2 i 8
ובאו: **177** 12–13 i 10
יבוא: **159** 1 ii 5 **174** 1–2 i 3
תבוא: **169** 3–4 iv 6 **184** 6 2
בואו: **163** 12 1
בוא: **163** 4–7 i 4
לבוא: **158** 3 3 **161** 5–6 10 **169** 3–4 i 2
הבא: **159** 1 ii 3
הבאה: **163** 36 4 **171** 1–2 ii 18 **174** 1, 3 ii 1
ובאֵי: **179** 1 i 11
הביאמה: **174** 4 6
להביא: **184** 1 16
כתבואתו: **158** 10–12 7
בור: **184** 1 6
בבור: **186** 1 ii 7
בשתם: **163** 4–7 i 11
בז: **169** 3–4 ii 5
לבזרמה: **174** 4 5
יבחן: **185** 3 2
לבוחנם: **177** 10–11 10
ובחר: **177** 14 1
ובחרתי: **160** 7 4
בחרו: **171** 1–2 i 19
ולבחורֵי: **184** 1 14
בחירו: **164** 1 3 **171** 1–2 ii 5 1, 3–4 iii 5 3–10 iv 12
בחירֵי: **165** 6 1 **169**:1–2 8 **171** 3–10 iv 14 11 2 **174** 1–2 i 19 **177** 27 2
בטן: **185** 1–2 iii 12
בין: **186** 2 i 1
ובין: **186** 2 i 1
יבינו: **160** 3–4 ii 6 **169** 3–4 iii 4
ובינה: **158** 1–2 8
בינותם: **169** 3–4 ii 5
בנותם: **169** 3–4 iii 1
בית: **161** 8–10 3 **169** 3–4 iv 1 **173** 5 2 **176** 16 3 **179** 1 ii 7
הבית: **174** 1–2 i 2, 3
בבית: **171** 1–2 ii 13 **186** 1 ii 7 iii 5
לבית: **174** 4 4
מבית: **186** 1 iii 6
ביתו: **159** 1 ii 5
לביתו: **185** 1–2 iii 11
ביתה: **184** 1 10
בכא: **163** 30 2
תבכה: **179** 2 9
בכו: **179** 2 9
בבכורו: **175** 22
בל: **175** 20 **184** 1 16
בליעל: **171** 1–2 ii 10 **174** 1–2 i 8 (2x) 1, 3 ii 2 4 3 **175** 23 **176** 8–11 15 **177** 1–4 10 10–11 4 12–13 i 4, 6, 7, ii 2, 7 **178** 10 1
לבליעל: **174** 1–2 i 9 **177** 12–13 i 4
בלע: **163** 1 3
המבלעים: **174** 4 1
לבלתי: **159** 2–4 3
בן: **184** 4 4
ובן: **174** 1–2 i 4
בנֵי: **159** 5 2 **161** 2–4 1 **163** 22 3 **174** 1–2 i 8 (2x), 17 **177** 10–11 7 12–13 i 7, 11 **179** 1 ii 5 **181** 1 1, 2 **184** 1 17 **185** 1–2 i 9

בבני: **175** 28
מבני: **181** 1 3
בניה: **179** 2 9
בנַי: **185** 1–2 ii 3
לבניכם: **185** 1–2 ii 2
בת: **175** 29 **176** 25 5
ובת: **179** 1 ii 4 **186** 2 i 2
בנות: **179** 1 ii 13
בנותיה: **179** 2 5, 8
ובנו: **175** 25
יבנה: **174** 1–2 i 10 **175** 22
לבנות: **171** 1, 3–4 iii 16 **174** 1–2 i 6
בעוך: **164** 1 1
יבעה: **158** 10–12 7
בעלן: **179** 2 8
בוערת: **172** 4 4
להבער: **176** 20 3
מבקעת: **161** 5–6 11
ובקרוה: **159** 2–4 8
בקר: **177** 5–6 15
בקש: **169** 3–4 i 2 **177** 21 3 **178** 1 4
ובקש: **174** 4 5
יבקש: **177** 1–4 5 21 2
ויבקש: **171** 3–10 iv 14
יבקשנה: **185** 1–2 ii 14
יבקשו: **163** 13 4 **171** 1–2 ii 17 **173** 1 3 **177** 7 2
יבקשוהו: **185** 1–2 i 12
ברא: **176** 22 2
בראם: **169** 1–2 2 **180** 1 2 2–4 ii 10
בראתה: **160** 3–4 ii 5
בריאותיה: **181** 2 10
ברית: **185** 3 3
הברית: **171** 1–2 ii 13
בריתו: **176** 16 5 **179** 1 i 4
בבריתו: **183** 1 ii 3
ברחו: **172** 4 2
בברחו: **161** 8–10 9
וברכם: **177** 1–4 10
יברכם: **177** 1–4 10
לברכה: **158** 14 i 3
בברכו: **158** 1–2 10
וברקי: **174** 16 3
הברורים: **177** 9 3
הבר: **184** 3 2
ולהבר: **160** 2 1
הברושים: **163** 8–10 3
בשר: **171** 1–2 ii 11
בבשר: **181** 1 2
בשרם: **169** 3–4 ii 6
בתולת: **159** 2–4 8
והבת: **159** 1 ii 13
גאל: **185** 1–2 ii 10
וגאלתים: **158** 14 i 5
גבול: **161** 5–6 13 **169** 5 2
תגביר: **160** 3–4 ii 4
גבר: **159** 2–4 6
גברים: **180** 1 8
גבורים: **181** 2 2
וגבורים: **161** 8–10 4
גבורַי: **161** 8–10 5 **169** 3–4 iii 11
גבוריו: **169** 3–4 iv 4
גבורות: **181** 1 2
גדאו: **159** 2–4 1
גדודַי: **169** 3–4 i 10
גדול: **176** 20 2
גדולו: **161** 8–10 8
גדולה: **175** 28
הגדולה: **177** 12–13 i 9
גדולים: **181** 1 1
גדולות: **177** 1–4 15
גדולַי: **169** 3–4 iii 9
גדוליו: **169** 3–4 i 11
בגדוליו: **169** 3–4 i 5
ומגדלים: **175** 26
בגוית: **169** 3–4 ii 6
גום: **166** ii 4
גואים: **171** 1–2 ii 19 3–10 iv 10
גוים: **169** 3–4 i 1 3–4 ii 5
הגוים: **169** 3–4 iii 1
בגוים: **169** 3–4 ii 1
הגואים: **161** 8–10 4 **166** ii 13, 16 **167** 10 3
הגויים: **159** 2–4 2
גרתי: **160** 7 2
גר: **169** 3–4 ii 9
וגר: **174** 1–2 i 4
גלה: **165** 1–2 3
וגלה: **177** 5–6 9
יגלו: **169** 3–4 iii 3
ובהגלות: **169** 3–4 iii 4
וגלות: **169** 3–4 ii 5
ונגוללה: **179** 1 ii 2
יתגוללו: **177** 19 4
וגלגלים: **186** 1 i 5
גלוש ?: **186** 2 ii 3
וגם: **172** 4 4 **176** 22 1
גמול: **177** 1–4 9
גמולו: **171** 3–10 iv 9
הגמריות: **186** 2 i 1
נגעלַי: **184** 1 3
גורל: **174** 1, 3 ii 2 17 1 **176** 16 2 **177** 1–4 8
ובגורל: **181** 1 4
גורלו: **164** 1 8 **177** 12–13 i 11 **181** 1 5

גורן: **159** 1 ii 3
לגורן: **159** 1 ii 3
לגרנות: **167** 3 4
גרה: **159** 1 ii 7

דובר: **180** 2–4 ii 9
דבר: **159** 2–4 5 5 7 **171** 1, 3–4 iii 16 3–10 iv 4 **178** 2 2
דברה: **185** 1–2 iii 13
וידבר: **175** 1
וידברו: **177** 1–4 14
הדבר: **159** 5 5 **162** i 2 ii 1 **163** 4–7 ii 4, 14 22 1 23 ii 10 **165** 1–2 3 5 2 **171** 1, 3–4 iii 19 **174** 1–2 i 14, 19 13 3 **177** 1–4 6 10–11 9
דבֵרי: **158** 6 6 **176** 8–11 13 **185** 1–2 ii 3 3 3
דבריה: **184** 1 1
לדבריהם: **177** 1–4 1
המדבר: **171** 1, 3–4 iii 1
כמדבר: **179** 1 i 12
ממדבר: **161** 5–6 2
ובדֶבֶר: **171** 1–2 ii 1 1, 3–4 iii 4
דויד: **161** 8–10 17 **174** 1–2 i 11, 12, 13 **177** 12–13 i 2
לדויד: **174** 1–2 i 7
דומה: **184** 1 7
מדור: **179** 1 ii 7
דור: **166** i 10 **171** 1, 3–4 iii 1
בדור: **177** 9 8
הדור: **176** 20 2
דורות: **158** 1–2 9
מדור: **169** 3–4 i 1
נדכה: **184** 2 4
דלתיה: **175** 23
בדל: **179** 1 ii 6
דם: **176** 1–2 i 2
דמיטרוס: **169** 3–4 i 2
דניאל: **174** 1, 3 ii 3 **178** 12 1
דקות: **186** 1 ii 6 2 i 3, 4
ודקות: **186** 1 ii 5
דרך: **162** i 5 **163** 1 3 **180** 2–4 i 1 5–6 3 **184** 1 14 **185** 1–2 ii 1
מדרך: **174** 1–2 i 14 **183** 1 ii 5
לדרכו: **158** 1–2 10
דרכֵי: **176** 18 2 **184** 1 8, 9
בדרכי: **184** 1 17
מדרכי: **184** 1 16
דרכיה: **184** 1 9
דרש: **163** 22 2
דרוש: **159** 5 6
לדרש: **163** 23 ii 13
דורש: **174** 1–2 i 11 23 1 **176** 14 6 **177** 10–11 5
ודורש: **179** 1 i 13
דורשֵי: **169** 3–4 i 2 ii 2, 4 iii 3, 6 **177** 9 4
בדורשי: **169** 3–4 i 7
מדרש: **174** 1–2 i 14
והתדשנו: **171** 1–2 ii 10

הבל: **184** 1 1
והגתה: **179** 2 10
וההידד: **174** 9–10 1
הוא: **159** 2–4 7 **162** iii 4 **163** 4–7 ii 6 12 11 14 3 20 4 **169** 3–4 i 11 **176** 22 2 **180** 2–4 ii 1 **185** 1–2 ii 7
והוא: **180** 1 3 **185** 1–2 i 13 iii 9
הואה: **160** 3–4 ii 3, 6 **163** 1 2 4–7 i 4 30 4 **174** 1–2 i 2, 3, 11 5 3 **177** 1–4 13, 14 **186** 1 ii 8 (2x) 2 i 8, 9
ההואה: **158** 1–2 12 **163** 13 4 22 5
והואה: **177** 14 5 **186** 1 ii 6 2 i 3, 4
הוה: **184** 1 3, 8
הוי: **179** 1 i 10 **184** 1 8
הון: **183** 1 ii 5
ההון: **169** 3–4 i 11
והון: **160** 7 3
היא: **162** ii 10 **163** 2–3 4 29 2 **169** 1–2 7 3–4 ii 2 **177** 5–6 10 12–13 i 8
והיא: **184** 1 11
היאה: **161** 1 2, 4 **163** 8–10 7 **172** 1 3 **174** 1–2 i 12 1, 3 ii 1, 3 4 3
והיאה: **184** 1 8 **186** 2 i 2
היה: **160** 3–4 ii 2 **177** 1–4 8 (2x) **179** 1 i 5
והיה: **162** ii 1
היתה: **179** 1 i 12
היו: **167** 11–13 4 **179** 1 i 7
והיו: **176** 1–2 i 1 **177** 1–4 7
הייתם: **176** 22 3
יהיה: **186** 1 i 4 ii 9 iv 2
יהי: **160** 7 1
ויהי: **174** 1–2 i 15 **176** 20 2
תהיה: **160** 6 1
יהיו: **159** 2–4 6 **171** 1, 3–4 iii 5 **173** 3 2
להיות: **166** ii 12 **167** 33 1 **171** 1, 3–4 iii 4 **174** 1–2 i 6 4 6 **175** 24, 25 **176** 23 2
בהיותו: **172** 4 1
ונהיה: **180** 1 2
וילך: **158** 1–2 10 **177** 5–6 10
ילכו: **163** 4–7 ii 15 **169** 3–4 iv 4
וילכו: **167** 7–9 2
ללכת: **158** 1–2 17 **177** 1–4 13 **183** 1 ii 4
וללכת: **184** 1 3
והולכֵי: **184** 1 15
יתהלכו: **169** 3–4 ii 2
להתהלך: **180** 1 1
יוליכו: **166** ii 16
יתהללו: **185** 1–2 ii 9
הוללים: **171** 1–2 i 14

ההוללים: **177** 5–6 1, 4
הולל[: **176** 35 2
להלל: **175** 21
תהלתכה: **160** 3–4 ii 3
בתהלותיהו: **175** 21
הם: **162** ii 6, 7 **169** 1–2 3 3–4 i 10 (2x) ii 1 iii 9 (2x), 11 iv 1.
המה: **158** 1–2 17 **161** 8–10 5 **163** 20 3 23 ii 1 **171** 1–2 ii 5 1, 3–4 iii 12 3–10 iv 1, 23 **174** 1–2 i 16, 17 14 3 19 2 **177** 1–4 16 5–6 13, 14 9 4 10–11 5 **180** 2–4 ii 4
והמה: **166** ii 13 **177** 1–4 7
להמה: **158** 4 7 6 6 **177** 7 6
מהמה: **164** 1 6
הִנֵּה: **177** 1–4 12 **185** 1–2 i 9
והִנֵּה: **158** 1–2 17 **186** 1 ii 4
]הנה: **167** 21 1
הֵנה: **184** 1 13
והנה: **184** 1 13
והפכה: **179** 1 i 5
נהפכה: **166** ii 17
והרג: **185** 1–2 ii 11
הרוג: **177** 5–6 15
הר: **171** 1, 3–4 iii 11 **180** 5–6 4
ההר: **163** 57 1 **177** 8 4
בהר: **163** 24 1
הרי: **177** 14 6
מהותלות: **172** 10 1

הזאת: **163** 11 i 5
זואת: **160** 3–4 ii 1
הזואת: **163** 35 1
זות: **186** 2 i 10
הזות: **158** 3 2 **175** 22, 26
זבח: **174** 9–10 1
מזבח: **158** 4 4
המזבח: **173** 5 3
זה: **180** 1 4
הזה: **158** 1–2 9
וזה: **186** 1 ii 8, 9
הזיד: **171** 3–10 iv 15
זדון: **169** 3–4 iii 4 **184** 16
להזע: **163** 40 2
זרים: **174** 1–2 i 5
בזרים: **159** 2–4 2
יזכרו: **185** 1–2 i 14
זכריה: **163** 8–10 8
יזומו: **171** 1–2 ii 14
זמות: **177** 5–6 6
ובזעם: **160** 3–4 ii 4
וזקנו: **186** 2 i 1
מזוקק: **177** 20 3
המזרח: **169** 3–4 ii 12
וזרם: **163** 25 3
זרע: **174** 15 3
ולזרעו: **177** 1–4 13
לזרעם: **171** 1, 3–4 iii 2

לחבל: **177** 7 2
חבל: **163** 4–7 ii 4
חבורת: **185** 1–2 i 14
חדרי: **185** 1–2 iii 12
לחובת: **162** ii 1
חילה: **169** 3–4 iii 11 iv 1
חילו: **161** 1 3 **169** 3–4 i 10
חל: **175** 29
חוק: **184** 1 15
וחוק: **184** 5 5
החוזים: **174** 5 4
ויחזק: **177** 12–13 i 6
יחזקו: **169** 3–4 iii 8
יחזיקנה: **185** 1–2 ii 14
חטאת: **184** 1 9
בחטאת: **181** 1 1
חטאתמה: **180** 2–4 ii 5
בחטאתמה: **174** 1–2 i 6
חטאותינו: **179** 1 i 15
יחיה: **163** 31 1
יחיו: **171** 1, 3–4 iii 1
יחים: **171** 1, 3–4 iii 3
חי: **169** 3–4 i 8
חיים: **169** 3–4 i 7
לחיים: **185** 1–2 ii 2
לחיֵי: **181** 1 4, 6
לחיה: **179** 1 i 9
מחלה: **160** 3–4 iii 1
ומחלים: **181** 1 1
חללו: **179** 3 2
להחל: **182** 1 3
תחלת: **165** 9 1
חלליהם: **169** 3–4 ii 6
תחלץ: **184** 3 1
תחליק: **184** 1 2
חלקות: **186** 2 i 5
החלקות: **163** 23 ii 10 **169** 3–4 i 2, 7 ii 2, 4 iii 3, 7
בחלקות: **184** 1 17
ובחלקות: **185** 1–2 ii 14
מחלקות: **171** 3–10 iv 23
מחמד: **163** 32 1
חומה: **175** 26
חמס: **158** 1–2 8 **175** 25
חמשה: **159** 1 ii 9
ולחמשים: **159** 1 ii 9

חונני: **177** 12–13 i 3
התחנן: **184** 2 4
חנופה: **175** 28
חסדו: **185** 1–2 i 10
חסדיו: **185** 1–2 ii 1
וחסדיו: **185** 1–2 ii 13
חסנכה: **163** 27 3
וחפץ: **179** 1 ii 10
ויחפש: **185** 1–2 iii 12
וחצי: **171** 13 5
מחצית: **159** 1 ii 6, 8, 9, 12
חצים: **177** 5–6 8
כחציר: **185** 1–2 i 10
חצרות: **179** 1 i 7
חקק: **185** 1–2 ii 4
ובחוק: **175** 29
חקות: **163** 4–7 ii 5
בחוקות: **167** 7–9 2
חקרו: **185** 1–2 ii 1
חקר: **181** 2 6 **185** 1–2 ii 15
וחריבות: **173** 5 5
חרב: **169** 3–4 ii 5
החרב: **162** ii 1 **177** 1–4 16
בחרב: **163** 21 4 **169** 3–4 iv 4 **171** 1–2 ii 1 **176** 19 2 **177** 1–4 16
חרה: **162** ii 8
חרון: **166** i 12 **177** 19 5
החרון: **167** 2 2 **169** 3–4 i 5, 6
בחרונו: **177** 12–13 i 4
בחרי: **171** 1–2 i 14
חורף: **179** 1 ii 6
וחרפה: **166** ii 13
וחרחור: **169** 3–4 ii 5
חרות: **180** 1 3
יחשב: **163** 21 2
ולחשוב: **174** 1–2 i 9
להתחשב: **181** 1 3
במחשבת: **174** 1–2 i 8
מחשבות: **174** 1–2 i 9
במחשבות: **185** 1–2 iii 15
ובמחשבות: **178** 2 5
במחשבל: **177** 12–13 i 6
מחשבותיהם: **180** 2–4 ii 10
חושך: **184** 1 4, 6
חשך: **185** 1–2 ii 6
החושך: **186** 1 ii 8
חתימה: **185** 1–2 ii 4
יחתו: **161** 8–10 4
ומחתה: **175** 24

טהור: **185** 1–2 i 4
טוב: **174** 9–10 2 **179** 1 ii 11 **185** 1–2 ii 4 iii 14
הטוב: **178** 9 3
טב: **185** 1–2 ii 10
הטבים: **185** 1–2 ii 1
טובו: **181** 1 3
ולטובו: **181** 2 6
מטיט: **160** 5 1
טמא: **186** 1 ii 1
ויטמאו: **183** 1 ii 1
טמא (n.?): **177** 7 6
וטפו: **169** 3–4 iv 4
טרם: **176** 22 3
בטרם: **180** 2–4 ii 10
כטרם: **180** 1 2
טרף: **167** 38 8 **169** 3–4 i 4
בטרפו: **167** 3 3
וטרפו: **169** 3–4 i 11

יאל: **185** 1–2 ii 13
והיארים: **169** 3–4 iii 9
נואש: **176** 8–11 13
תבל: **169** 1–2 9 **177** 1–4 7 **181** 1 3
ויבש: **185** 1–2 i 11
וגת: **159** 1 ii 3
הגתות: **177** 1–4 15
יד: **171** 1–2 ii 17
יַד: **158** 14 i 5
ביד: **159** 2–4 6 **161** 8–10 8 **171** 1–2 i 16 ii 19 3–10 iv 10, 15 **172** 3 1 **182** 1 3
ויד: **177** 12–13 i 9
מיד: **171** 3–10 iv 21 **177** 12–13 i 7
ידו: **167** 2 3 **176** 18 1
בידו: **161** 8–10 20
ובידו: **161** 8–10 24
בידם: **171** 1–2 ii 15
ידנו: **179** 1 i 2
מידם: **171** 1–2 ii 19
ידים: **185** 1–2 iii 13
ידיו: **186** 1 iii 4 2 i 4
ידַי: **179** 1 ii 12
ידיהם: **177** 15 1
ידיהן: **179** 1 ii 6
ולהודות: **175** 21
ידע: **174** 5 3 **180** 2–4 ii 10
ידעתי: **185** 1–2 ii 7, 15
אדע: **180** 2–4 ii 2
וידעו: **160** 3–4 ii 5
יודע: **185** 1–2 iii 13
יודעיו: **181** 2 5
הודיענו: **160** 1 5
וידיעהו: **177** 1–4 12

דעת: **171** 1–2 i 19
לידעתיכהו: **175** 16
מדע: **181** 2 7
הבו: **175** 14
יהודה: **167** 25 1 **169** 3–4 iii 4 **171** 1–2 ii 13 **174** 1, 3 ii 1 4 4 **177** 1–4 9 **179** 1 i 3
וביהודה: **175** 27
מיהודה: **177** 9 6
יהוה: **158** 1–2 16, 18 4 8 7–8 3 10–12 11 **162** ii 7, 8 **174** 21 1 **185** 1–2 ii 3 𐤉𐤄𐤅𐤄 **171** 1–2 ii 4, 12, 24, 1, 3–4 iii 14, 15 3–10 iv 7, 10 **183** 2 1 3 1 . . . . **175** 1 91
יום: **167** 25 2 **185** 1–2 ii 4
היום: **158** 1–2 9
ביום: **158** 1–2 12 **163** 13 4 **167** 4 1
וביום: **163** 4–7 i 5
ימים: **163** 49 2 **180** 5–6 3
הימים: **161** 5–6 10 **162** ii 1 **163** 13 3 14 2 23 ii 10 **169** 3–4 ii 2 **174** 1–2 i 2, 12, 15, 19 **177** 1–4 5 7 4 12–13 i 2 **178** 2 3 3 4 9 2 **182** 1 1 2 1
היומים: **175** 4
ימיו: **159** 1 ii 7 2–4 10
בימיהם: **169** 3–4 ii 6
יון: **169** 3–4 i 2, 3
יונים: **176** 34 2
יחד: **171** 11 1 **174** 22 2 **177** 19 3 **184** 1 2
היחד: **164** 1 2 **165** 9 3 **171** 1–2 ii 14 3–10 iv 19 **174** 1–2 i 17 **177** 5–6 1, 16 14 5
ביחד: **181** 1 1
ליחד: **181** 1 2
ליחידיהן: **179** 2 9
יחזקאל: **174** 1–2 i 16 **177** 7 3
יהלתי: 160 7 3
אוכל: **163** 57 1
יוכל: **170** 1–2 2
וילדו: **180** 1 8 **181** 2 2
ילוד: **186** 1 ii 8 2 i 8
הוליד: **180** 1 5
ילדים: **177** 5–6 4
המולד: **186** 1 ii 8
מולדו: **186** 2 i 8
ים: **158** 14 i 7
הים: **169** 1–2 3
לים: **169** 5 2
ובימים: **160** 3–4 ii 4
תימינו: **163** 23 ii 19
הונו: **171** 1, 3–4 iii 7
יסדו: **164** 1 2
יוסדנה: **175** 23
מוסֵדי: **184** 1 4
ממוסדי: **184** 1 6
יוסיפו: **169** 3–4 iii 7
העדה: **161** 5–6 3
עדת: **162** ii 10 **163** 23 ii 10 **164** 1 3 **171** 1–2 ii 5, 9 1, 3–4 iii 5, 10, 16 3–10 iv 19 **177** 9 4
לעדת: **181** 1 4
עדתם: **169** 3–4 ii 5
מועד: **171** 1–2 ii 9 **179** 1 i 11
במועד: **171** 1, 3–4 iii 3
מועדי: **160** 7 2
במועדי: **166** ii 16
תועפות: **184** 1 4
יעץ: **177** 5–6 6
עצת: **164** 1 2 **177** 14 5
בעצת: **169** 3–4 i 2 ii 6 **171** 1–2 ii 14
לעצת: **174** 1–2 i 17
עצתו: **169** 3–4 i 5 **171** 1–2 ii 18 **177** 1–4 14, 16
עצתם: **169** 3–4 iii 7, 8
עצתמה: **174** 1–2 i 17
בעצתם: **169** 3–4 ii 9
יעקוב: **158** 3 1 **175** 29 **185** 1–2 ii 4
ויעקוב: **177** 1–4 15
ליעקוב: **173** 5 6
יפה: **180** 2–4 ii 2
יצאו: **159** 5 5 **171** 1, 3–4 iii 4
יֵצא: **161** 8–10 24
תצא: **185** 1–2 ii 8
תוציא: **184** 1 1
יוצו: **159** 2–4 8
בהוציאכה: **158** 1–2 16
צאצאֵי: **174** 4 1 **177** 1–4 12 **178** 4 4
לצאצאיו: **185** 1–2 ii 15
תתיצב: **184** 1 12
יצוע: **160** 7 4
יצועֵי: **184** 1 5
יצועיה: **184** 1 5
מוקדֵי: **184** 1 7
היקרים: **179** 1 ii 13
יקוש: **175** 24 **185** 1–2 ii 5
לירא: **175** 3
יראתו: **185** 1–2 ii 5
יראתכה: **160** 5 3
מיראות: **186** 1 iii 3
ירדו: **184** 1 3
יֵרדו: **184** 1 11
רדת: **177** 1–4 15
ברדתו: **174** 1, 3 ii 5
יורו: **169** 3–4 iv 2
יורוהו: **161** 8–10 23
מורה: **163** 21 6 **171** 1, 3–4 iii 15, 19 3–10 iv 27 **172** 7 1 **173** 1 4 2 2
מוריהם: **167** 5–6 2
תורה: **174** 1–2 i 7 **178** 2 4

התורה: **159** 5 6 **161** 8–10 18 **163** 23 ii 14 **165** 6 7 **171** 1–2 ii 14, 22 3–10 iv 2, 8 **174** 1–2 i 11 1, 3 ii 2 **176** 17 7, 8 **177** 1–4 14 5–6 16 10–11 5

התרה: **163** 2–3 4

בתורה: **163** 23 ii 12

ובתורה: **184** 2 2

לתורה: **171** 1–2 ii 3 11 1

תורת: **162** ii 7 **165** 1–2 3 **177** 5–6 5

ירושלמ: **175** 30

ירושלים: **161** 5–6 13 **169** 3–4 i 2, 11 **176** 1–2 i 3 **179** 1 i 8 **180** 5–6 4

בירושלים: **162** ii 7, 10 **163** 23 ii 11

ויירושלים: **177** 12–13 i 10

ירמיה: **182** 1 4

ירשנה: **185** 1–2 ii 14

ירשו: **171** 1, 3–4 iii 11

ויורישנה: **185** 1–2 ii 15

יורשֵׁי: **173** 1 7

מוריש: **163** 31 4

ישחק: **180** 1 5 **181** 2 1

לישחק: **185** 1–2 ii 4

ישראל: **159** 1 ii 17 2–4 2, 8 **161** 1 2 8–10 3 **162** ii 8 **163** 4–7 ii 7 **164** 1 1, 7 **165** 6 1 **169** 3–4 i 12 iii 3, 5 5 2 **171** 1, 3–4 iii 11, 12 11 2 **174** 1–2 i 6, 13, 19 4 7 5 2 **177** 1–4 9 5–6 7 **181** 2 3

בישראל: **159** 2–4 5 **169** 3–4 i 8 **175** 27

לישראל: **185** 1–2 ii 10

יישבו: **158** 14 i 8

שבת: **184** 1 7

יושבת: **176** 8–11 16

יושבות: **186** 2 i 6

ויושבות: **186** 2 i 3

יושבֵי: **169** 1–2 9

ישוע: **175** 21

הושיע: **183** 1 ii 3

יושיעם: **171** 3–10 iv 21

יושיעום: **166** ii 14

להושיע: **172** 8 1 **174** 1–2 i 13

וישועות: **185** 1–2 ii 13

ישעיה: **174** 1–2 i 15 **176** 1–2 i 4

ישר: **171** 1, 3–4 iii 17 **176** 38 1

לישרם: **177** 9 8

ישר: **184** 1 15

ישרים: **184** 1 14

בישרה: **171** 1, 3–4 iii 1

יושר: **184** 1 17

יותר: **163** 12 4

יותיר: **177** 12–13 i 4

ויתר: **163** 12 4

כמוהו: **161** 5–6 12

וכארום: **169** 3–4 iii 4

כאורה: **169** 3–4 iii 2

ויכבדום: **166** ii 5

נכבדים: **169** 3–4 ii 9

נכבדֵי: **169** 3–4 iii 9

ונכבדיו: **169** 3–4 iv 4

כבוד: **161** 8–10 19 **169** 3–4 iii 4

הכבוד: **177** 14 1

וכבוד: **169** 3–4 ii 4 **176** 8–11 13

כבודו: **181** 1 3

כוהן: **167** 2 3

הכוהן: **171** 1, 3–4 iii 15

בכוהן: **171** 1–2 ii 18

כוהנים: **163** 12 6 **169** 3–4 ii 9

הכוהנים: **161** 1 4 **164** 1 2

וכוהנים: **159** 2–4 4

מכוהנֵי: **161** 8–10 24

כוהניכה: **176** 1–2 i 3

כוח: **160** 3–4 ii 1

כח: **185** 1–2 i 7

כוחו: **174** 4 5

כחו: **185** 1–2 ii 15

יכילה: **185** 1–2 ii 12

יכלכל: **185** 1–2 i 8

יכין: **184** 1 2

הכין: **180** 1 2

הכינו: **171** 1, 3–4 iii 16

תוכן: **172** 2 2

כוסם: **169** 3–4 iv 6

הכזב: **171** 1–2 i 18 3–10 iv 14

כזביהם: **169** 3–4 ii 8

אכזריה: **179** 1 ii 4

כחש: **159** 2–4 9

בכחש: **169** 3–4 ii 2

כיא: **159** 2–4 7 **160** 3–4 ii 1, 3, 6 **161** 1 4 **164** 2 2 **166** i 12 **171** 1–2 i 19 ii 3, 23 3–10 iv 25 **174** 1–2 i 4 5 3 8 2 14 3 15 3 **176** 22 2 41 1 **177** 1–4 10 5–6 4 8 3 10–11 5 12–13 i 5 (2x) 15 2 20 2 **180** 2–4 ii 9 **184** 1 9

כי: **159** 2–4 8 **167** 2 2 **169** 1–2 6 3–4 i 8 ii 12 **176** 18 1 32 2 **179** 1 i 2 ii 1 **185** 1–2 i 8 ii 6 iii 1

כלה: **163** 8–10 1 **175** 21

לכלות: **171** 1–2 ii 14

כלותו: **185** 1–2 iii 12

כלותם: **176** 23 3

ולכלותם: **169** 1–2 4

לכלותמה: **174** 1–2 i 8

תכלת: **179** 1 ii 12

כלֵי: **159** 2–4 6 **163** 25 3 **175** 25

וכליותיה: **184** 1 2

כול: **158** 10–12 7 14 i 2 **159** 1 ii 7 2–4 6, 10 5 8 **160** 3–4 ii 5 **161** 8–10 4 **164** 1 1 2 2 **167** 26 1 **169** 5 2

171 1–2 ii 2, 3, 6, 7, 10 1, 3–4 iii 1, 4, 10 **172** 1 1 5 3 7 2 12 1 **174** 1, 3 ii 2 11 2 (2x) 12 2 **176** 17 3 18 2 22 2 54 1 **177** 12–13 i 11 **179** 1 i 14 2 7 **181** 2 5 **183** 1 ii 5 **184** 1 8, 12
הכול: **159** 1 ii 9 **177** 1–4 12 **180** 2–4 ii 9
בכול: **164** 1 6 **167** 7–9 2 **171** 1–2 ii 10 **174** 4 5 5 4 **176** 21 2 **177** 9 6 **181** 2 9 **184** 1 7 **185** 1–2 ii 15
ובכול: **161** 5–6 12 8–10 20
וכול: **167** 21 2 **177** 10–11 4 12–13 i 11 **184** 1 11
לכול: **159** 1 ii 2 **169** 3–4 iii 3 **175** 24 **177** 1–4 7 12–13 i 7 **184** 1 8
מכול: **158** 1–2 8 **171** 1–2 ii 9 **177** 12–13 i 9
כל: **169** 1–2 3 **179** 1 i 2, 3, 10, 11 2 5, 6 **180** 1 9 2–4 ii 7 **185** 1–2 iii 12 3 2
וכל: **179** 2 5, 8 **185** 1–2 ii 10
ובכל: **185** 1–2 ii 15
לכל: **185** 1–2 ii 8
כולם: **177** 5–6 4
וכולם: **164** 2 1
לכלל: **169** 3–4 ii 6
כן: **161** 8–10 23 **162** ii 8 **171** 1–2 ii 19 **177** 5–6 3 **185** 1–2 ii 14 (2x)
כנס: **163** 55 1
וכנס: **159** 1 ii 4
כנסתם: **169** 3–4 iii 7
בכנפיה: **184** 1 4
ובכנורות: **163** 25 2
כסא: **161** 8–10 19 **174** 1–2 i 10
יכס: **159** 2–4 7
מכסיה: **184** 1 5
כסף: **159** 1 ii 6, 11
כפים: **160** 2 1
כפיכה: **184** 3 3
כפות: **158** 1–2 13
וכפות: **186** 2 i 5
לכפר: **159** 1 ii 2
כפר: **159** 1 ii 6
כפרם: **163** 14 5
כפיר: **167** 2 2 **169** 3–4 i 5, 6
וכפיריו: **169** 3–4 i 10
לכרמל: **163** 21 3
ככר: **159** 1 ii 8
הככר: **159** 1 ii 8
יכרתו: **171** 1–2 ii 4 1, 3–4 iii 12 (2x)
ונכרתו: **171** 3–10 iv 18
בכשו: **176** 14 1
יכשולו: **169** 3–4 ii 6
מכשול: **173** 5 2
ותכשילהו: **184** 1 14
להכשיל: **174** 1–2 i 8
המכשילים: **174** 1–2 i 8 **177** 10–11 7
כתוב: **163** 1 4 2–3 5 4–7 i 1, ii 18 47 2 **165** 1–2 2 **174** 1–2 i 2, 12, 15, 16 1, 3 ii 3 **176** 8–11 13 **177** 1–4 7, 12 5–6 11 7 3 10–11 1, 3 **178** 3 2 **180** 5–6 2, 5 **182** 1 4
כתיאים: **161** 8–10 5, 7
כתיים: **169** 3–4 i 3
הכתיאים: **161** 8–10 3, 8
וכתם: **179** 1 ii 11
כתונת: **159** 2–4 7
יכתו: **161** 8–10 3

לו: **158** 1–2 7 **159** 1 ii 4 (2x) **160** 3–4 ii 2 7 2 **171** 1, 3–4 iii 16 **185** 1–2 ii 8 **186** 1 ii 7 iii 5 2 i 6
לוא: **174** 1–2 i 6 (2x) 11 **176** 14 6
לה: **175** 26 **177** 5–6 10
לכה: **160** 6 1
לי: **185** 1–2 i 14 ii 10
להם: **163** 22 4 **166** ii 17 **177** 1–4 10 5–6 6 **180** 1 8 **183** 1 ii 4
ולהם: **171** 1, 3–4 iii 1
להמה: **160** 3–4 ii 3 6 1 **174** 1–2 i 7 4 2 **181** 2 2
לאהםה: **175** 5
למו: **178** 1 2
לכם: **185** 1–2 ii 1
לנו: **167** 4 2 **176** 17 6 **179** 1 i 4 ii 1
מלאך: **177** 12–13 i 7
במלאך: **176** 17 4
מלאכים: **180** 2–4 ii 4
והמלאכים: **180** 1 7
מלאכיו: **163** 20 2 **185** 1–2 i 8 ii 6
ומלאכיו: **169** 3–4 ii 1
לאומים: **163** 50 2 **179** 2 5
לב: **163** 23 ii 13 **177** 10–11 9 **183** 1 ii 4 **184** 2 4, 5
לבה: **184** 1 2
לבב: **158** 14 i 7 **184** 2 6 **185** 1–2 ii 12
לבבם: **172** 4 5
לבבכם: **185** 1–2 i 15
לבנון: **163** 8–10 4 **169** 1–2 7 (2x)
הלבנון: **163** 21 2
ילבש: **159** 2–4 7
הלבושים: **179** 1 ii 11
ומלבשיה: **184** 1 4
להבה: **185** 1–2 i 9
ונלויתי: **160** 7 2
ונלוו: **169** 3–4 iii 5
נלוה: **169** 3–4 ii 9
הנלוים: **169** 3–4 iv 1
וילווו: **166** i 5
בלוחות: **177** 1–4 12
לוי: **159** 5 2
ללוי: **175** 14
התלוננו: **177** 19 3

מלונותיה: 184 1 6
לחיה: 179 1 i 9
לחיה: 179 2 9
ללחם: 161 5–6 11
והלחם: 165 5 6
מלחמה: 163 25 3
מלחמכי: 176 50 1
למלחמת: 161 8–10 7
מלחמתה: 169 3–4 iii 11
למלחמות: 183 1 ii 2
לילה: 167 3 2 184 1 4, 6
ולהליץ: 184 1 2
למליץ: 171 1–2 i 19
הלצון: 162 ii 6, 10
בתלמוד: 169 3–4 ii 8
להלעין: 177 5–6 7
לקח: 177 24 2
בקחת: 159 5 4
קחתו: 159 2–4 8
לשון: 169 3–4 ii 8 171 3–10 iv 27 185 1–2 iii 13
ובלשון: 183 1 ii 6
לשונם: 169 3–4 ii 10 177 1–4 11

מאת: 159 1 ii 8
מאות: 159 1 ii 8
ימאנו: 171 1–2 ii 3
מאסו: 162 ii 7 163 23 ii 14
ומגוג: 161 8–10 20
ימדה: 185 1–2 ii 10
וממדת: 185 1–2 ii 10
מה: 185 1–2 ii 8
למה: 185 1–2 ii 2
ומואבי: 174 1–2 i 4
תמד: 177 12–13 i 9
תמיד: 174 1–2 i 5 184 1 1 3 2
ימוש: 169 3–4 ii 5
ימשו: 179 1 ii 12
וימותו: 159 5 1
המתים: 179 1 ii 2
ולהמית: 165 6 4
להמיתו: 171 3–10 iv 8
והומתה: 159 2–4 9
יומת: 159 2–4 6
מות: 184 1 9, 10
ממזר: 174 1–2 i 4
ומחיר: 160 7 3
מים: 176 36 1 179 1 ii 8
כמים: 175 29 184 4 3
ימכר: 159 2–4 3
ממכרת: 159 2–4 3
מ]לאו: 181 1 5
ימלא: 184 4 3
ומלאות: 186 1 iii 4
וימלט: 183 1 ii 3
וימלטם: 171 3–10 iv 20
מלך: 165 9 2
מלך: 163 25 1 169 3–4 i 2
מלכים: 169 3–4 ii 9
מלכֵי: 169 3–4 i 3
מלכותו: 169 3–4 iv 3 172 3 2
וממלכה: 160 3–4 ii 5
ממלכות: 176 1–2 i 2
מילת: 176 16 3
ממרה: 180 2–4 ii 4
ממכה: 184 3 4
מהם: 166 ii 6 183 1 ii 2
ממנו: 169 1–2 10
ממנה: 159 1 ii 3
ימנה: 185 1–2 ii 9
המנה: 159 1 ii 9, 10
מנים: 159 2–4 9
המנים: 159 1 ii 10
מנשה: 169 3–4 iii 9 (2x) iv 1, 3, 6 171 1–2 ii 17
ונמס: 161 8–10 4
מעט: 171 1–2 ii 5
למעוט: 163 4–7 ii 8
למיעט: 163 4–7 ii 17
מעל: 184 4 5
מועלם: 166 i 9
ומצאה: 185 1–2 ii 12
ימצאהו: 185 1–2 i 12
ימצא: 171 1–2 ii 7 185 1–2 i 12
מצרים: 158 14 i 4, 5 159 2–4 3 163 28 1 167 17 1
במצרים: 158 14 i 6 185 1–2 i 15
מרדתם: 181 1 2
תמרו: 185 1–2 ii 3
מרה: 163 46 2
ימרה: 159 2–4 5
הממרים: 171 1–2 ii 3
מרורים: 179 2 7
מושה: 158 7–8 3 159 1 ii 17 5 4, 7 174 1, 3 ii 3 175 1
ימשול: 161 8–10 20
ומושלים: 169 3–4 ii 9
מושלֵי: 169 3–4 i 3
ולמושליו: 169 1–2 7
ממשלת: 169 3–4 ii 4
בממשלת: 177 1–4 8
ממשלתם: 169 1–2 5a
ממשלותם: 180 1 4
ממשלותיה: 184 1 6

נא: 185 1–2 i 13

נאצו: **162** ii 8
ונצה: **175** 28
הנבואות: **165** 1–2 1
נביא]: **158** 6 6
הנביא: **174** 1–2 i 15, 16 1, 3 ii 3
הנביאים: **166** ii 5
נביאֵי: **177** 1–4 9
הבטתה: **176** 14 4
להביל: **184** 1 15
נבלת: **176** 1–2 i 3
יבע: **167** 20 2
נגד: **167** 1 2
הגיד: **171** 3–10 iv 5 **177** 1–4 10
נוגה: **184** 1 8
נגועֵי: **184** 1 5
בנגיעיהם: **183** 1 ii 7
מגיר: **179** 1 ii 8
הגיש: **181** 1 3
ונדיבה: **185** 4 ii 2
ידוד: **177** 12–13 i 9
ידודו: **169** 3–4 iii 5
ידח: **177** 29 3
ינדפ]: **178** 2 4
נוח: **180** 2–4 i 7
ינודו: **177** 5–6 8
יניח: **174** 1–2 i 7
להניחו: **159** 1 ii 5
וניחוח: **179** 1 i 6
נזר: **161** 8–10 19
וינזרו: **183** 1 ii 5
]נחל: **159** 1 ii 1
נוחליה: **184** 1 8, 11
וינחילהו: **177** 1–4 12
ולהנחיל: **180** 1 9
ומנחילֵי: **181** 2 4
הנחלה: **173** 1 7
נחלת: **171** 1, 3–4 iii 1, 10 **176** 18 1
בנחלת: **171** 3–10 iv 12
נחלתה: **184** 1 7
נחלתנו: **179** 1 i 12
תנחומים: **176** 1–2 i 4 8–11 13
נחרו: **163** 56 1
להטות: **184** 1 14
ולהטות: **184** 1 16
נוטרים: **174** 4 2
הכם: **166** ii 12
יכה: **169** 3–4 i 5
להכות: **167** 2 3
להכותם: **182** 2 2
מכה: **176** 14 5
למכתינו: **179** 1 i 14
נכר: **174** 1–2 i 4
יפולו: **169** 3–4 ii 6, 10
הנופלת: **174** 1–2 i 12, 13
הפיל: **181** 1 5
הִפיל: **176** 16 2
לפיל: **171** 1–2 ii 15
נפש: **159** 2–4 5 **163** 4–7 i 12
נפשו: **159** 1 ii 6 **163** 14 7 **174** 1–2 i 9
נפשכה: **184** 2 1
נפשי: **177** 26 1
נפשכם: **185** 1–2 ii 1
יציב: **175** 23
נציות: **186** 1 ii 4
לנצח: **177** 10–11 9
ונצלו: **171** 1–2 ii 9
יצל: **185** 1–2 ii 3
ויצילכה: **158** 1–2 8
ויצילם: **171** 3–10 iv 21
להציל: **174** 9–10 6
מנצור: **184** 1 15
נקמות: **169** 3–4 i 7
ישאנה: **185** 1–2 ii 11
תשא: **185** 1–2 i 11
נושאים: **179** 1 ii 11
המשא: **160** 1 4
נשיא: **161** 5–6 3
נשבה: **185** 1–2 i 10
נשף: **184** 1 5
ונתיבותיה: **166** i 7 **184** 1 10
נתנו: **159** 1 ii 6
ינתן: **175** 3
ויתן: **183** 1 ii 4
תתן: **185** 1–2 ii 14
תתנו: **185** 1–2 ii 2
יתננו: **159** 1 ii 7
יתנוהו: **169** 3–4 i 12
ולתת: **176** 16 3
לתתו: **171** 3–10 iv 9
נתנה: **185** 1–2 ii 8
ינתן: **169** 3–4 i 12
ינתנו: **171** 1–2 ii 19

סוד: **180** 1 10
מסוד: **181** 1 2
לסוף: **171** 1–2 ii 6
יסור: **161** 5–6 3
סרֵי: **174** 1–2 i 14
סרה: **177** 1–4 14
במסורת: **185** 3 4
בסירים: **166** i 7
וכמסככה: **179** 2 7

סוכת: **174** 1–2 i 12 (2x)
מסך: **167** 3 3
המסלאים: **179** 1 ii 9
ונסלו: **177** 1–4 10
מסלה: **185** 1–2 ii 2
סלע: **160** 3–4 ii 3
בסמחה: **177** 12–13 i 10
יסומכנו: **161** 8–10 18
סמוכֵי: **184** 1 15
הספיר: **164** 1 3
הספון: **174** 11 1
האספסוף: **177** 10–11 4 30 2 (?)
ספר: **176** 1–2 i 4 **177** 1–4 13, 14 18 2
בספר: **163** 8–10 8 **174** 1–2 i 2, 15, 16 1, 3 ii 3 **177** 5–6 5, 9, 11 7 3 **182** 1 4
מספר: **177** 1–4 12
ספרֵי: **171** 3–10 iv 26
במספר: **177** 1–4 8
למספר: **158** 4 3
סרך: **180** 1 4
סרכ]: **186** 2 i 1
סרכמה: **186** 2 i 3, 6
במסתרים: **184** 1 11

עבדו: **177** 7 5
יעבודו: **159** 2–4 2
עובדי: **163** 11 i 2
עבד: **159** 2–4 3
עבדכה: **160** 3–4 ii 1
עבדים: **158** 1–2 17
עבדיו: **166** ii 5 **176** 8–11 15
עבות: **186** 1 iii 4 (2x), 5
עברו: **173** 5 1
בעבור: **176** 28 2
במעגלֵי: **184** 1 17
מעגלותיה: **184** 1 9
עד: **158** 1–2 9 (2x) **160** 3–4 ii 1 **161** 5–6 13 **169** 3–4 i 3 **171** 1, 3–4 iii 2 **174** 1–2 i 4 **176** 8–11 13 **177** 5–6 3 **181** 1 2 **185** 1–2 i 11
ועד: **185** 1–2 i 6
לעד: **177** 12–13 i 11
ועֶדיה: **184** 1 5
עֵדים: **179** 1 ii 11
עדות]: **166** ii 16
הנעדרות: **164** 1 6
עדריהם: **171** 1, 3–4 iii 6
עוד: **169** 3–4 ii 1 iii 7, 8 **174** 1–2 i 5 **176** 8–11 14
ועוד: **171** 1–2 ii 5
עון: **163** 23 ii 20
עוונם: **183** 1 ii 7, 8
בעוונם: **169** 3–4 iii 4
מעונם: **171** 1–2 ii 4
עוונותינו: **179** 1 i 2
עוז: **175** 26
עול: **184** 1 2, 8, 10 3 4
העול: **172** 4 2
בעול: **184** 1 3
עולה: **180** 1 9 **181** 2 4
לעוליהן: **179** 1 ii 4
ועפעפיה: **184** 1 13
ובעורון: **166** i 8
בעורונם: **166** ii 6
עזבו: **167** 7–9 2
ועזבו: **169** 3–4 iii 5
עזבם: **162** i 2
יעזבם: **171** 1–2 ii 14
עזובה: **179** 2 6
כעזובה: **179** 2 5
עזובות: **179** 2 5
וכעזובת: **179** 2 6
עוז: **160** 5 2 **185** 1–2 ii 15
עזזאל: **180** 1 7, 8
יעזור: **177** 12–13 i 7
לעוזרם: **177** 12–13 i 9
ועזרתה: **160** 3–4 ii 2
עינים: **184** 2 5 **185** 1–2 ii 12
לעינֵי: **159** 2–4 2 **166** ii 13 **181** 2 5
עיניו: **186** 2 i 1
עיניה: **184** 1 13
עיניהם: **162** i 6
עיצים: **176** 24 2
עיר: **169** 3–4 ii 2 **179** 1 i 8 **184** 1 12
העיר: **175** 22, 26
בעיר: **169** 3–4 iv 7, 8 **177** 12–13 i 5
ערים: **169** 3–4 ii 9
עָרֵי: **161** 5–6 12 **169** 3–4 ii 12 **179** 1 i 11
עכו: **161** 5–6 11
עלי: **179** 1 ii 10
עליו: **174** 1–2 i 5 **177** 1–4 14 12–13 i 6 **184** 2 3 **186** 1 ii 8
עליה: **159** 2–4 9 **174** 17 3
עליהם: **166** ii 13 **171** 1–2 ii 18 **177** 1–4 7 5–6 5, 11 7 4 10–11 3 **182** 1 4
עליהמה: **174** 1–2 i 9, 16 **176** 19 3
עליהים: **176** 20 3
עליהיהם: **159** 2–4 3
מעל: **169** 1–2 4
מעלהם: **161** 5–6 3
עלה: **179** 1 ii 1
בעלותו: **161** 5–6 11
והעלהו: **160** 3–4 ii 2
עלי: **160** 1 3

התעוללו: **177** 1–4 7
עילוליו: **169** 3–4 iv 4
עילוליה: **169** 3–4 iv 2
עלומיה: **179** 1 ii 5
עולם: **158** 1–2 9 4 8 **165** 6 2 **171** 1, 3–4 iii 2 **174** 1–2 i 4 (2x), 5 **177** 1–4 13 **181** 1 4, 6 **184** 1 7
לעולם: **171** 1, 3–4 iii 13 **177** 1–4 10 (2x) **185** 4 i 1
עולמים: **176** 17 2
עלמיה: **185** 1–2 ii 13
תתעלף: **184** 1 12
עִם: **174** 1–2 i 11 **176** 1–2 i 2 **177** 8 3 **179** 1 ii 2 **181** 1 1, 4 **184** 3 5
ועם: **171** 3–10 iv 11
מעם: **169** 3–4 ii 10
עמו: **160** 7 2 **161** 8–10 24 **181** 1 3
עמה: **185** 1–2 ii 12
עמהמה: **177** 12–13 i 9
עמם: **172** 4 1 **179** 1 ii 13
ועמד: **175** 24
יעמוד: **174** 1–2 i 13 **177** 1–4 6 5–6 3 **180** 2–4 ii 5
עמוד: **164** 2 2 **169** 3–4 i 3
לעמוד: **171** 1, 3–4 iii 16 **185** 1–2 i 7, 8
ולעמוד: **178** 1 1
בעומדם: **177** 10–11 6
עומד: **175** 24 **177** 1–4 15
העומד: **161** 8–10 17 **174** 1–2 i 11
והעמד: **160** 3–4 ii 3
במעמד: **181** 1 4
מעמדם: **177** 1–4 11
מעמדֵי: **164** 1 8
עמוד[: **186** 2 i 7
העמוד: **186** 1 ii 6
ועמוני: **174** 1–2 i 4
עמורה: **172** 4 3
עם: **171** 1, 3–4 iii 7 **177** 9 7 **185** 1–2 ii 8
העם: **159** 1 ii 16 **163** 25 8 27 2
ועם: **169** 3–4 ii 9
והעם: **164** 1 2
עמו: **185** 1–2 ii 10
בעמו: **162** ii 8
לעמו: **175** 24
עמכה: **160** 3–4 ii 4, 6 5 2
בעמכה: **176** 1–2 i 1
לעמכה: **160** 3–4 ii 2
עמי: **179** 1 ii 4 **185** 1–2 i 13
ולעמי: **185** 4 ii 1
עמים: **163** 4–7 ii 5
העמים: **161** 8–10 21 **165** 5 6 **177** 9 6
בעמים: **167** 11–13 4
עמֵי: **160** 3–4 ii 5
ולעומת: **181** 1 2, 3
עמק: **167** 1 1
עמוקי: **184** 4 2
מעמקֵי: **184** 1 6
יתענגו: **171** 1–2 ii 10 1, 3–4 iii 11
תענוג: **171** 1–2 ii 10
ויען: **160** 1 4
במענֵי: **171** 3–10 iv 27
ענה: **159** 2–4 9
לענות: **176** 8–11 15
ולענוי: **178** 11 2
ענוים: **184** 1 16
וענֵי: **161** 8–10 3
]ענוי[: **165** 7 2
עני: **186** 1 ii 9
ענות: **177** 12–13 i 8
וענות: **178** 6 3
עניה: **186** 2 i 2
העונה: **177** 5–6 13
עת: **174** 1, 3 ii 1 **177** 5–6 3 12–13 i 8
העת: **174** 4 3
בעת: **162** ii 2 **171** 1–2 ii 18 **172** 1 2 **175** 21 **177** 1–4 5
מעת: **176** 8–11 14
העתים: **163** 27 1
לעתת: **185** 1–2 ii 5
עתה: **177** 1–4 12
ועתה: **185** 1–2 i 13
למען: **158** 1–2 1 **171** 1–2 i 19
למעאן: **175** 4
ונענש: **159** 2–4 9
כעצובה: **179** 2 6
העץ: **169** 3–4 i 8
בעץ: **163** 23 i 17
עצום: **184** 1 14
עצרתי: **160** 3–4 ii 1
יעקוב: **158** 3 1 **175** 29 **185** 1–2 ii 4
כעקרה: **179** 2 7
מעורב: **186** 2 ii 2
מעורבים: **186** 1 i 6
ובערום: **166** ii 12
הערכים: **159** 1 ii 6
ערוכים: **184** 1 16
ערל: **184** 2 5
ערלות: **177** 9 8
ערומי: **177** 8 2
עורפם: **182** 1 2
יערץ: **185** 1–2 i 15
עריצֵי: **171** 1–2 ii 13, 19 1, 3–4 iii 12 3–10 iv 1, 10
ערשיה: **184** 1 5
עשה: **159** 2–4 6 **180** 1 1 **185** 1–2 i 14 iii 11, 13 3 3
ועשה: **159** 1 ii 3
עשו: **174** 11 2

ועשה: **176** 1–2 i 1
ועשו: **174** 1, 3 ii 2 **175** 28 **185** 1–2 ii 1
יעשנה: **185** 1–2 ii 13
לעשות: **169** 1–2 4 **171** 3–10 iv 10, 15 **175** 26
עושה: **171** 1–2 ii 22 **176** 21 4
עושֵׂי: **171** 1–2 ii 5, 14 **177** 5–6 16
מעשֵׂי: **174** 1–2 i 7 **176** 20 2
למעשי: **178** 6 2
מעשיהם: **169** 3–4 iii 3
עשר: **164** 1 4 **185** 1–2 i 6
עשרה: **177** 12–13 i 5
העשר: **159** 2–4 4
מעשרה: **185** 1–2 ii 5
לעשרת: **159** 1 ii 10
עשרים: **159** 1 ii 7, 9 **180** 1 5
העשרונים: **159** 1 ii 14
מעשר: **159** 1 ii 11
כעשן: **171** 1, 3–4 iii 8
עש: **163** 31 3
עתרות: **173** 1 4

תפארת: **160** 3–4 ii 4
תפארתנו: **179** 1 i 6
פגרֵי: **169** 3–4 ii 6
יפדם: **171** 1–2 ii 18
בפיהו: **159** 1 ii 5
כפיך: **164** 1 1
פיהם: **159** 2–4 5 **161** 8–10 23
לפי: **181** 1 2 (2x), 3, 5
ולפזרם: **177** 12–13 i 8
פחדו: **185** 1–2 i 15
יפחדו: **166** ii 6
מפחד: **169** 3–4 ii 5 **185** 1–2 ii 5
פוחזים: **177** 1–4 7
פחז: **172** 4 3 **184** 3 5
בפחז: **184** 1 13, 15
פחוז: **184** 1 2
מפַּח: **185** 1–2 ii 5
פחֵי: **171** 1–2 ii 9
פלאכה: **176** 1–2 i 1
נפלאים: **185** 1–2 i 14
נפלאֵי: **181** 2 7
והפלא: **181** 1 3
פלג: **169** 3–4 iv 1
בפליליים: **158** 9 5
בתפלה: **184** 3 3
פנֵי: **169** 1–2 4 **185** 1–2 iii 1
לפני: **158** 10–12 10 **159** 2–4 4 **160** 1 3 7 4 **167** 33 2 **178** 1 1 **185** 1–2 i 8
מלפנים: **169** 3–4 i 8
מלפני: **161** 8–10 9 **169** 1–2 8 **179** 1 ii 6
ומלפנֵי: **169** 1–2 10
מפנֵי: **162** ii 1 **185** 1–2 i 15
פניו: **167** 2 6 **180** 2–4 i 2
לפניו: **174** 1–2 i 7 **185** 1–2 ii 8
פניה: **160** 7 3
לפניה: **185** 1–2 i 7
פעולותיהם: **180** 1 2
פעמים: **185** 1–2 i 6
פעמיהם: **184** 1 16
פקדת: **162** ii 2
הפקודה: **166** i 10
ונפרדה: **169** 3–4 iii 7
יפרכה: **158** 1–2 7
הפרי: **173** 2 1
ופרח: **185** 1–2 i 10
ופֶרַח: **169** 1–2 7
ויפרעו: **182** 1 3
פרע: **171** 1–2 i 15
פרעה: **180** 5–6 5
פרוש: **184** 3 3
מפורשים: **177** 1–4 11
להפשיע: **184** 1 15
פשעים: **184** 1 4
פשעיהם: **159** 1 ii 2
פשעינו: **179** 1 i 15
פשר: **159** 5 1, 5 **162** i 2 ii 1 **163** 4–7 ii 4, 14 22 1 23 ii 10 **165** 1–2 3 5 2 **167** 19 1 **172** 14 1 **174** 1–2 i 14, 19 **177** 1–4 6 10–11 9 **180** 1 1, 7
פשרו: **161** 8–10 22 **163** 4–7 ii 8, 17 29 3 **164** 1 4, 7 **165** 6 6 **166** ii 12, 15 **167** 7–9 1 10 2 11–13 4, 9 16 1 **169** 1–2 3 3–4 i 6 ii 2, 4, 8, 11 iii 3, 6, 9, 11 iv 1, 3, 5, 7 **170** 1–2 2 **171** 1–2 ii 2, 4, 6, 8, 13, 17 1, 3–4 iii 3, 5a, 7, 10, 15 3–10 iv 8, 16 **173** 2 1
פיתאום: **178** 5 2
פתאום: **185** 1–2 i 14
ופתאים: **169** 3–4 iii 7
פתאֵי: **169** 3–4 iii 5
פתגם: **161** 5–6 10
ולפתות: **184** 1 17
ופתי: **177** 9 7
יפתח: **174** 4 3
בפתח: **184** 1 10

צואן: **177** 5–6 15
צון: **171** 1, 3–4 iii 6
ואצבעות: **186** 1 ii 5 iii 3, 5 2 i 4
צדוק: **163** 22 3 **174** 1–2 i 17
יצדק: **176** 18 1
צדיק: **177** 9 7 **184** 1 14
צדיקים: **173** 5 4 **177** 12–13 i 5
וצדיקים: **174** 1, 3 ii 4a

צדק: **184** 1 14, 16
הצדק: **165** 1–2 3 **173** 1 4 2 2 **174** 9–10 1 **176** 1–2 i 1
צדקה: **178** 4 3
בצדקה: **176** 20 1
צהרים: **171** 1–2 i 12
צוה: **178** 1 2
צונו: **174** 11 2
ויצו: **159** 2–4 3
מצוה: **184** 1 15
מצוות: **167** 23 1
מצוותיו: **166** ii 4
במצלות: **158** 14 i 7
וציצו: **185** 1–2 i 11
כציץ: **185** 1–2 i 10
בצוקה: **159** 5 6
מצורו: **177** 10–11 6
צי: **184** 3 4
ציה: **177** 12–13 i 8
ציון: **175** 29 **176** 24 3 **177** 12–13 i 10 **179** 1 ii 13 **180** 5–6 4
בציון: **174** 1–2 i 12
צירו: **169** 3–4 ii 1
כצל: **185** 1–2 i 13
צמח: **174** 1–2 i 11
יצמח: **185** 1–2 i 10
צונם: **186** 1 ii 2
תצעד: **184** 1 10
תצעדו: **185** 1–2 ii 4
ובצעירו: **175** 23
צופה: **171** 3–10 iv 8
כצפור: **177** 5–6 9
ויצטרפו: **174** 1, 3 ii 4a
ולצורפם: **177** 10–11 10
מצרף: **174** 24 2
המצרף: **171** 1–2 ii 18 **174** 1, 3 ii 1 **177** 5–6 3
יצור: **166** i 3
בצר: **178** 1 2
מצרותיהם: **166** ii 14

יקבלו: **171** 1–2 ii 9
קבצו: **169** 3–4 i 11
אקבוץ: **177** 19 5
יקבצו: **177** 7 4
ונקבצו: **171** 13 6
קובר: **176** 1–2 i 4
הקדשתה: **160** 3–4 ii 7
קדוש: **162** ii 7
וקדוש: **185** 1–2 i 4
וקדושו: **177** 12–13 i 10
קדושַי: **174** 1–2 i 4
קדושיו: **181** 1 4
קודש: **171** 3–10 iv 25 **176** 16 3 **181** 1 4 **185** 4 i 3
הקודש: **159** 1 ii 12
קודשו: **171** 1, 3–4 iii 8, 11
קודשנו: **179** 1 i 7
קדשים: **158** 13 2
במקדוש: **176** 22 1
מקדש: **174** 1–2 i 6 (2x)
במקדש: **167** 20 1
מקדשכה: **176** 1–2 i 2
מקדשם: **183** 1 ii 1
הקהל: **169** 3–4 iii 7
קהלם: **169** 3–4 iii 5
קוו]: **160** 3–4 ii 2
מקוה: **185** 1–2 i 7, 12
קול: **158** 6 6
קולו: **186** 2 i 2
קולם: **169** 3–4 ii 1
יקום: **174** 16 2 **185** 1–2 i 11
ויקום: **160** 1 3 **177** 1–4 13
ויקומו: **183** 1 ii 2
קמה: **179** 1 ii 12
והקימותי: **174** 1–2 i 12
ממקומו: **177** 5–6 9
מקטירים: **174** 1–2 i 6
לקלון: **166** ii 12
קללת: **176** 21 2
בקלות: **171** 1–2 i 19
וקלס: **184** 1 2
בקנאתמה: **174** 4 2 **177** 9 5
קצף: **176** 20 2
קץ: **169** 3–4 ii 6 **180** 1 1, 3
וקץ: **166** i 9 **177** 1–4 11
הקץ: **169** 3–4 iii 3 **173** 1 5
לקץ: **169** 3–4 iv 3
לקצו: **180** 1 3
קצה: **181** 1 3
קצים: **177** 1–4 10
הקצים: **180** 1 1
בקצי: **166** i 12
לקצי: **180** 1 4
קצותם: **181** 2 9
קצר: **186** 2 i 4
וקצרות: **186** 1 iii 5
קרא: **177** 5–6 6
יקרא: **169** 3–4 i 8
ויקרא: **158** 3 1
מקרב: **169** 3–4 ii 5
לקרותנו: **179** 1 i 3
קריות: **184** 1 12
קרן: **174** 6–7 1
יקשו: **182** 1 2

קשות: **174** 4 4

ראו: **177** 5–6 12
יראה: **174** 1–2 i 5
ואראה: **180** 2–4 ii 9
יראו: **171** 3–10 iv 11
וראה: **176** 1–2 i 3
לראות: **184** 1 13
היראתי: **158** 4 6
מראה: **160** 1 5 3–4 i 6
בראש: **163** 12 2
וראושו: **186** 1 iii 2
רשים: **171** 1, 3–4 iii 5
ראשֵׁי: **164** 1 7
לראשי: **177** 1–4 9
למרואש: **160** 3–4 ii 3
בראישונה: **174** 1–2 i 5
למרישונה: **160** 6 2
ראשית: **184** 1 8
רב: **176** 8–11 13
רבים: **160** 3–4 ii 6 **163** 4–7 ii 6 **169** 1–2 6 3–4 ii 8 **171** 1–2 i 18
ורבים: **161** 2–4 4 **169** 3–4 iii 4 **171** 1, 3–4 iii 3
רוב: 184 1 4
ורוב: **169** 3–4 ii 5
ברוב: **177** 9 3
רובכה: **169** 3–4 i 10
תרבות: **172** 3 2
ארבעים: **171** 1–2 ii 7
תרגל: **186** 2 i 2
ברגל: **186** 1 ii 9
רגליו: **186** 1 ii 5 iii 5 2 i 5
רגליה: **184** 1 3
להרגיעה: **184** 1 12
רוח: **177** 12–13 i 5 **183** 1 ii 6 **185** 1–2 i 11 **186** 1 ii 7
הרוח: **178** 1 6
ורוח: **186** 1 iii 5 2 i 6
מרוח: **185** 1–2 i 12
רוחו: **185** 1–2 i 10
ורוחו: **184** 4 4
ברוחֵי: **177** 1–4 7
רוחות: **177** 12–13 i 9
הרוחות: **158** 14 i 2
רוחתיו: **185** 1–2 i 9
ורוחותיהם: **176** 21 3
תרים: **184** 1 13
ארים: **176** 8–11 16
רום: **184** 2 6
רם: **176** 27 2
רמה: **159** 2–4 6 **171** 3–10 iv 15 **182** 1 3
רום: **169** 1–2 6
רומות: **186** 1 iii 3
מרום: **171** 1, 3–4 iii 11
רזֵי: **176** 16 2
רחבים: **186** 1 i 5
ברחובות: **184** 1 12
ורחובותיה: **179** 1 i 9
ברחובותיה: **184** 6 1
הרחמים: **177** 1–4 9
רחמֵי: **181** 1 3
הרחקות: **163** 13 2
וריבה: **176** 1–2 i 2
הרכות: **179** 1 ii 13
רכוש: **160** 7 3
מרמה: **169** 3–4 ii 8 **185** 1–2 ii 14
תרמס: **169** 3–4 i 3
מרנן: **177** 7 1
רעב: **163** 56 1 **172** 1 2
והרעב: **162** ii 1
ברעב: **166** ii 12 **171** 1, 3–4 iii 3, 4
וברעב: **171** 1–2 ii 1
רעות: **163** 12 9
רע: **159** 2–4 8
רעה: **185** 1–2 ii 8
רעים: **181** 1 1
הרעים: **169** 3–4 iii 3
ברוע: **179** 1 i 3
לרעות: **171** 1–2 ii 23
מרעתם: **171** 1–2 ii 3
ומרפה: **176** 30 3
רצה: **167** 16 3
וירצו: **166** i 4 **183** 1 ii 7
רצון: **171** 1–2 i 13 **183** 1 ii 4
רצונו: **171** 1–2 ii 5, 25
רצין: **163** 2–3 4
רוקמות: **161** 8–10 19
רקיעֵי: **169** 1–2 2
רק: **159** 1 ii 7
להרשיע: **174** 1, 3 ii 3 **184** 1 3
רשע: **171** 1–2 ii 8 **173** 4 3 **175** 26 **177** 9 7
רשעים: **185** 1–2 ii 9
רשעה: **169** 1–2 6 **171** 1–2 i 16 3–10 iv 11 **180** 1 9 **181** 1 2 **183** 1 ii 5
רשעם: **181** 1 2
הרשע: **163** 30 3 **171** 3–10 iv 8
הרשעה: **171** 1–2 ii 6
רשעֵי: **167** 10 3 **169** 3–4 iv 1, 5 **171** 1–2 ii 17 1, 3–4 iii 12
לרשעי: **169** 3–4 i 1
ורשף: **185** 1–2 ii 12

וישבעו: **166** ii 3

השביע: 181 2 3
בשבעים: 181 2 3
השדה: 158 10–12 7 159 1 ii 5
שמו: 177 12–13 i 10
]שמתיה: 176 23 2
ובמשטמתמה: 177 9 5
ישכילו: 184 1 13
והשכילו: 185 1–2 i 13
ושמח: 177 1–4 15
ישמח: 176 8–11 16
ישמחו: 171 3–10 iv 12
שמחה: 179 1 i 13
ושמחת: 185 1–2 ii 12
בשמלות: 159 2–4 7
שנא: 176 40 1
ושנאום: 169 3–4 iii 4
שונאנו: 176 14 3
שונאַי: 160 3–4 ii 4
כמשונאה: 179 1 ii 3
שנאית: 176 14 2
שער: 186 1 iii 4
ושפת: 169 3–4 ii 8
בשפת: 171 12 1
שפיח: 177 5–6 2
השפיח: 177 5–6 2
שרף: 159 1 ii 17
לשרפת: 179 1 i 5
שרים: 169 3–4 ii 9
ושרים: 171 1, 3–4 iii 5
שרֵי: 171 1, 3–4 iii 7
שרתי: 179 2 5

שואגים: 172 9 2
שאולה: 184 1 10
שאלו: 179 1 ii 8
ישאלו: 159 2–4 5
ונשאר: 174 1, 3 ii 2
לשארית: 185 1–2 ii 2
שאר: 186 1 i 6
שבי: 166 i 16 169 3–4 ii 5
בשבי: 169 3–4 iv 4
שבט: 171 13 5
שבטֵי: 164 1 7
שבילֵי: 184 1 9
שבע: 171 3–10 iv 23
שבר: 163 47 1
שברנו: 176 14 3
]שבת: 163 46 5
ישבת: 163 4–7 i 16
לשבית: 171 3–10 iv 14
ותשיגהו: 184 1 14
להשגות: 184 1 17
משגות: 184 1 9
במשגת: 174 1–2 i 9
שודד: 165 5 7
ושדדה: 184 1 8
שש: 186 1 ii 7
לשש: 159 1 ii 8
בשוא: 184 1 2
ושבו: 163 21 3
ישוב: 167 18 2
ישובון: 177 19 6 184 1 11
שוב: 177 1–4 9 185 1–2 ii 15
בשוב: 166 i 16
לשוב: 171 1–2 ii 3, 4 11 1
]שובם: 172 9 1
בשובם: 161 5–6 2
השבים: 171 1–2 ii 2
שבי: 171 1, 3–4 iii 1 3–10 iv 24
ושבי: 175 25 178 3 3
שוח: 184 1 3
שוחה: 184 1 17
שחת: 184 1 5 (2x), 11
השולים: 169 3–4 ii 12
ושוקיו: 186 1 ii 5 iii 4 2 i 5
שור: 186 1 ii 9
השור: 186 1 ii 9
ושחוט: 177 5–6 15
תשחר: 184 1 1
שחורות: 186 2 i 1
שחת: 184 1 5 (2x)
לשוטמם: 174 4 4
לשכוב: 160 7 4
משכבֵי: 184 1 6
וישכחו: 166 ii 3
כמשכלות: 179 2 8
שכן: 180 2–4 ii 1
ותשכון: 184 1 7
שכניו: 175 24
שלוג ?: 186 2 ii 3
שלח: 166 ii 4 171 3–10 iv 9
ושלח: 159 2–4 10
ישלח: 167 2 3
לשלוח: 171 1–2 ii 17
ילח = ישלח ?: 158 10–12 10
השליכו: 166 ii 4
ישלם: 171 3–10 iv 9
שלום: 171 3–10 iv 17 177 5–6 14
השלום: 178 1 5
ושלוש: 186 1 ii 7
שלושים: 158 1–2 17
שלושת: 159 1 ii 14 180 2–4 ii 3

שלשת: **163** 39 2
לשלישית: **159** 1 ii 8
שם: **159** 2–4 8
השם: **161** 8–10 24
שמות: **177** 1–4 8
בשמות: **177** 1–4 11
שָׁם: **158** 1–2 10 **174** 1–2 i 4
שָׁמָּה: **158** 1–2 3 **159** 5 5 **174** 1–2 i 3 **177** 1–4 4
משמה: **177** 1–4 13
ונשמדו: **171** 1, 3–4 iii 12
שמואל: **160** 1 2
השמים: **160** 3–4 ii 3
שמיו: **169** 1–2 2
שממו: **179** 1 i 10
שוממו: **179** 1 ii 5
שוממה: **179** 2 5
השמו: **174** 1–2 i 5
ישמוהו: **174** 1–2 i 5
שמות: **173** 5 5
ושממה: **177** 12–13 i 8
שמונה: **176** 17 5 **186** 1 iii 6 2 i 7
השמינית: **177** 5–6 13
שמע]: **160** 1 2
שמעו: **166** ii 5 **167** 2 7
שמעתי: **185** 1–2 ii 3
שמענו: **179** 1 i 2
שְׁמְעוּ: **185** 1–2 i 13
נשמעה: **179** 1 i 13
שׁוֹמְרֵי: **176** 16 4
ישמע: **169** 3–4 ii 1
כשמש: **164** 1 6
להשנות: **184** 1 15
השנה: **177** 5–6 2
שנים: **159** 2–4 4 (2x) **164** 1 4
שני: **159** 2–4 9 **180** 5–6 3
השני: **186** 1 ii 6 2 i 7
שניהמה: **175** 25
שנותיהם: **177** 1–4 11
שנית: **177** 1–4 14
שתי: **158** 1–2 13
השנה: **171** 1–2 ii 7
לשנן: **184** 1 1
ושניו: **186** 1 iii 3 2 i 2
נשענו: **166** ii 13
השער: **173** 5 4
שַׁעֲרֵי: **184** 1 10
ובשערי: **184** 1 12
שעריה: **184** 1 10
ושערוריה: **175** 27
אשפותות: **179** 1 ii 7
משפחה: **159** 2–4 1
ומשפחות: **169** 3–4 ii 9
שפט: **185** 3 4
שפטו: **176** 27 1
ישפוט: **161** 8–10 23
תשפוט: **161** 8–10 21
ישפטו: **185** 1–2 i 9
ונשפטו: **159** 2–4 4
בהשפטו: **171** 3–10 iv 9
משפט: **169** 1–2 4 **171** 3–10 iv 15 **184** 5 5 **185** 1–2 ii 3
ומשפט: **180** 1 10
במשפט: **159** 5 3 **171** 3–10 iv 11
כמשפט: **164** 1 5
למשפט: **171** 1–2 ii 19
ולמשפט: **176** 19 2
משפטים: **180** 1 10
ולמשפטים: **181** 1 1
שפל: **161** 7 2
תשפל: **169** 3–4 iv 3
שופר: **177** 12–13 ii 4
השופר: **177** 1–4 13
שוקד: **159** 2–4 1
שקל: **159** 1 ii 9
השקל: **159** 1 ii 7
למשקלת: **163** 12 7
שקוצי: **169** 3–4 iii 1
שקר: **171** 1–2 i 19 **172** 6 2
שקרם: **169** 3–4 ii 8
ושקרים: **169** 3–4 ii 2

תוך: **186** 1 iv 2
בתוך: **164** 1 3 **171** 1, 3–4 iii 6 **184** 1 7 (2x)
מתוך: **169** 3–4 iii 5 **171** 3–10 iv 19
תוכה]: **176** 27 3
תכנם: **181** 2 8
תכון: **159** 1 ii 13
יתלה: **169** 3–4 i 7
לתלוי: **169** 3–4 i 8
תולע: **179** 1 ii 10
ובתמהון: **166** i 8
תמכו: **184** 1 3
תּוֹמְכֵי: **184** 1 9
תתם: **169** 1–2 5a
יתמו: **171** 1–2 ii 7
להתם: **174** 1, 3 ii 1
תמו: **185** 1–2 i 14
תומים: **163** 14 1
והתומים: **164** 1 5 **174** 6–7 7
תועבה: **159** 2–4 7
תועבותיהם: **169** 3–4 iii 1
לתעות: **169** 3–4 iii 7
תוֹעֵי: **183** 1 ii 6

התעה: **171** 1–2 i 18
יתעו: **169** 3–4 ii 8
ומתעים: **171** 1–2 i 15
מתעֵי: **169** 3–4 ii 8
התעות: **171** 1–2 ii 9 1, 3–4 iii 3
מתעיהם: **169** 3–4 iii 5
ולמתעיהם: **166** ii 5
תועות: **184** 1 1
בתופים: **163** 25 2
יתפושו: **167** 16 2

158. Biblical Paraphrase: Genesis, Exodus

PLATE II

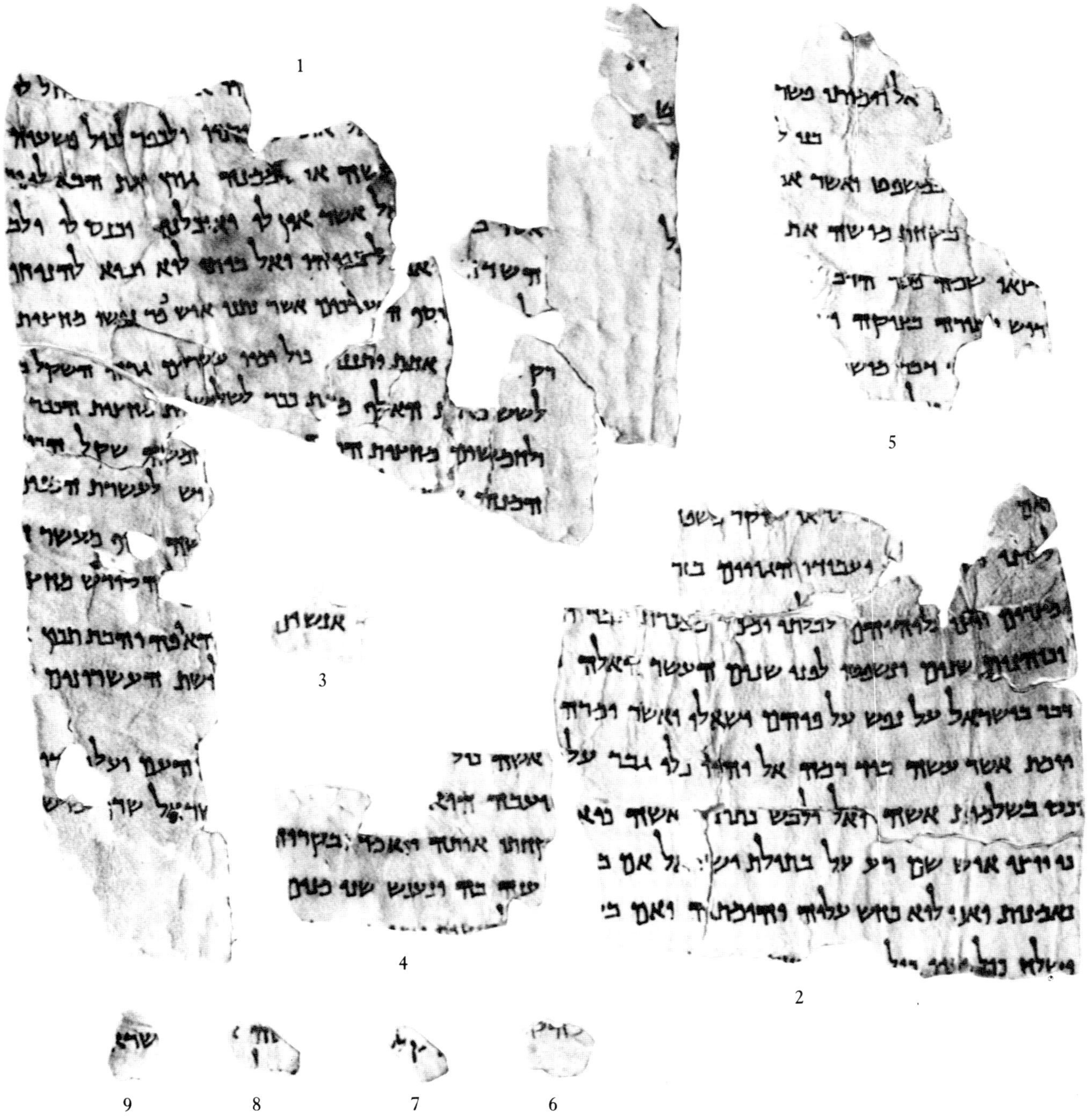

159. Ordinances

2

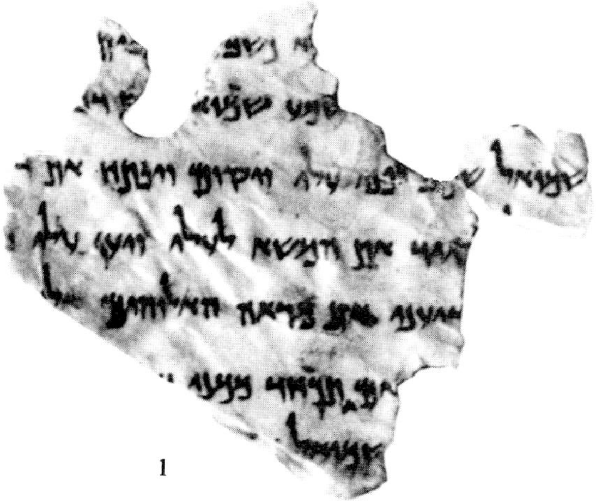

1

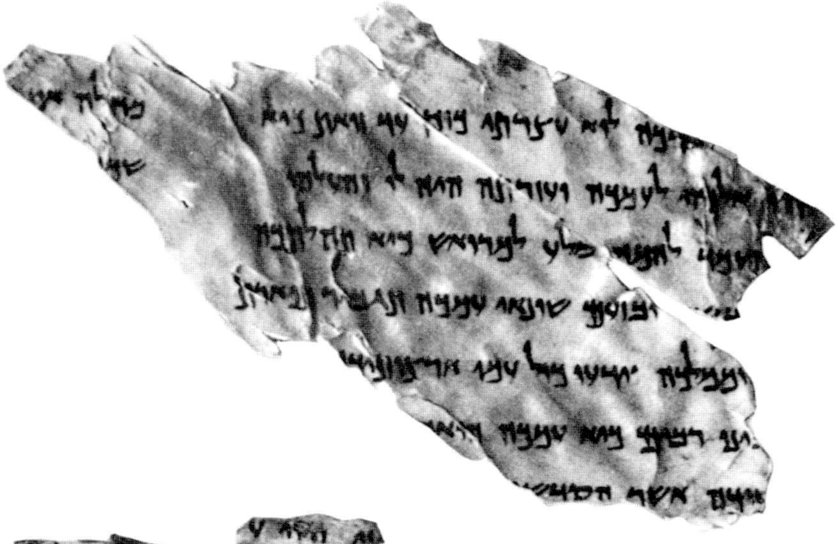

4

3

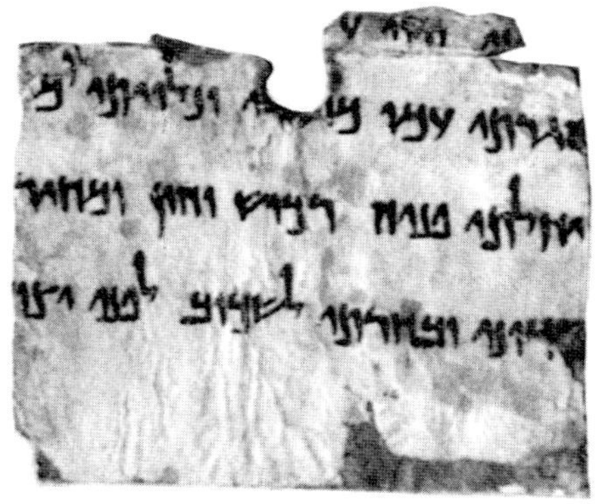

7

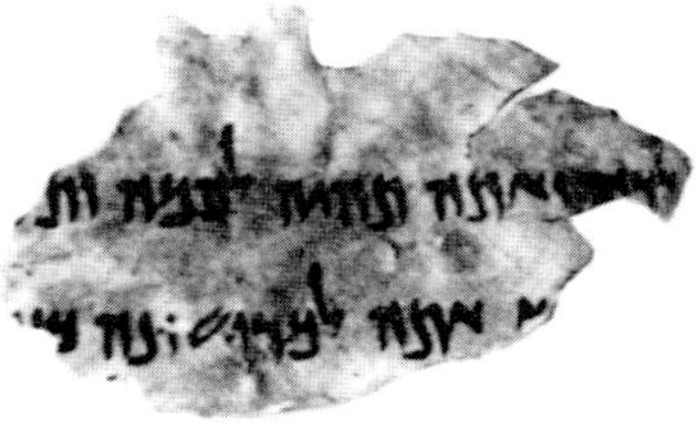

6

5

160. Vision of Samuel

161. p Isa[a]

8

7

9

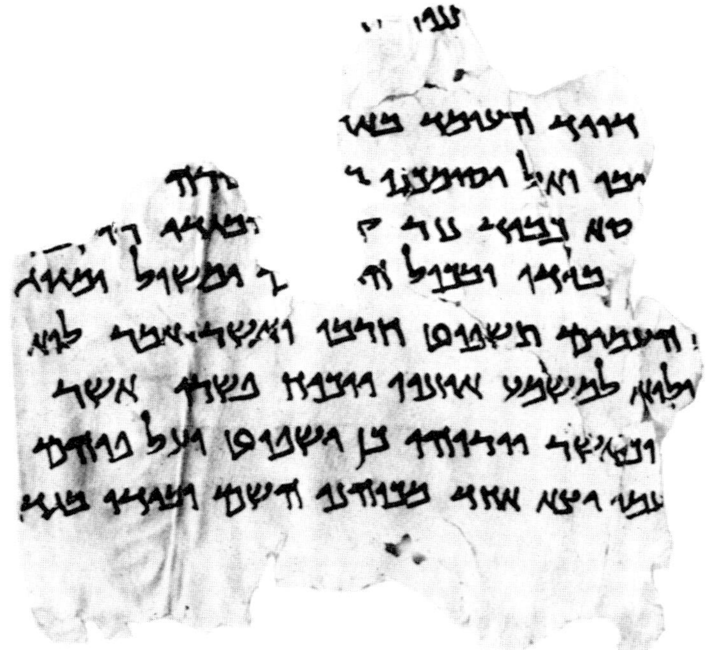

10

161. p Isa[a]

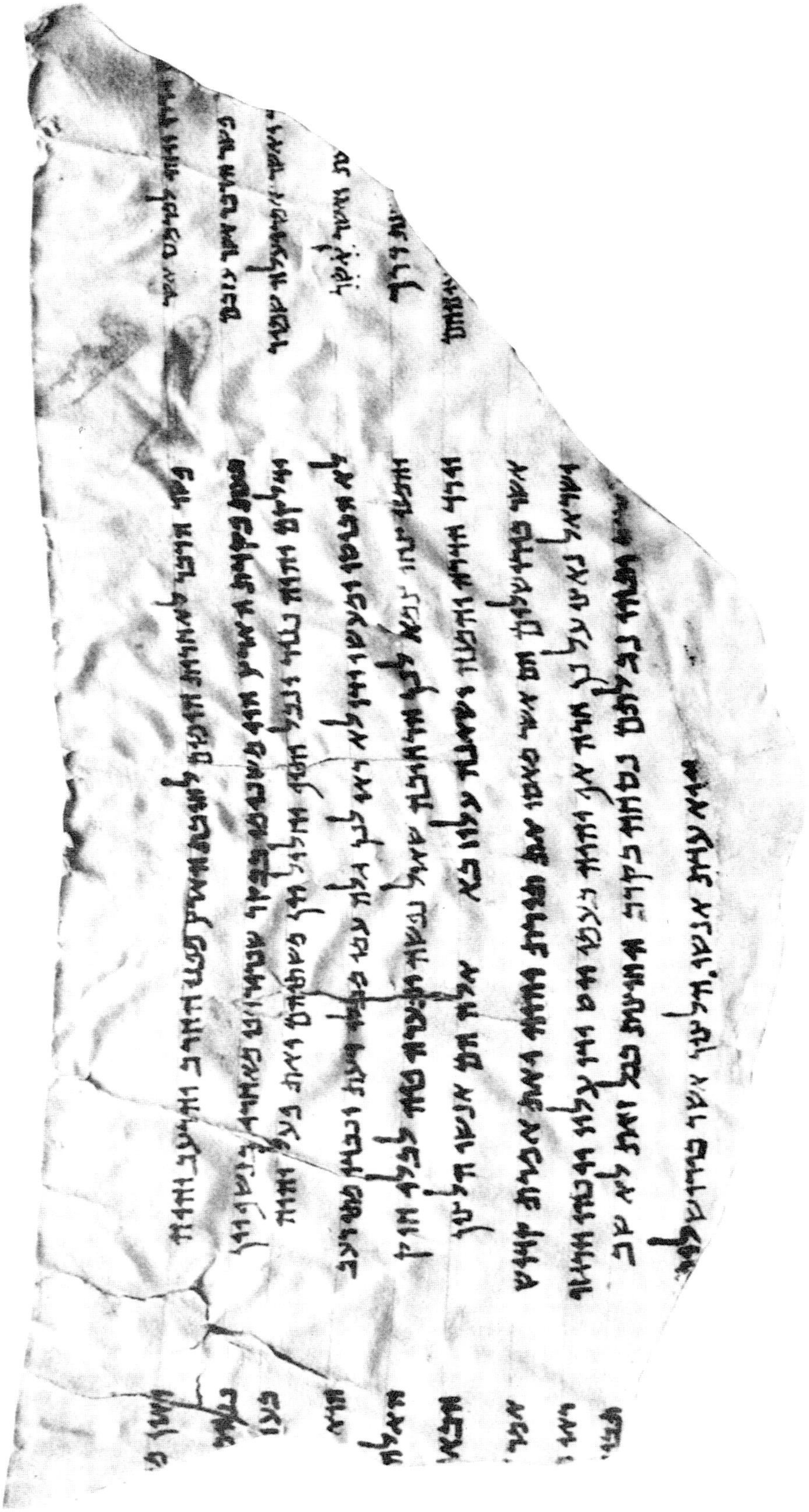

162. pIsa^{b}

163. pIsa^{c}

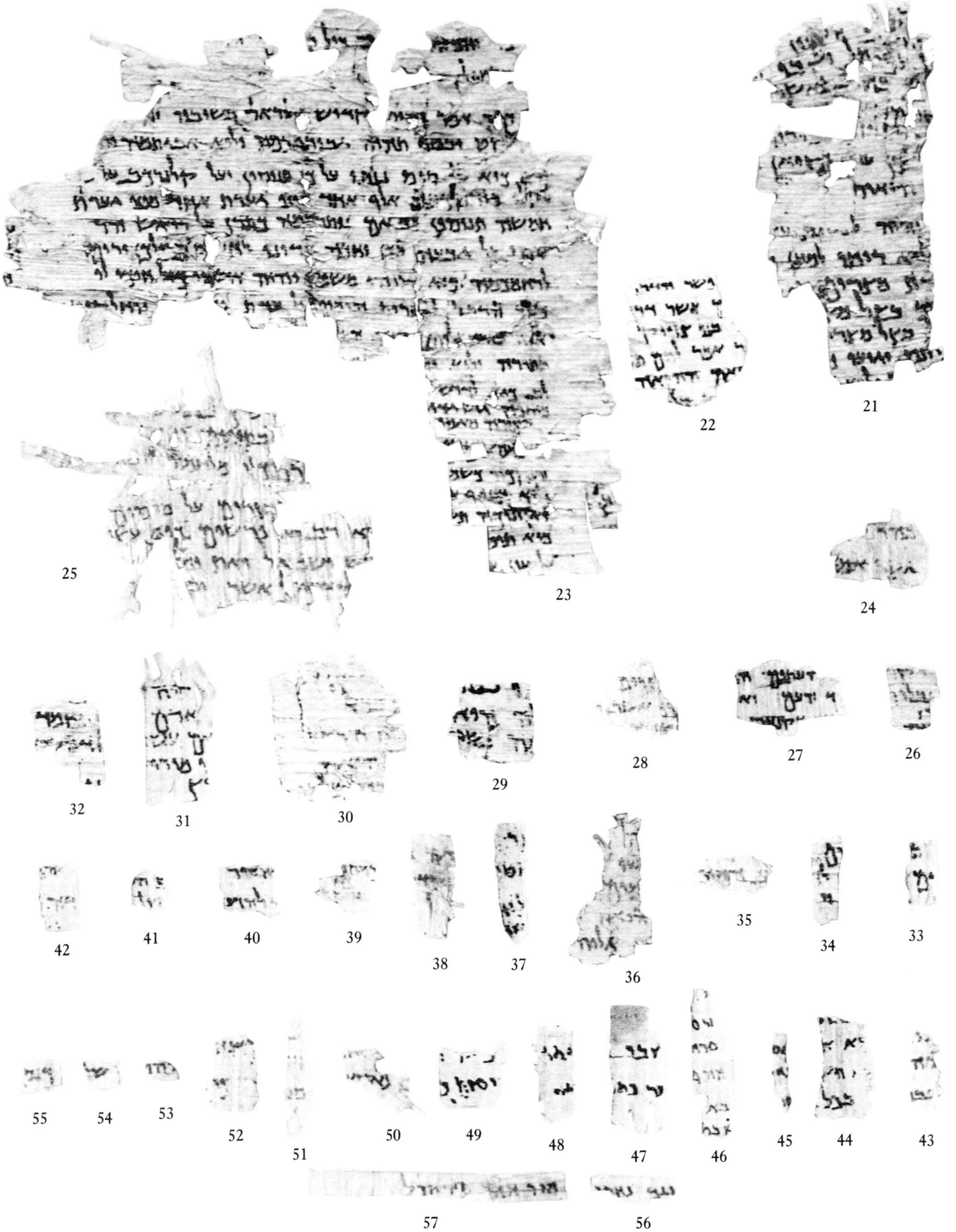
21
22
23
24
25
26
27
28
29
30
31
32
33
34
35
36
37
38
39
40
41
42
43
44
45
46
47
48
49
50
51
52
53
54
55
56
57

163. pIsa

164. pIsa^{d}

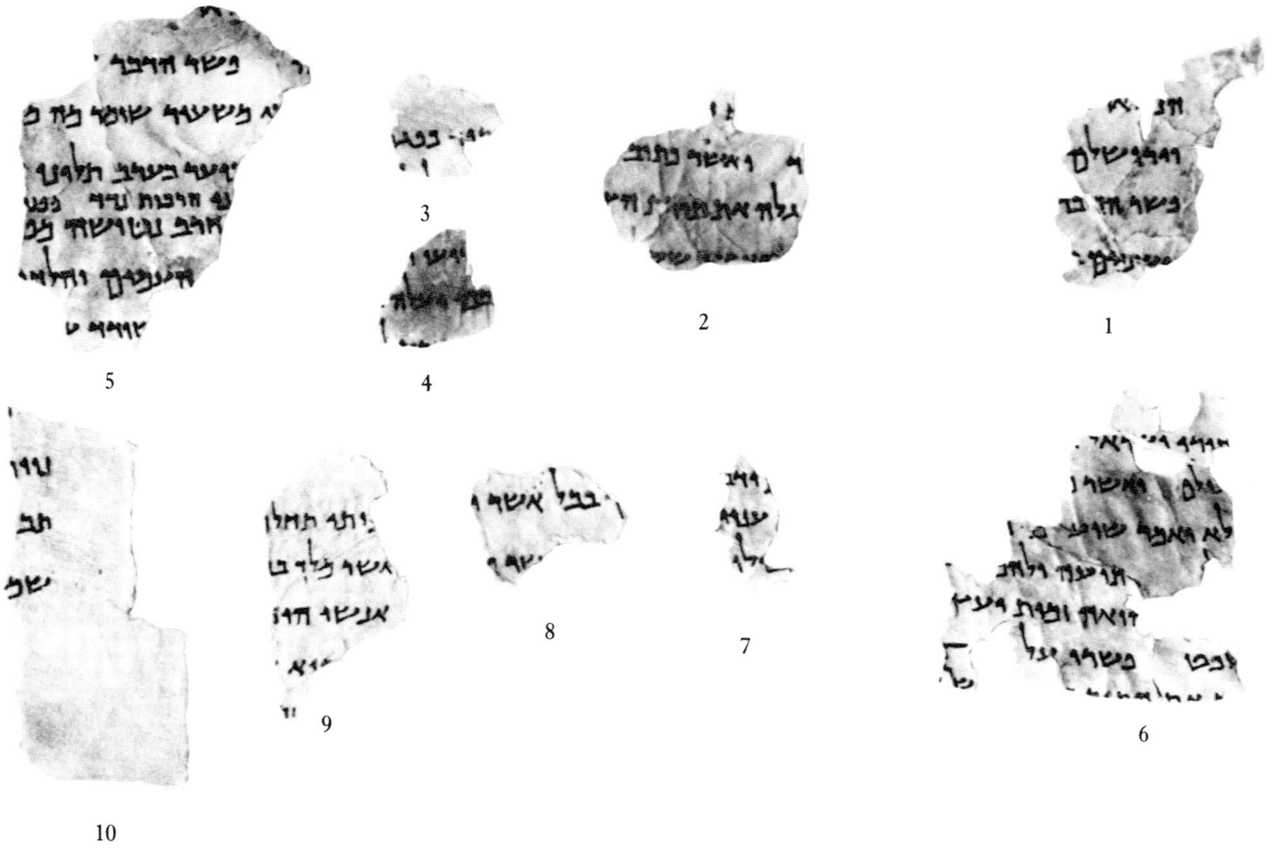

165. pIsa^{e}

PLATE X

166. pHos[a]

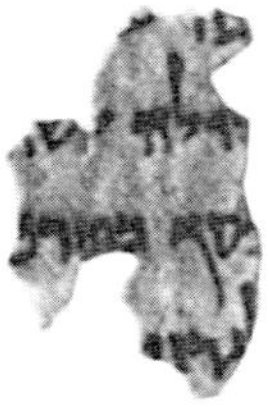

3

2

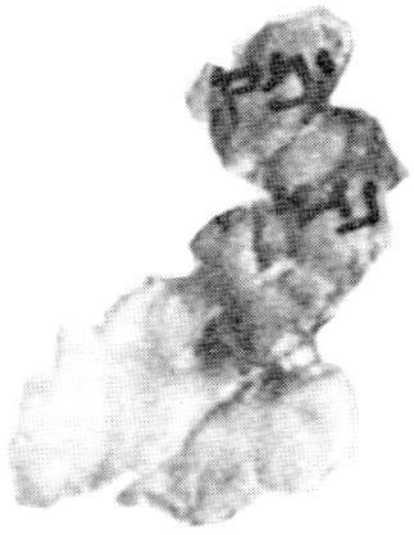

1

167. pHos[b]

7
6
5
4
13
12
10
9
8
11
16
15
14
21
20
19
18
17
38
25
24
23
22
31
30
29
28
27
26
37
36
35
34
33
32

167. pHos^{b}

1

2

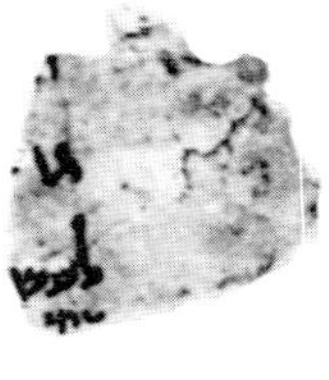

1

4

3

2

168. pMic

4

col. I

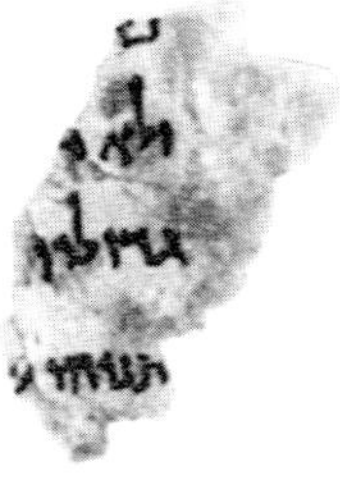

3

169. pNah

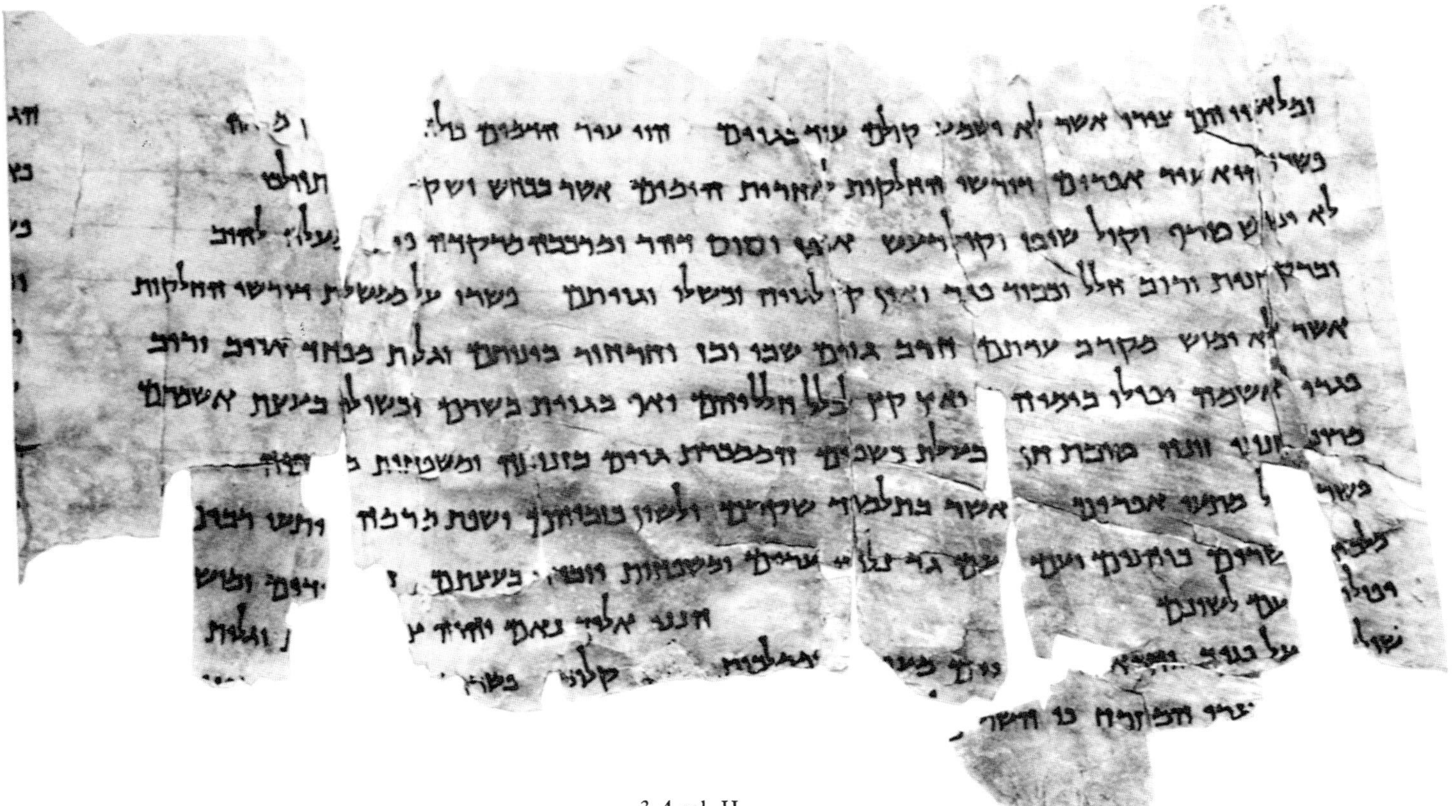

3–4 col. II

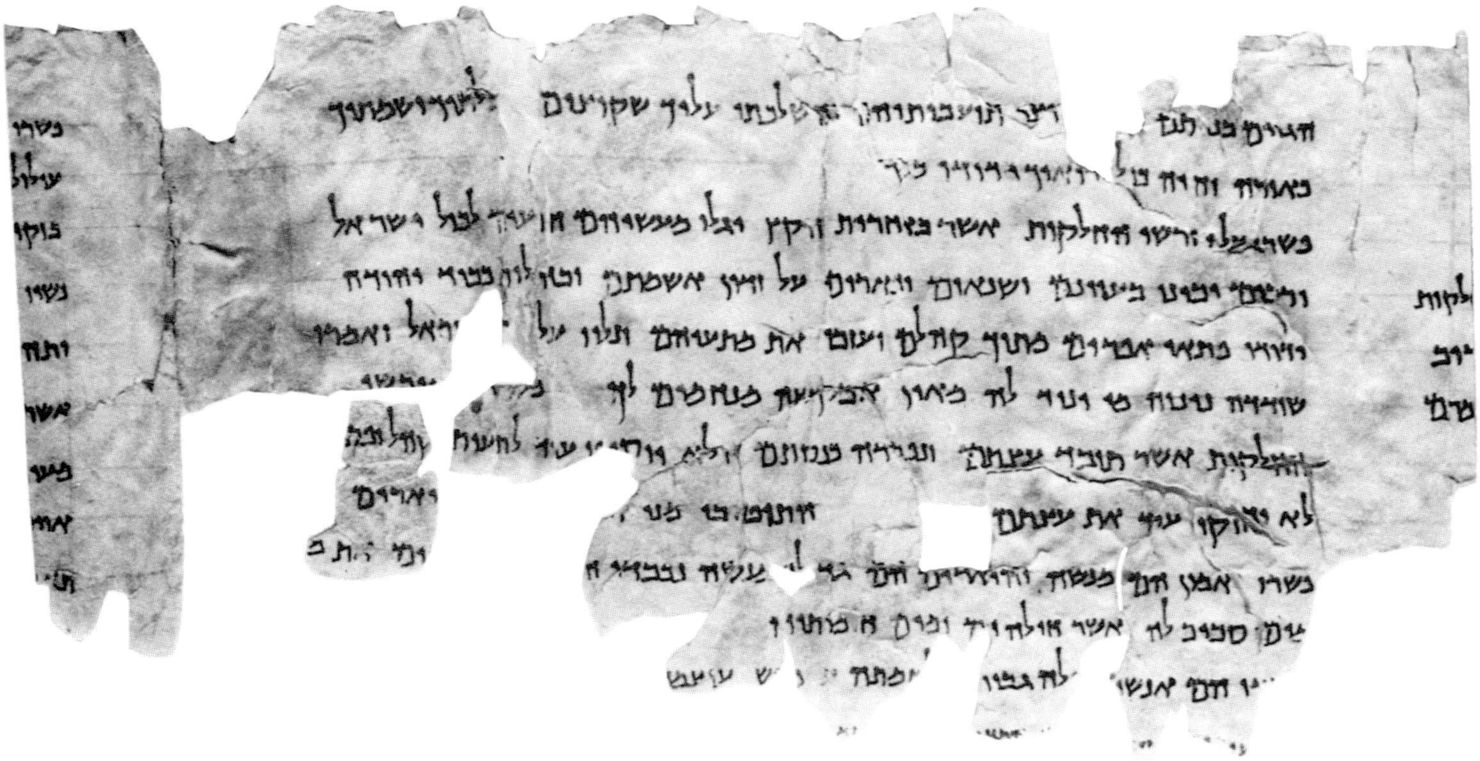

3–4 col. III

169. pNah

5

4 col. IV

169. pNah

2 1

170. pZeph

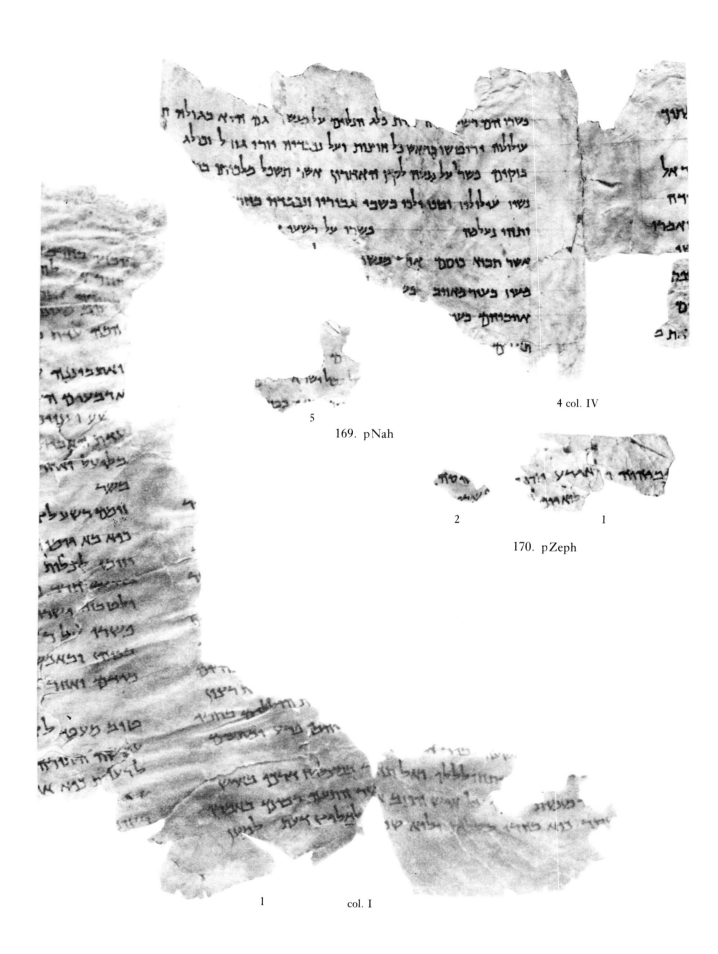

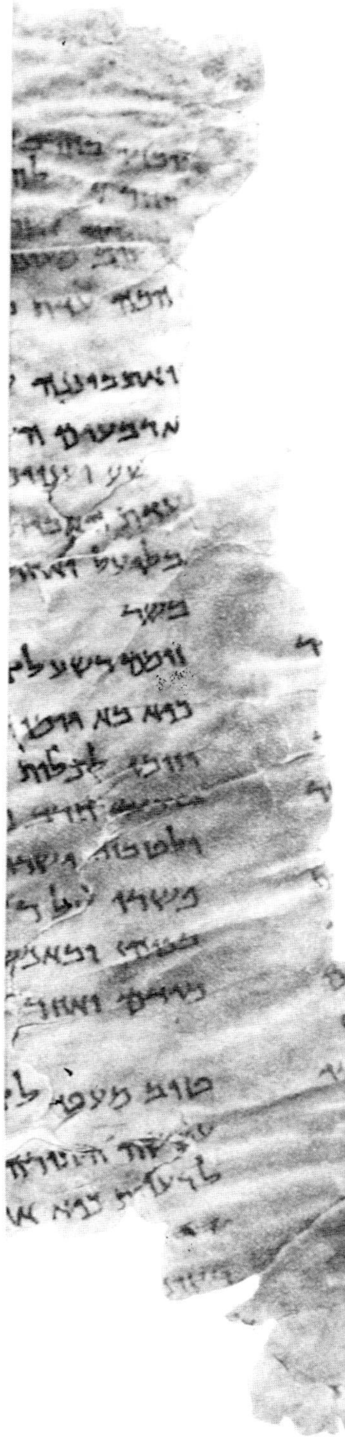

1 col. I

171. pPss[a]

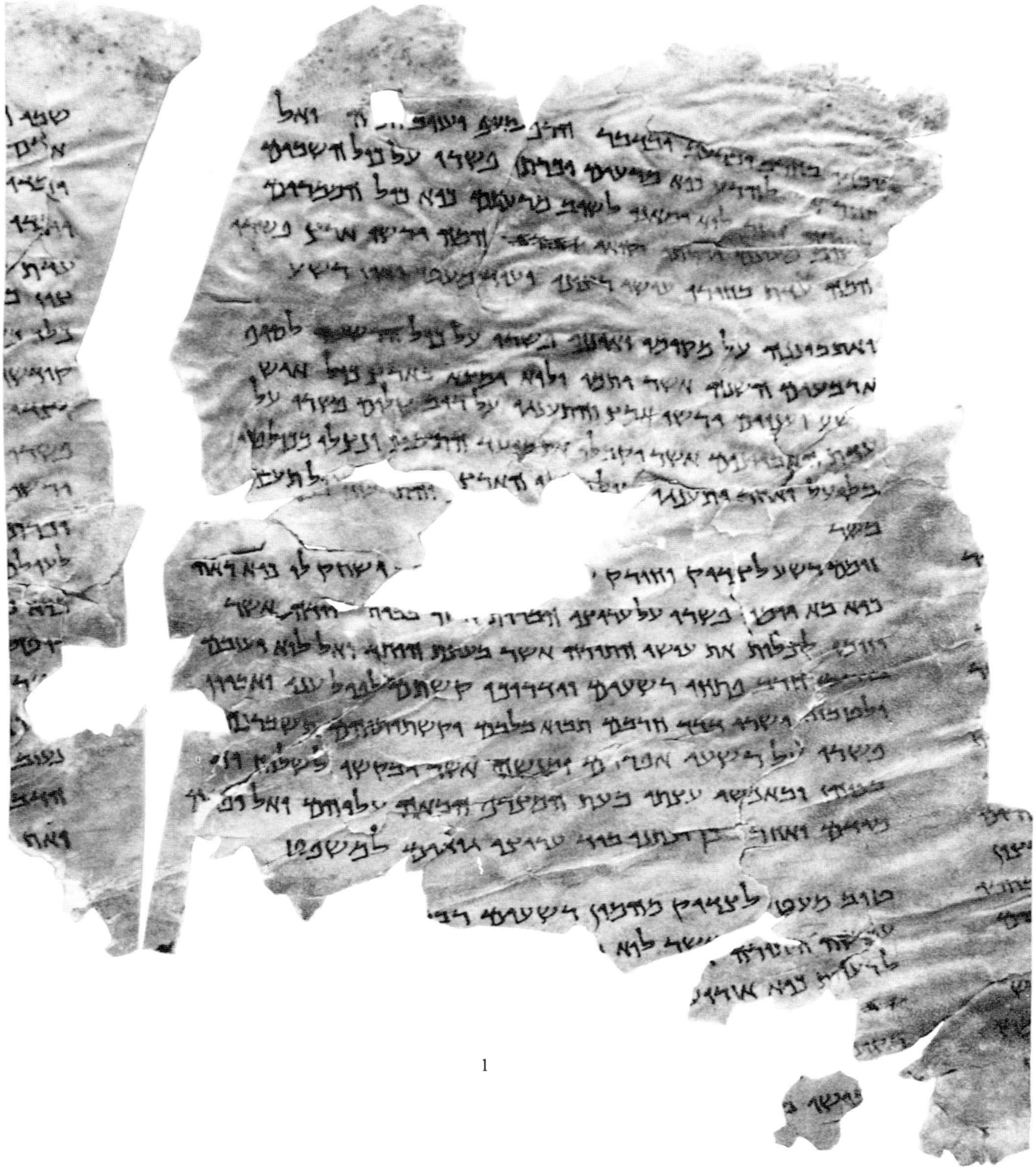

1

2

171. pPss^{a} col. II

171. pPss[a] col. III

171. pPss[a] col. IV

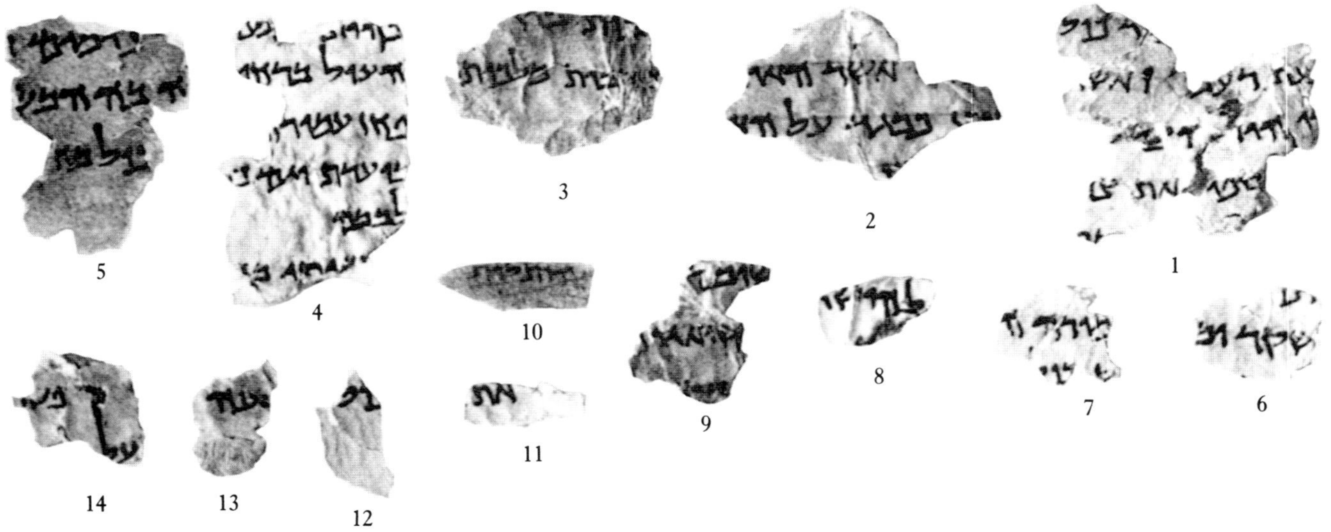

172. pUnid

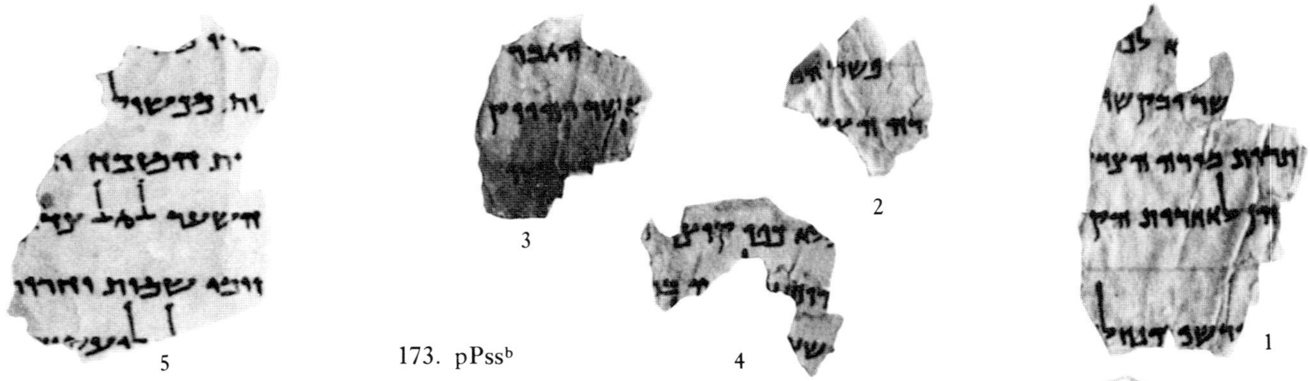

173. pPss[b]

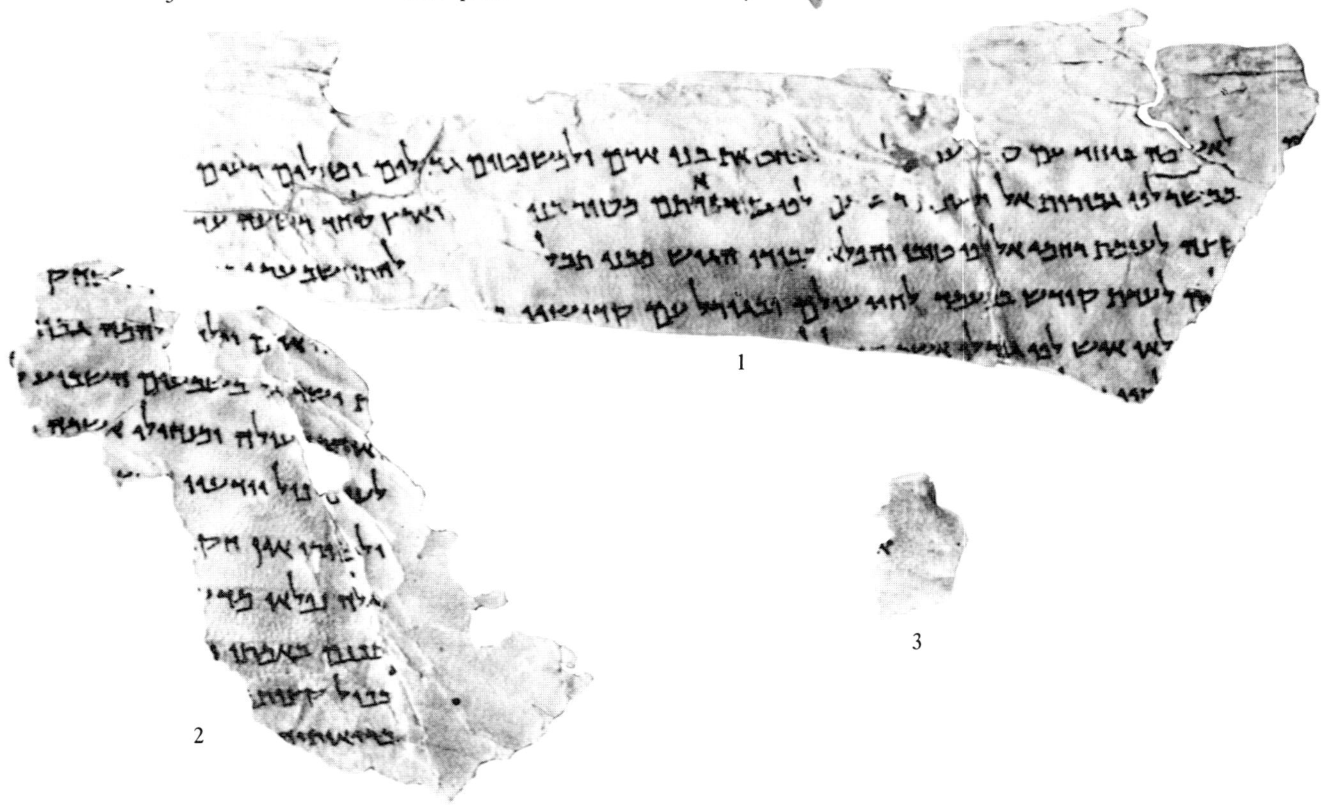

181.

2 1

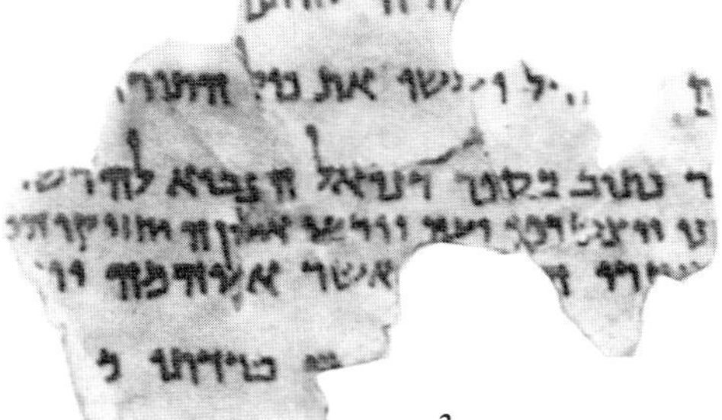

3

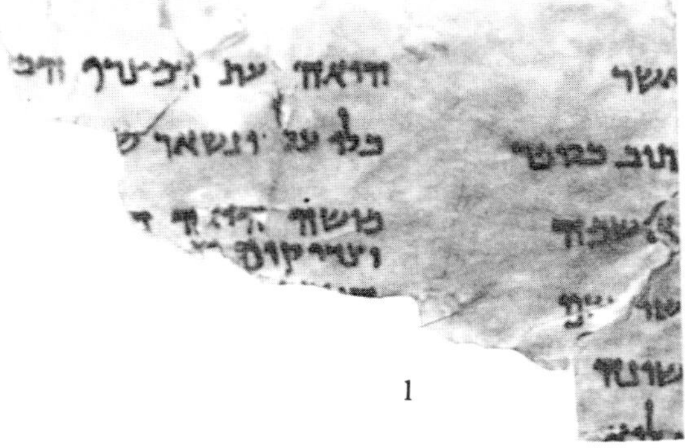

1

174. Florilegium

PLATE XX

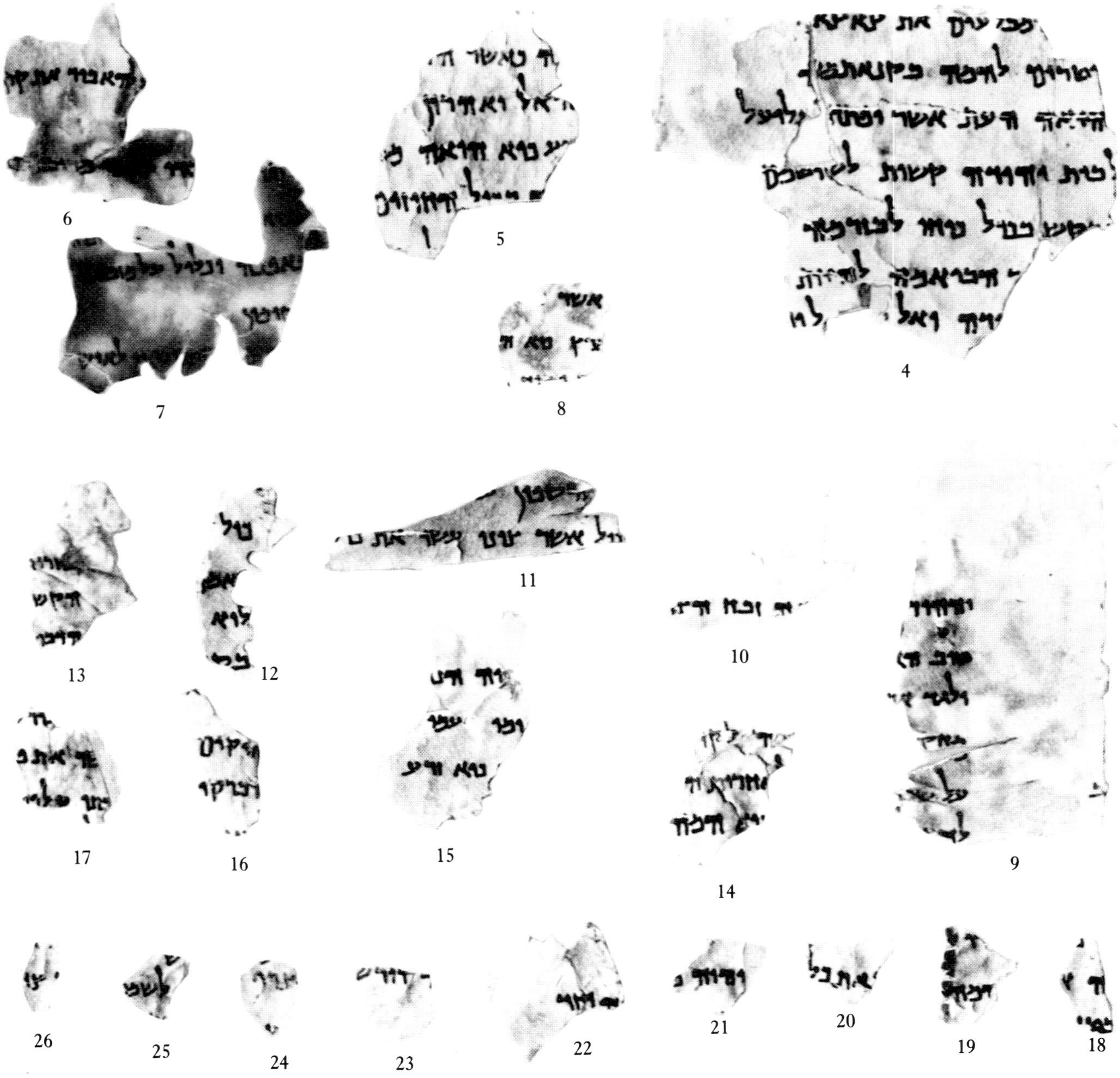

174. Florilegium

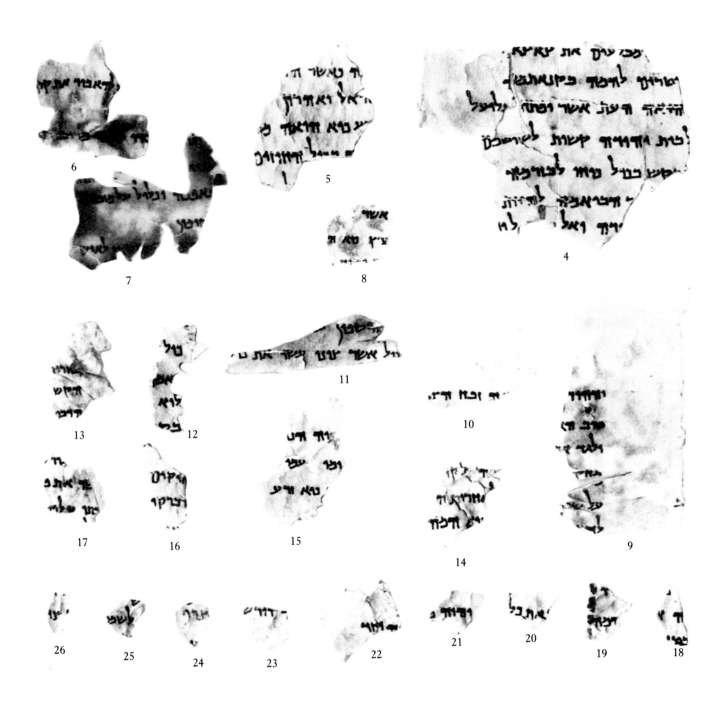

175. Testimonia

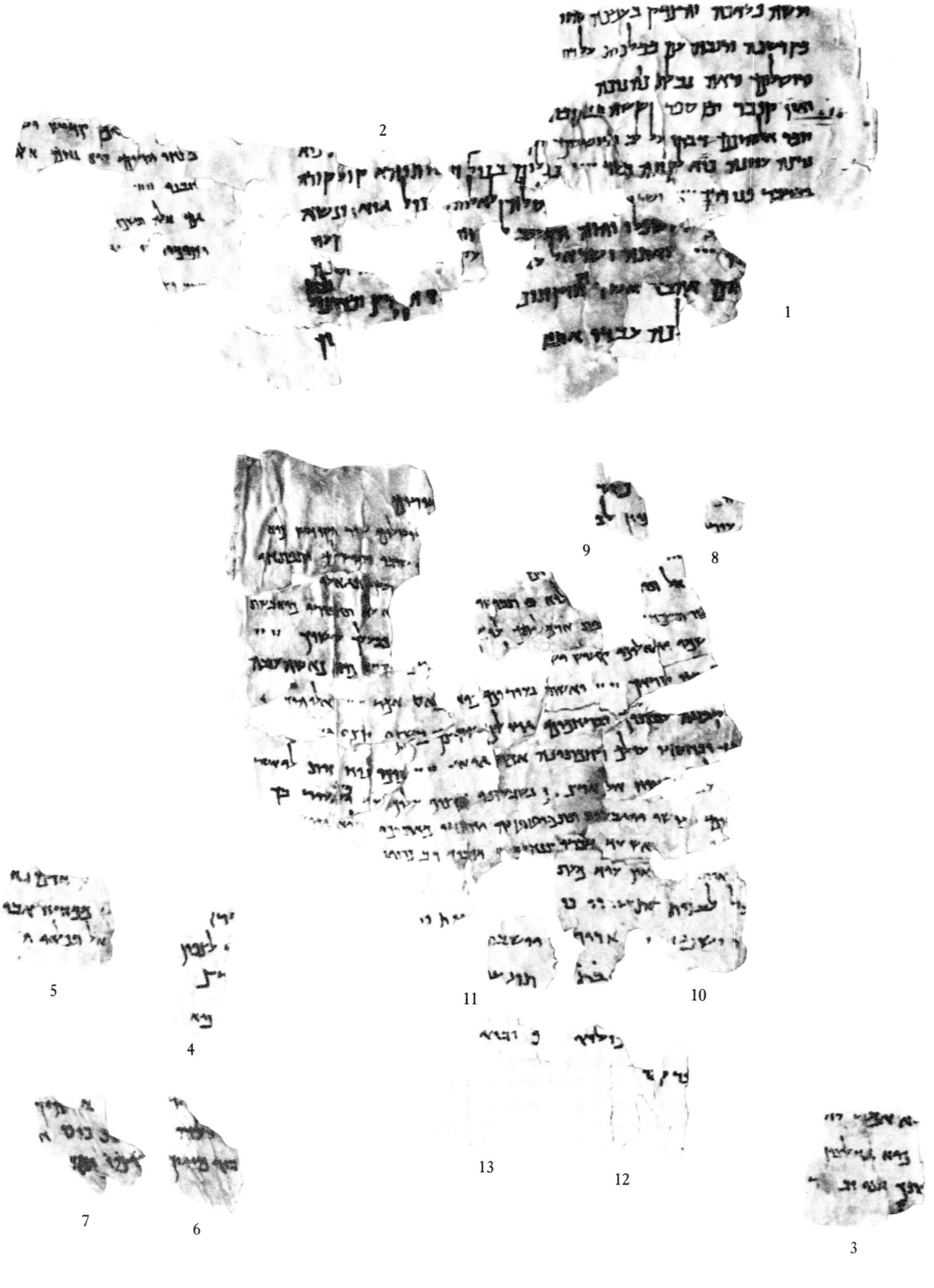

176. Tanḥûmîm

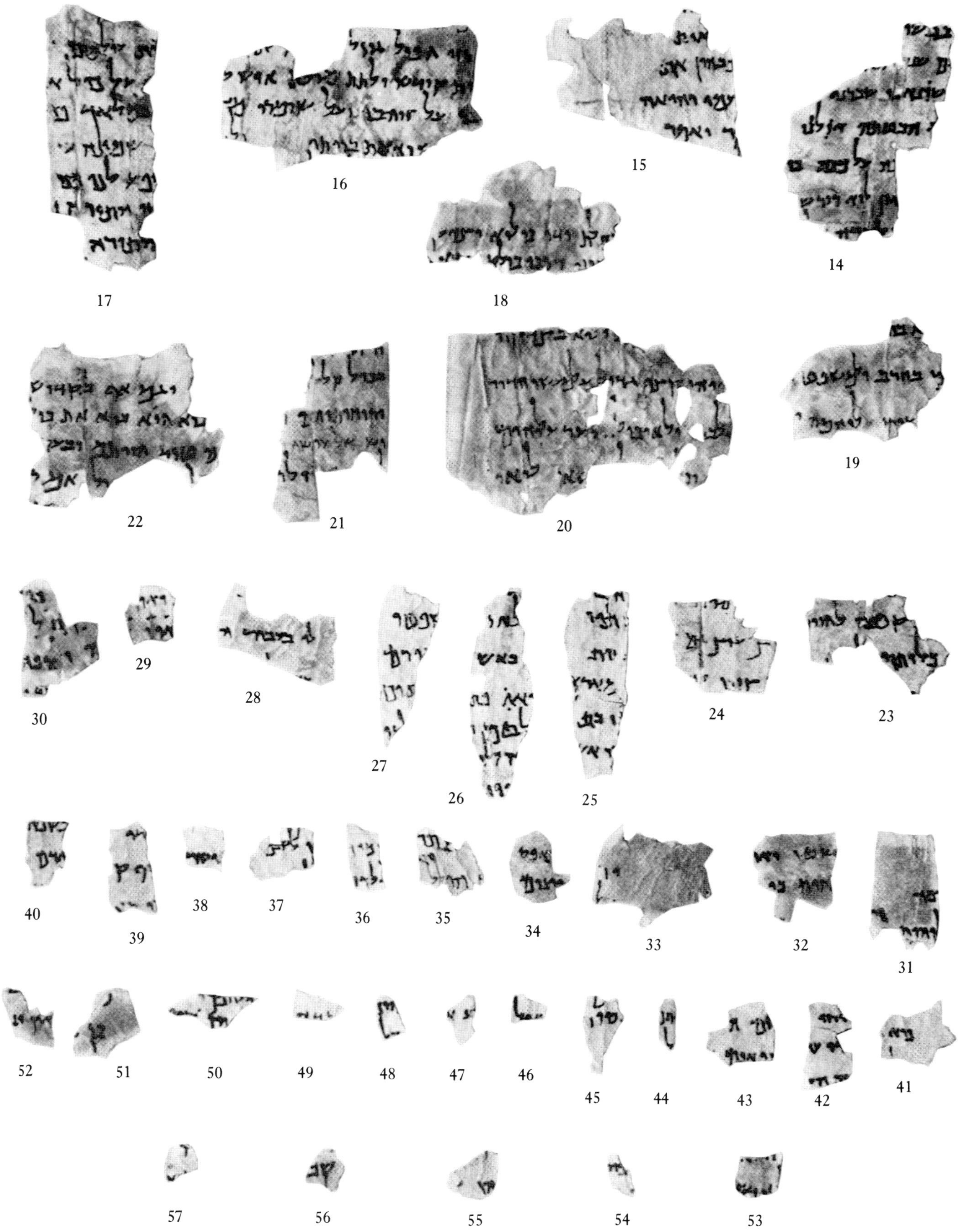

176. Tanḥûmîm

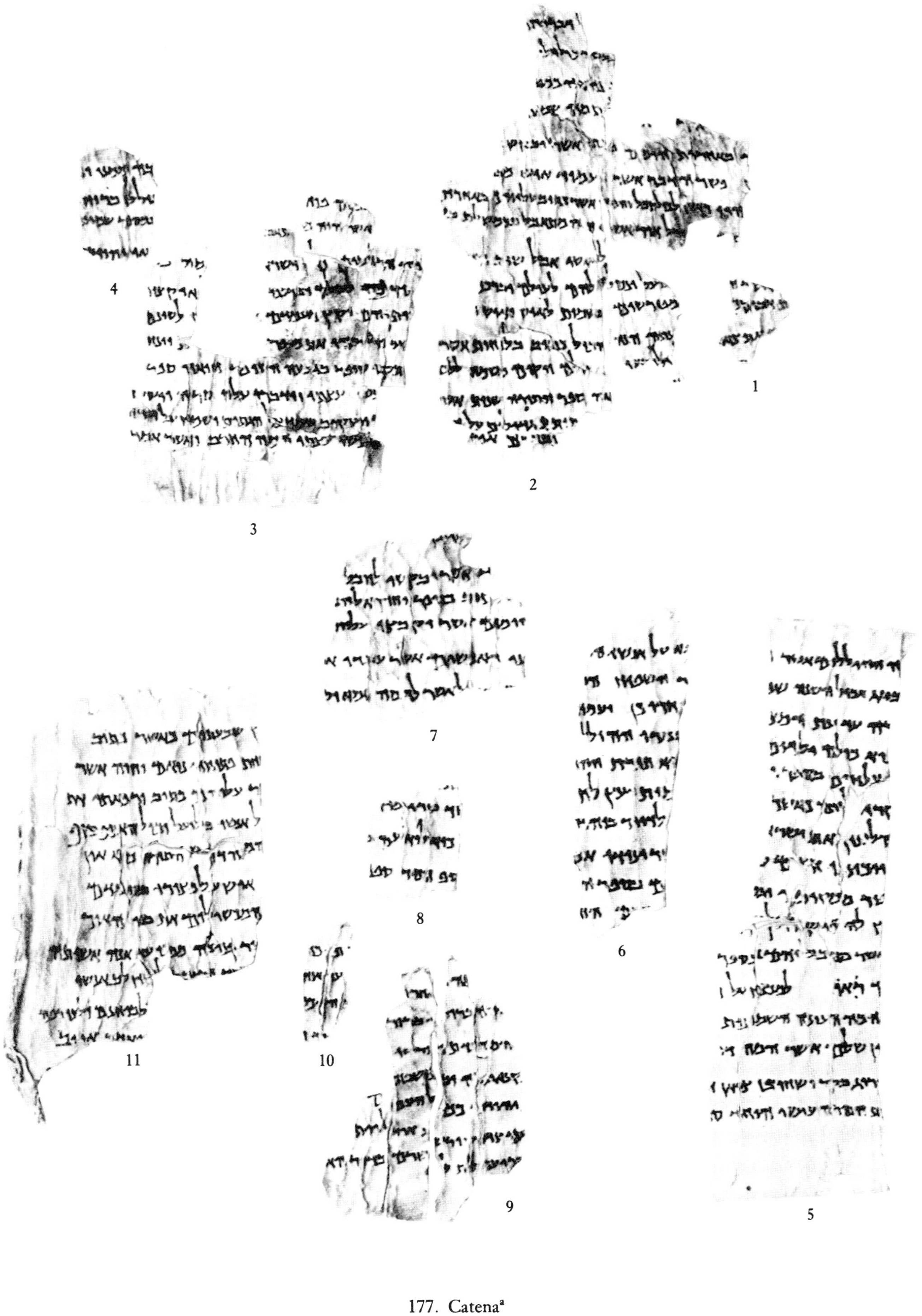

177. Catena[a]

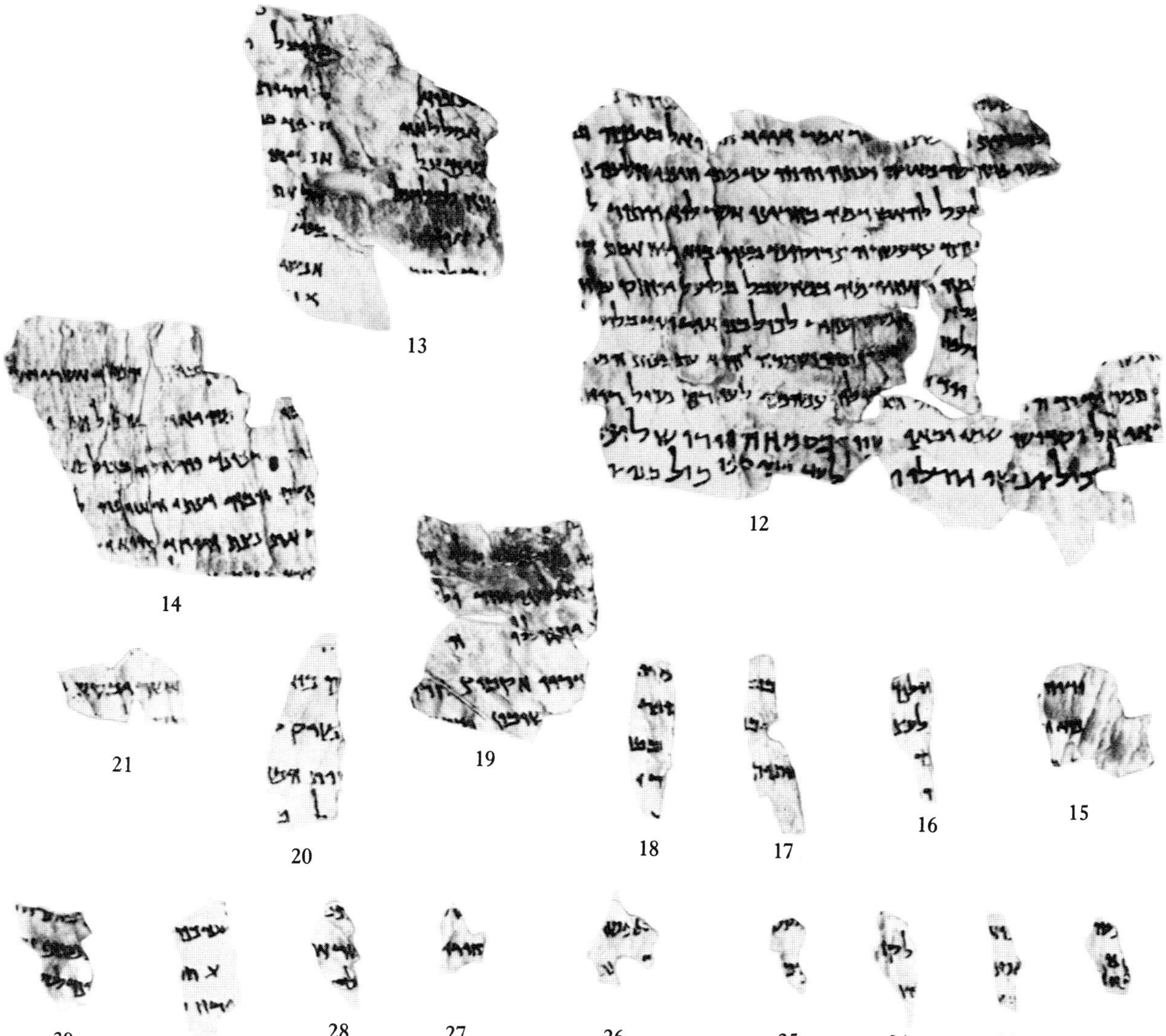
13
12
14
21
20
19
18
17
16
15
30
29
28
27
26
25
24
23
22

177. Catena[a]

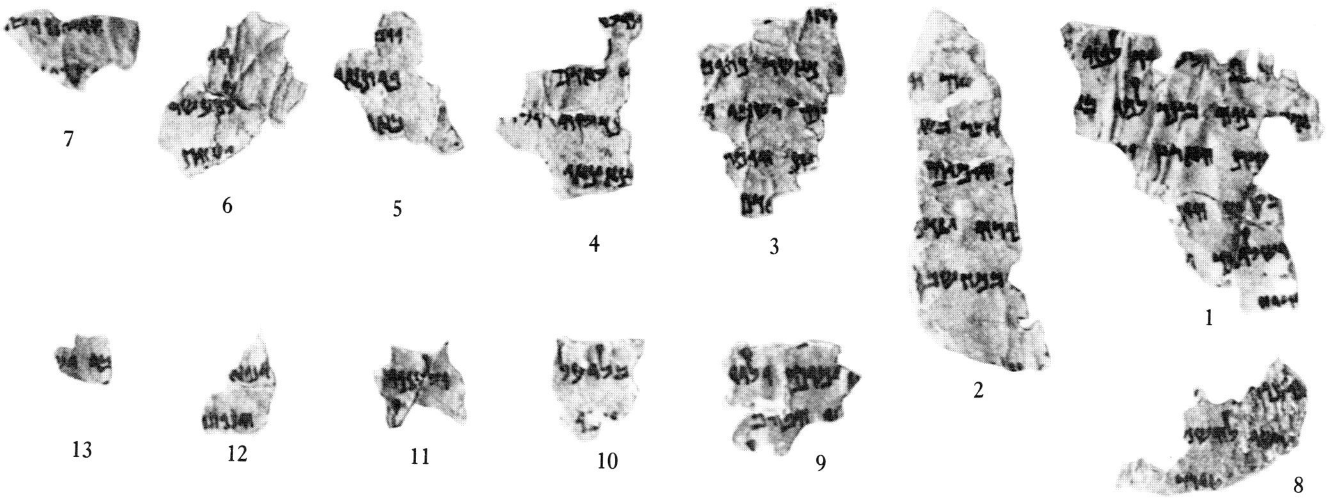
7
6
5
4
3
2
1
13
12
11
10
9
8

1

5

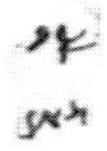

4

3

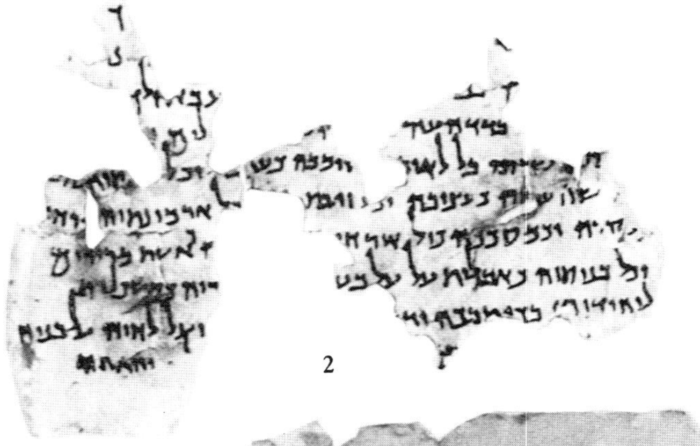

2

179. Lamentations

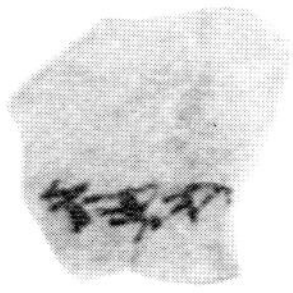

3

2

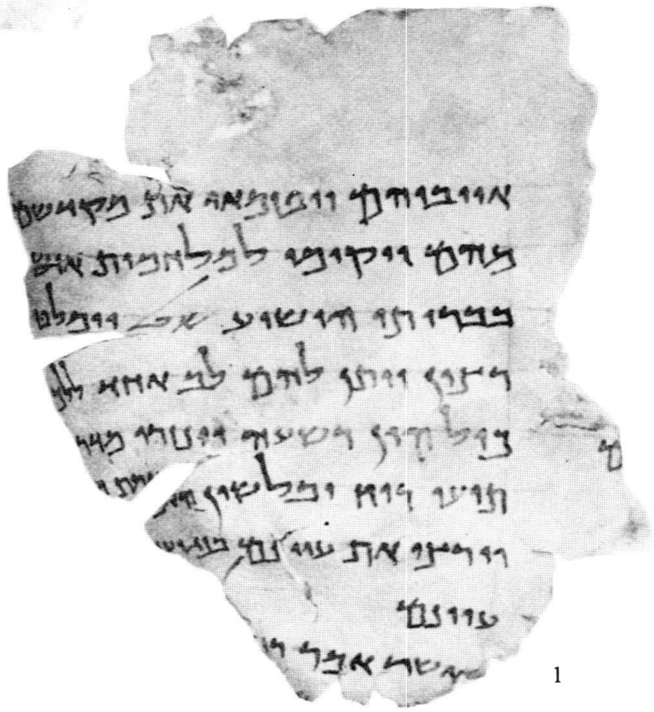

1

5

6

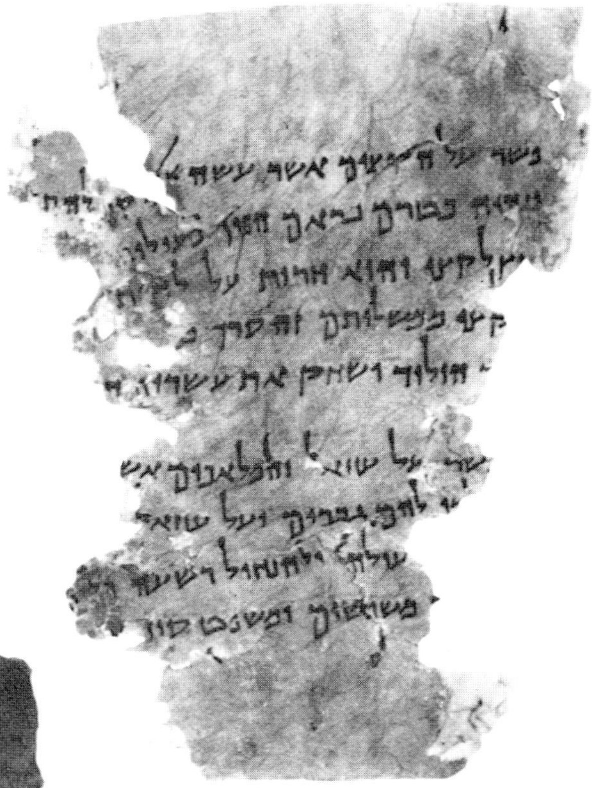

1

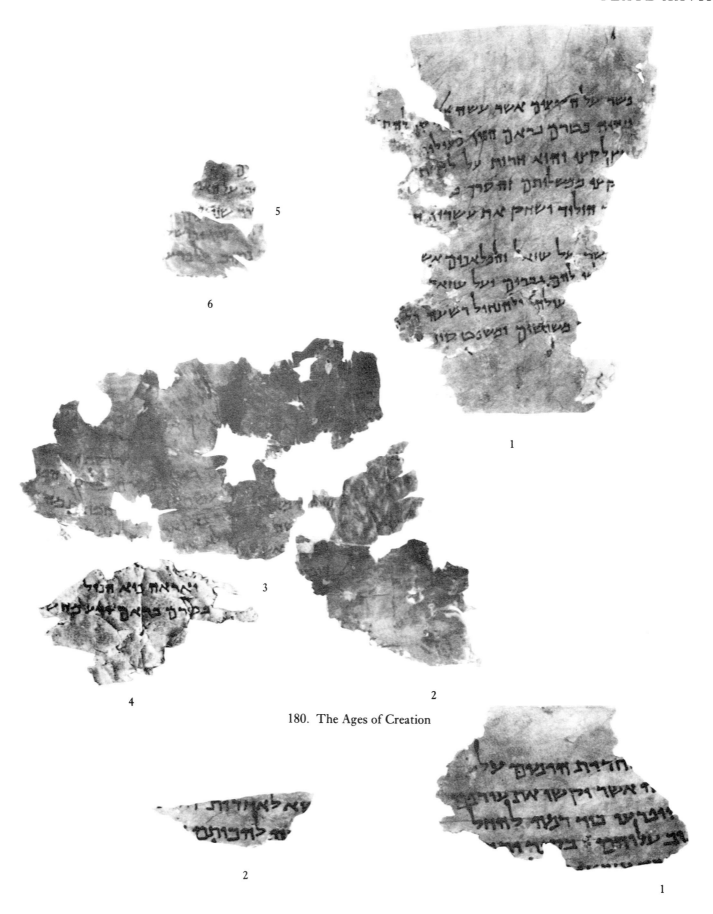

3

4

2

180. The Ages of Creation

2

1

182. Catena[b]

1

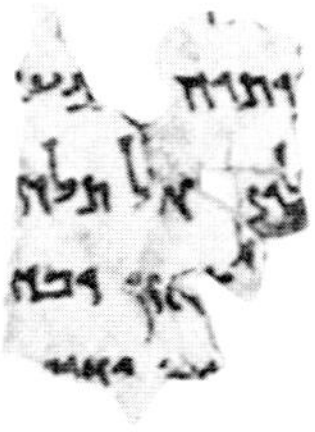

5

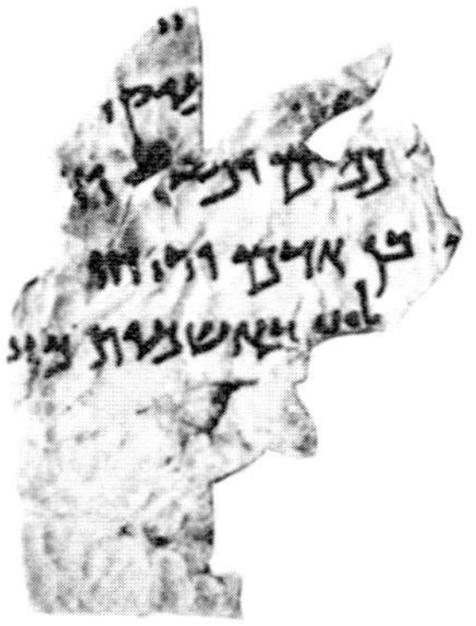

4

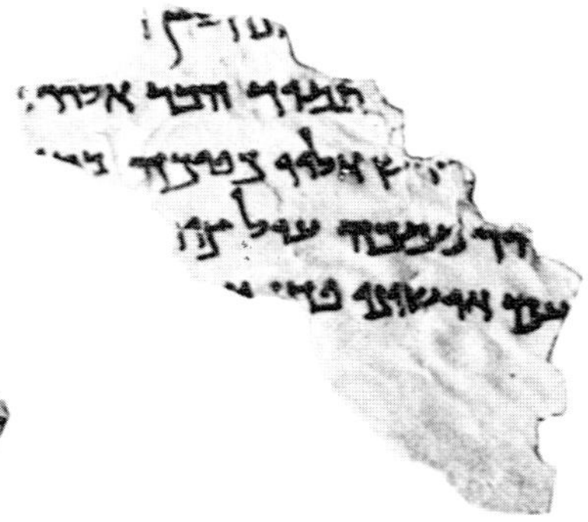

3

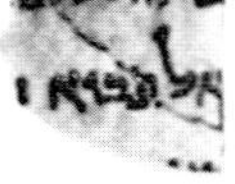

6

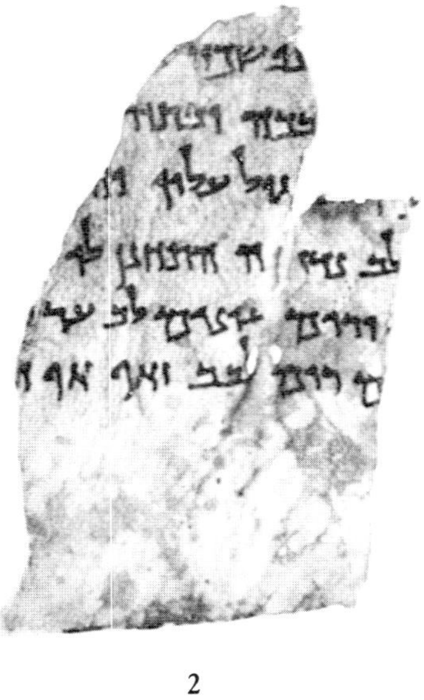

2

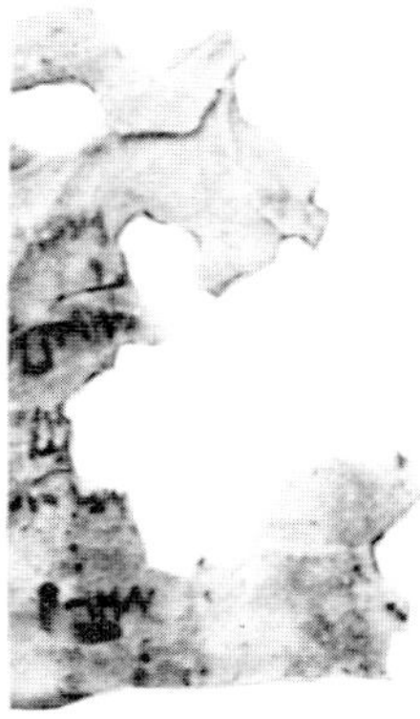

2

1

6

5

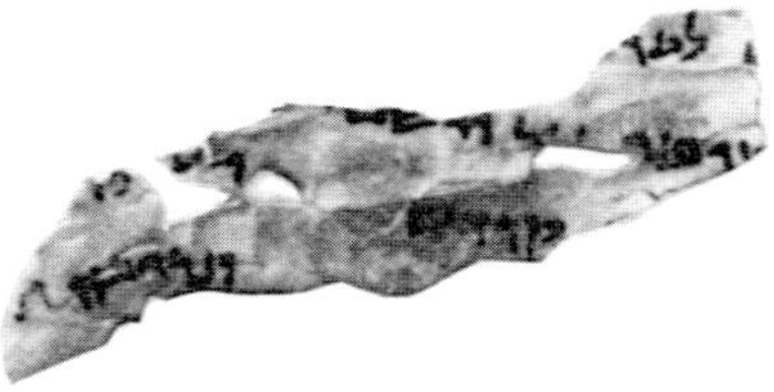

4

3

PLATE XXX

2

1

2

1

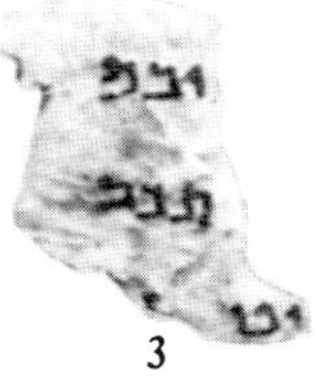

3

1